FORBIDDEN *Love*

THE TRUE LOVE STORY OF
A BLACK PRIEST and A WHITE NUN
Who Defied the Church and Society

Written by
LISA JONES GENTRY

As Told by Their Son
JOSEPH EDWARD STEELE

TUNSTULL STUDIO
PUBLISHING

Forbidden Love

Forbidden Love may be purchased for educational use.
For bulk purchase information please e-mail tstudiopubs@gmail.com
For Forbidden Love bulk purchase information please email
tstudiopubs@gmail.com.
First published in 2018 by Tunstull Studio Publishing
PO Box 264
Claverack, NY 12521

tstudiopubs@gmail.com
Distributed throughout the world by
Tunstull Studio Publishing

ISBN 978-0-692-19236-8
Library of Congress Control Number 2018950382

Art Direction: LaVon Leak-Wilkes
Production Design: Sandy Lawrence
Retouch Design: Sydney Williams
Cover Image: Glenn Tunstull
Lisa Jones Gentry Photo/Back Cover: Jane Love
Joseph Steele Photo/Back Cover: Uli Rose
Cover Models: Nyell Segura
Jolynn Carpenter
Interior Photos courtesy of Joseph Edward Steele and William Grau

Printed in USA
First Printing, 2018

We would like to dedicate
this book to our mothers who have passed on
but whose love endures always.

FORBIDDEN LOVE

Author's Foreword

When Joe first told me the story of his birth parents, Sister Sophie, a white Catholic nun, and Father William Grau, a black Catholic priest, I was immediately captivated. I knew that it was a true love story that should be shared with the world. And when Joe recounted how he sat by Sophie's side in her hospital room as she told him of her love for Father Grau and how, after Joe's birth and adoption, that love continued as Sophie and Father Grau lived together in the Rectory, where Sophie worked as Father Grau's housekeeper until his death in 1964, I sensed that this story was truly very special and one that would resonate with anyone who has been touched by adoption, whether as an adopted child, a birth parent or an adoptive parent.

I also believe strongly that all people, regardless of race, religion or gender, will connect with the love story of these two people—because their story is, at its core, about courage and the determination to love, regardless of the seeming restrictions that society may place upon you. In crafting the book, I went through the voluminous notes that Joe had taken while sitting at Sophie's side, as well as his own recollections of his childhood, and audio tapes that he'd recorded of some of his family members recounting special moments during Joe's childhood. Joe's personal stories are poignant, and at times hilarious, and add a dimension to the book that gives the reader a complete view of the three lives that intersected at Joe's birth, only to be rejoined again when Joe reunited with Sophie in 1991.

The events in this book span from 1909, the year that Joe's birth father, Father Grau, was four years old, himself a bi-racial child raised in Cleveland, Ohio by his Irish-American mother and her German-American husband, continuing through 1955 when Father Grau and Sophie first met at the Catholic Parish in Lackawanna, New York, to Sophie's death in 2007. One of the unique things about this book is the personal window that it affords into one of the most turbulent times in our country's history. Sophie's detailed recollections of the challenges that they faced, including threats to their lives, sheds new insight into this critical period.

I chose to write the book from the unique viewpoints of Joe, and of each of his birth parents, and the tremendous amount of detail that Joe had amassed through his conversations with Sophie, made this possible. As a writer, I journeyed through the lives of Joe, Sophie and Father Grau, and often felt as if each was speaking through me as I wrote, so much so, that I found it difficult to write the end of the book where Father Grau dies. But in so doing I became aware that his presence still lives on through Joe and through each of you who will read this story.

My sincerest hope is that you enjoy the book, that you feel the lives of the characters, and that their story connects with your personal story in a way that will both inspire and empower you, as it did me.

Lisa Jones Gentry
June 2018

CHAPTER

1

It Began
Hudson, New York; 2006

I had the dream again. I'm trying to force my eyes open and wake up from the horror of what just won't go away. The images are swirling, like the bodies in the air being knocked back and forth as if they were no more than feathers floating lightly in the wind. I can still smell the burning flesh. I can still see the gaping hole in the huge tower, flames consuming it, licking the sides hungrily until one giant explosion levels it. Yet, I can't pull away, my face presses against the glass of the building that by a few feet missed the same fate as the one in front of me. The World Trade Center, an icon of power and strength, now nothing more than a mass of rubble before my eyes. I want to wake up but, yet I cannot, something lays the hard hand of sleep on me and instead I twist and turn trying to escape the memory that won't go away.

And now I'm in a different place and seeing through different eyes. I look at my hands; the same but not quite. Something is scratching my throat. It's uncomfortable and stiff, some type of collar. My clothes are heavy and bulky. I can feel that they're wet; I can smell the mustiness around me. The same sound, the same bombing. Bodies flying through air, but this time my face is not pressed against a glass skyscraper—this time the bodies are just feet in front of me. In the distance I see the outlines of what seem to be cavernous Renaissance villas barely standing, pock marked with holes. I hear voices, I recognize it as Italian and as I gaze deeper, my eyes grow accustomed to the darkness. I can hear the sound of airplanes circling overhead and as one comes closer and closer, it's followed by the sound of more explosions and crashing and crying and men running back and forth. My feet are wet. I'm in a pool of muddy water and as I look down, I see what I expect to be my face, but it's not. I expect to see my eyes but they're not. Similar, but not the same. And I look through those eyes that are not mine but yet feel like mine, and I hear a voice. *"You must tell them, you must tell them my story."* And a shudder goes through me as another bomb explodes, and I wake up.

Everything is quiet now, the only sound is the ticking of the clock. Rubbing my eyes trying to get the memories out of my head, the memories that won't go away. I lie back on my bed, my heart is still pounding. It's 2006, but for a moment, just a moment, I was back there on September 11, 2001. Then to another time—a time before there was a me. A time that I'd only read of, but yet I experienced in that dream as real as if I were there. And I know that it was him. He has spoken to me like this before over the years, but never with such clarity and force.

I lie back longing for the comfort of an empty mind, one that is not fraught with images of death and dying. But somehow, I know that unless I know the story that he's been trying to tell me in bits and pieces, these images will never leave me. I fumble for the light and pick up a creased newspaper article reading it again, but this time knowing that I must go.

"Local Group to Honor Famed World War II Buffalo Soldiers Regiment"

I fold the newspaper carefully and, again, this sense as if I'm on a moving conveyor belt pushing me forward. Yet, as I look at the passing scenes that are in fact the scenes of my own life, I know that this inexorable forward movement must continue. The parts of my life that have been like empty slots waiting to be filled, a patchwork quilt not yet done, now laid out before me. But I must be the quilt maker; I must be the one who completes the picture.

CHAPTER

2

J looked around the large room. We were in a conference room at a non-descript hotel, the kind of place where family weddings and reunions took place with the same standard issue red and blue carpet, the same comfortable yet decidedly unstylish furniture clustered in small groups around the room. As I walked in, I felt suddenly uncomfortable, but before I could lose my nerve and turn back, an older gentleman caught my eye and smiled warmly.

"So, young man, you look much too young to have been one of us."

The older black man who appeared to be in his early seventies smiled warmly, slapping me gently on the back. His face was creased, though not heavily lined, and his clothes and his demeanor suggested someone who had done well, someone who had taken advantage of what had been offered to him and had claimed that which others may have sought to deny, solely because of who he was and was not. His shoes were shiny and of soft leather and subtle craftsmanship, his dark blue blazer, with a crest on the pocket, gray flannel pants firmly creased of almost the same color as his hair. His skin was a little darker than mine but not by much; one might say café au lait, brown enough to know, but in his day probably considered not too brown.

He introduced himself to me, shaking my hand firmly, putting his arm around my shoulder in a fatherly way. "Did you have a dad or an uncle who served with us?"

I hesitated, not quite knowing what to say, feeling uncomfortable as if I were somehow masquerading at a ball to which I had not been invited. "No, no. I'm just doing some research." I didn't know if my words sounded as hollow as they felt, but I still wasn't ready to tell anyone, much less admit to myself why I was here.

"Well, that's just fine. It was a good group of men, we lost too many of them, way too many of them. Guys that I was in school with, we all left together, but only a few came back. But we served, and we served proudly, and those of us who were fortunate enough to have been given a chance to return to our families…well, I think we did OK. I think we did just fine."

I smiled, still feeling uncomfortable, but sensing the man's pride and wanting to be part of that, I asked hesitantly, "Did you know someone, a chaplain, he was a Catholic priest, a Father William Grau?"

The man leaned back on his fine shoes, but not too much to leave a crease mark. thinking, then shaking his head, "No, no, I don't believe that I did, but hold on. Harry over there, he's Catholic, maybe he knew the man." He motions for his friend to come over. "Introduce yourself again, young man."

"Joe…Joe Steele." I held out my hand which the other man pumped warmly.

"Well, Joe, this is my friend, Harry Flynn. Harry and I fought together, in fact, we fought together, we drank together, and we escaped with our lives together, been friends ever since. So, Harry, Joe here is doing some research and there's a… tell him the name again, Joe."

"Father William Grau."

"He was a Catholic priest and one of our Chaplains. Harry, I know that you're Catholic, thought maybe you knew him, do you remember a Father Grau?"

Harry was a tall man with nut-brown skin smooth and well cared for, still a full head of hair, although all gray, wavy and thick. I could sense that he must've been the Casanova of the group in his time. Even now, I caught his eyes lingering on some of the younger women in the crowd.

He reluctantly pulled his gaze away from the young woman, now walking out of his line of sight and turned back to me, "Father William Grau, now that does ring a bell, I didn't know him personally, but I do believe that some of the other boys talked about him. I remember something about a Christmas Eve Mass, yeah something like that, just been too many years to remember everything, but that does…that does remind me of something that I heard about."

Trying to hide my excitement, I asked eagerly, "Did they say anything about him? What kind of man he was... Anything... I'm trying to put together as much as I can."

Suddenly realizing that I may have said too much, Harry, or Casanova as I like to think of him, leaned against the wall closing his eyes for a moment smiling, saying, "I do believe, yes, I do believe that I heard about him, fine man, a good man." Then he chuckled. "Not like any priest I knew and now, mind you, I grew up in the Catholic church and I love my church, but some of them were a little stiff, but Father Grau, from what I heard as I don't remember him myself, but from what I heard, he had a good relationship with the men. He was a little older than the rest of us and I remember some of the men affectionately called him 'Pops.' He went that extra mile, wasn't sitting up in his ivory tower. Yeah, I remember them talking about him. He was well-liked."

"Do you think..." Before I could finish my sentence, another man came up to him cutting me off.

"Harry Flynn, why I can't believe it's you!"

Before I could say anything else, the men were embracing heartily, slapping each other on the back, reminiscing. Feeling suddenly awkward again, I excused myself, walking over to the other side of the room towards the punch bowl. As my eyes traveled around the small group, I saw men who had served their country and come back to discrimination, but despite all of that had triumphed. The men in this room exuded a sense of success and one could feel the weight of the contributions that they had made to their families, to the community and, I dare say, to the world. I felt proud to have a connection with them even though it was one that I could not speak of openly, at least not yet. But somehow being in their presence made me feel closer to that part of me that I was now being allowed to discover.

It's late now and I'm driving home to Hudson, New York. After the World Trade Center tragedy, my husband Glenn and I decided that we had to get out of the city because the place that had given me so much pleasure in my younger days seemed only to cause me pain now. I couldn't erase the images, I couldn't shake the feeling that death seemed to hang like a pall over the once vibrant place. So, Glenn and I consolidated everything and moved out of the city to the picturesque Hudson River Valley. We bought a beautiful home and it was there that I began to feel a greater sense of peace than I had in many years. And now I wondered, was this peace to be short-lived? Was I now to experience the inner turmoil of not knowing a part of me that made me, but yet was closed to me? Meeting the men who had served with *him* had awakened that long dormant curiosity that I had long tried to deny. Because to acknowledge it almost felt guilty, as if somehow I was less than grateful for the loving family that adopted me as an infant. Mama, Daddy and my brother Billy, and Otis, or 'Pops' as I called him, who became like a father to me after my father's death when I was five. That cocoon of warmth enveloped me from my earliest memories. I remember the story of how Daddy and Mama and my brother Billy had gone to the orphanage and Billy had immediately gone to where I lay in my crib and he said, "*That's the one, that's my little brother.*"

Was I somehow betraying all that I have been given by seeking to know more? I know what Billy would say, that I had the right to know, the anger that only now was starting to subside in him for having found out about his own adoption as a teenager, an age where anger and confusion reign even in the best of us. But for me, I believe I viewed it in a different way, wasn't that I didn't want to know. I just didn't feel like I needed to, that is until now. I had been successful, Harvard College and Harvard Business School, an investment banker and an international consultant but now perhaps, as we mature we must know the complete self, the self that we present to the world and the self that was presented to us before we became aware of who we were. And so, it is that other self that I seek in this journey. It is that other self that seeks me.

I remember when I found out about her...my birth mother. I was in my 30s, and I remember contacting the agency and being told that the records were sealed. I remember having to jump through all sorts of hoops before, finally, I could get the information that I sought. And when I saw her name, I knew that I had to find out, was she living? Was she dead? Had she loved me, did she care? These thoughts tumbled back and forth in my head as I navigated the dark, inky black roads. On this moonless night, I wound around trees that were heavy with rain, with branches that bent like the curved backs of old men.

CHAPTER

3

The rain that had been my constant companion on my drive home had now subsided. The air was chill and crisp the way it always is on the cusp of winter, cold but not with the numbing bone cracking feel that turned you inside out, making you long for the hot, sticky days of summer. This was the pregnant cold; the cold that portended so much more. For me, it was a welcome respite from the endless days in muggy, clammy places where your clothes stick to you and the air always had a pungent, slightly rotting smell that never seems to leave you. Places in the far corners of the globe where I traveled in my work as a consultant in international development. But I wanted to rid my mind of thoughts of work so that I could better process the portals that I had opened by my recent trip.

I turned the key, the door making that familiar creak that it always did, my feet touching the warm familiarity of my home. Glenn's voice coming from the other room. "Is that you, Joe?"

"Yep, I'm home."

Glenn emerged from his art studio warming his hands around a cup of coffee. "You got a call." Before I could ask he said, "It's about Sophie. I think you better call them back; it sounds pretty serious." He handed me a piece of paper where he'd scribbled down the number.

I got my phone, quickly dialing, I don't remember much else after I said, "This is Joe Steele. I got a call about Sophie Legocki." I just listened and then said, "I understand...I understand." I hung up the phone slowly, turning back to Glenn, "She's really sick and they've asked me to come. But I don't know if I'm ready for this, it's just all too much. I mean, I wanted to know her. I wanted to have a relationship with her, but I didn't expect all of this."

Glenn, who probably knew me better than anyone else on this earth, said softly, "Joe, you've got to go, she's your mother." And then as clear as a bell I heard another voice, but a voice in my head that said, "*She's my lover and your mother.*"

I guess I must've looked like I was about to faint because Glenn shook me anxiously. "Are you OK? What happened?! For a minute you looked like you were about to black out!"

Still shaking, because the voice was as real as anything that I had ever experienced, I sat down weakly, "I'm OK. I'm OK."

CHAPTER

I never really liked hospitals, even though they're supposed to be places where people heal. They always seem to be more like the places where people go to die. Everything is so antiseptic and scrubbed shiny clean as if waiting to place yet more souls on the conveyor belt of death. Maybe because I had seen too many die, abandoned by hospitals and left to take their final sojourn in this body in places where they openly prepared you for the inevitable transition to the greater life beyond. I thought of all of those friends of mine who had died—my best friend, Chris, who passed away too young of AIDS, and so many others whom I've known, and so for me, hospitals were places that I avoided, that I ran from because they seem to stand as the gateway to death rather than life.

I was thinking these thoughts as I pushed open the swinging doors, my feet squeaking against the scuffed linoleum floors. Pale misshapen forms of what perhaps had been vibrant men and women, now shrunken into wheelchairs with the maze of tubes and bottles and miscellaneous strings and things dangling overhead. The endless chattering of nurses and hospital staff, seemingly oblivious to the walking carcasses, their patients. I often wondered why hospital workers didn't wear white anymore, why instead they had traded in the traditional uniform of caring for the sick for a series of multicolored pajama-like garb sporting everything from flowers to baby panda bears, all in faux cheery colors. An older man shuffled in behind me. I turned. His blue veined lined face, scraps of course hairs pressed against the side of his head, wide fleshy, pink hands, and heavy breathing made me wonder if perhaps he would be the next occupant of the parking lot of wheelchairs pushed haphazardly against the wall. He was carefully carrying a vase of daisies, the kind that were sold outside the hospital doors by those capitalizing on the guilt of relatives who visited not quite enough, but yet carry the flowers as a beacon of their devotion.

Something in those flowers, in those daisies, made me remember another day, a day not that many years ago, but feeling as if it was another time and place…

Flashback Through Joe's Eyes
Buffalo, New York; Several Years Earlier

It was a warm afternoon, the sun struggling to peek out from the mossy veil of fast-moving clouds overhead. A cacophony of Saturday afternoon sounds exploded around me. The squeaking of heavy shopping carts loaded with oversized boxes of cereal and beer, and Pampers and Cheetos, pushed by equally oversized hands leading to an even more oversized body draped in a shapeless shift and inevitably squeezed into pants that were never meant to stretch quite that far. Children scampered back and forth, some toddling on legs that barely looked as if they could support their round frames, others whizzing between parked cars and blaring horns and men oblivious to their families and women shouting names of children who ignored them. A nondescript parking lot in a nondescript part of a nondescript city filled with people whose lives were so different from mine that I wondered how could someone of whom I was a part, be a part of something with which I had so little in common.

I remembered at that moment Cincinnati in the sixties, the home that I grew up in, Mama and Daddy, my father a well-respected city worker, and Mama, serious and no-nonsense, but with a vein of love that ran deep, taking me on the bus to the library on Saturdays, a stern woman to some, and to me often of few words, but what she lacked in verbal expression she more than made up for where it counted. Mama never judged, she never made me feel as if I was anything less than her adored son. And so, I couldn't help wondering, would I have felt that same love from someone who at least on the surface appeared to be so different?

My eyes continued to roam over the crowd of Saturday afternoon shoppers, a sort of pushcart war unfolding before me, people jockeying for space for their large overstuffed baskets, space for the towering trucks and huge cars that they steered like ships on an uncertain sea. A war of littleness fought by those who clung to things that made them seem bigger than they really were. And among this mass of sameness, I saw a dusty car of no clear color with a rosary and St. Christopher's medal, dangling from the mirror. All manner of tchotchke slid back and forth on the dashboard with each tentative turn of the wheel. The driver was looking intensely as if she, too, were searching for someone, a small woman, pale skin, lightly furrowed like someone had taken a microscopic brush and carefully painted minute lines across her brow, blondish hair with a few random streaks of gray, watery blue eyes that were not unkind.

She clutched the steering wheel, white knuckled, swerving unsteadily to avoid the roiling masses of humanity as if on cue, belched forth periodically from the enormous doors of the shopping mall. When I looked at her again, I knew, and I think that she knew, as she pulled into a parking space stopping the car and then gingerly getting out herself, that each of us was who the other was seeking. She approached me her smock-like dress was covered in a simple pattern of blue and white, a few daisies thrown in around the cuff of the hem of her dress. She was a small woman, as I might've expected, and her eyes were kind and she looked at me with perhaps the same questions in her mind as I'd had. We approached each other wondering who would be the first to speak, then she said, *"Billy?"* and I said, *"It's Joe, remember?"* She said, *"Yes,"* hesitantly, *"Joe."* And I said, *"Sophie..."* and there wasn't anything else to say because that moment held all of the years that I had searched and had found my roots, but without the intensity that had inflamed my brother's odyssey for his own beginnings. And now here she was, the ultimate root—my mother.

We both stood there for a moment, feet of clay sticking to the hot blacktop parking lot. Then something drew us to each other, awkwardly at first, but then with a great force tears began overwhelming us both as we clung together.

CHAPTER

5

End Flashback
Buffalo, New York, Hospital; Present Time

Are you Joseph Steele?" A weary looking doctor with a chart tucked under his arm was standing in front of me. He asked again, this time a little more impatiently. "Excuse me, are you Joseph Steele?"

I realized that he had probably been standing in front of me for a few moments while I had been lost in my own thoughts. "Yes...yes...I am. I'm Joe Steele."

The doctor looked puzzled, saying, "Ms. Legocki listed you as next of kin. She's in intensive care so only next of kin are allowed to see her." His voice trailed off as if waiting for me to fill in the blanks.

"Yes, I am. I am next of kin."

The doctor, still puzzled, studied his chart again. "Well she doesn't have anyone listed here except a son. Is that you?"

I nodded yes. "Sophie Legocki is my mother."

The doctor hesitated. "She wouldn't tell me the name, she just said there was a son. Can you verify that for us? We're required, you know, with HIPAA and all."

"Why don't you just ask her?"

Snapping back, probably due to the lateness of the hour, but more likely impatient from having to spend his time tracing family trees when by rights the 15 minutes that he had been allotted to us by the HMO had probably long since passed. He walked briskly into a room a few feet away. I could see Sophie in the gray iron hospital bed, huddled under the blankets. He leaning over the bed. Sophie's eyes were closed, and she was breathing evenly, but her face was pale, and she looked smaller and more shrunken than I remembered.

He whispered loudly, "Miss Legocki can you hear me?"

Her eyes fluttered and then opened weakly.

"This gentleman here says that he's next of kin. Is that true?"

She turned away.

The doctor persisted. "We can't allow him to see you if he is not next of kin. You gave us his number and asked us to call him, but I need you to verify that he is next of kin since you did not put a name on the chart. So...again, is he your son?"

She hesitated and then nodded yes, but just barely.

Crisply turning back to me, "Well I guess you are then. She is doing better, although when we called we weren't quite sure that she would make it. But she seems to be much improved and I think, in fact, that we'll be able to move her out of intensive care tomorrow."

"That's good news." I didn't know quite what else to say.

"Yes, it is." And with that the doctor left, leaving Sophie and me alone.

Another awkward silence punctuated only by the sound of gurneys being rolled up and down the halls. Finally, she spoke, the color had started to come back in her face and even in the few moments that I had been there she seemed to be better than when I walked in the room.

"I'm glad you could come."

"It's OK. I wanted to."

"Were you far away?"

"It was a bit of a drive, I had just been clear across the state for something else and then when I got your call, I turned back around, otherwise it probably would've been closer."

"What was it...work?"

"Not exactly. It was just.... Well..."

"You don't have to tell me if you don't want to."

"No, no, it's nothing like that, it's just that well, I was at an event for the 92nd Regiment, the Buffalo Soldiers. You know, the black soldiers who fought in World War II." Trying to sound casual but feeling defensive, like she had no right to ask.

"Yes, he told me, he told me he was one of them. He was a Chaplain."

Silence again. I felt uncomfortable, now wondering why I had come.

She started coughing. I grabbed a cup of water, but she waved me away. "No, it's OK, he wants me to know…that's all, he just wants me to know…that I should tell you everything."

"Sophie, what are you talking about? *Who* wants you to tell me? And tell me what?" Secretly, I was starting to wonder if she was delirious.

She bolted straight up with a force that I had never seen, almost as if a greater energy was coming through her, and then she started talking. "I remember the first time that I saw him. I think I noticed him at first because I hadn't really seen a lot of colored people. I know that probably sounds ignorant, but that's the way it was where I lived, we just didn't see a lot of them. He was so confident, so different from what I'd expected."

Flashback Through Sophie's Eyes
Lackawanna, New York, Queen Of All Saints Catholic Church; 1955

The deep rumbling of the pipe organ filled the room so completely that I could barely hear someone whispering in my ear, "Sister Sophie, did you see the new assistant pastor?"

I was in the chapel at late afternoon Mass. Sister Gerta was sitting next to me, and as always, she was talking. She was an only child with much older parents and I used to think that she became a nun so that she'd never be alone. She was very plump, but not fat, and she had large green eyes and smooth pink skin. She was from Baltimore, one of the many things that she babbled about constantly. But today, Sister Gerta had a new topic of conversation, the same one that everyone seemed to be buzzing about, our new assistant pastor.

"So, what do you think of him?"

"I don't know, I really haven't had much of an occasion to speak with him." I had seen him just a few days earlier in the nursery where I spent most of my days working with the young children from the Parish. He came in just for a moment, introduced himself, asked about our work and then left as quickly as he'd come. Something about the way he walked and the way his gaze met yours, very straightforward and steady, made me feel something. I don't know what, but when Sister Gerta mentioned him, I got this funny feeling, almost a light-headedness, nothing I'd ever sensed before.

Sister Gerta cupped her hand over her mouth, presumably so that she could continue talking without disturbing the others around her. "I hear he was in the War and he was a hero; he got the bronze star." She sat back against the hard bench, "I didn't even know there were any colored soldiers in the War, I guess things have really changed." She whispered conspiratorially, "That's why he speaks all those languages. I hear he knows Italian fluently *and* French and Spanish!" she continued, seemingly unaware that I hadn't responded because, in spite of myself, I couldn't take my eyes off of him. He was walking down the aisle preparing for communion with the two altar boys flanking him at either side. He wasn't tall, but not short. He seemed to be well built, even under the voluminous priest's robes fanning behind him as he walked. He was a light brown color with wavy black hair with a few strands of gray framing his temples as if someone had taken a small brush and painted every hair individually. His eyes were large and seemed to miss nothing. Although his expression was serious, I could tell that he was someone who smiled easily, and he seemed to almost glow with a warmth and a kindness that I don't think that I'd ever seen before.

The men in my family and those I'd met in my home were rough and cold, as if the women around them were nothing more than a necessary inconvenience. I was thinking that as I watched him carefully take the chalice from the table, slowly wiping it with the starched white cloth so that the cup shone brightly, a few glints of sunlight playing off the intricate designs. He put the chalice down on the deep purple altar cloth then poured in a small amount of wine, placing the chalice on the altar, then taking out the small wafers. He broke one in half placing it in his mouth, lowering his eyes, making the sign of the cross, and then offered a wafer to each of the attendants.

Sister Gerta nudged me and I realized that she'd finally stopped chattering, only because it was our turn to approach the altar. I had gotten so caught up in my own thoughts that I didn't even realize that all the other parishioners had gone before us. I followed Sister Gerta quickly up the aisle.

Now standing in front of him, I lowered my eyes and he murmured softly, "The body and the blood of Christ, Amen." I raised my eyes, opened my mouth and he gently placed a wafer on my tongue, and then offered me the brass chalice. I took a small sip; the wine was dry, scratching the sides of my throat. *Why was I blushing?* As I handed the cup back to him, I looked into his eyes. They were a dark, warm brown, with laughter at the edges, and I thought, *"I've never really looked into the eyes of a colored man before."*

CHAPTER

6

he church bells were ringing, filling the air with deep resonant waves of sound, blocking out the few timid birds of winter that still remained. Gray squirrels scurried past us as we walked back to our residence.

"Lovely sermon, wasn't it?" Sister Gerta looped her arm through mine. I nodded, not really thinking about the words as much as the person saying them, but of course I couldn't say that to her. I don't even know why I was thinking those thoughts. I felt as if I almost needed to chastise myself, what had come over me? As those thoughts again danced through my mind, I sat down at the long wooden table, peering out the window. I could see huge drifts of snow starting to pile up. Here, inside it was warm, filled with the soft chatter of the other Sisters at our evening meal. As I took a piece of bread breaking it in half, I couldn't help thinking of earlier that day as a small wafer had been broken in half and placed in my mouth. Those thoughts again. I had to stop them, but they seemed to literally have a mind of their own. I almost laughed at my own joke. How could thoughts have a mind of their own?

But before I could continue my own internal conversation, I felt my shoulder being poked gently. I looked up into the solemn face of Sister Catherine. She and I had both started as young novitiates at the same time and we shared a special relationship because of that.

"Penny for your thoughts," she said, sitting down on the bench facing me.

I blushed slightly, wondering if she could read my mind, but knowing it was nothing but my own paranoia.

She curled her hands around a chipped cup and blew the steam off the top, taking a deep sip of warm tea, "You've been so quiet. Is everything OK?"

Turning away from her, "I'm fine, I guess I'm just a little tired. Some of the children were a handful today, especially the toddlers." I poured myself some tea and took another piece of the crusty bread, slowly spreading the butter around the edges.

She nodded. "I know what you mean." She gazed out at the billowing puffs of snow packed against the window. "I'm really *not* looking forward to shoveling that snow tomorrow morning."

Looking out at the steadily falling flakes of snow, "I don't really mind that much, it's quiet at least."

She laughed. "Yes…I'd say so." Sister Catherine coughed, covering her face which reddened as she coughed again.

"You still have that cold?"

She nodded, coughing again. "Yes, I can't seem to get rid of it."

Chiding her gently, "Well, the last thing you need is to be out shoveling snow. I'll do it for you tomorrow."

"I can't let you do that, it's my turn, you shoveled last week, you don't need to be out there any more than I do."

"Look, you can make it up to me when you're feeling better. I'll do it, I don't mind really."

She smiled, looking relieved, "You're sure?" I took another sip of my tea, "Absolutely, you stay in bed, you could probably use a couple more hours of sleep. I'm fine."

She hugged me, "Thanks, Sister Sophie you're the best!"

CHAPTER

7

turned over, my eyes still closed tightly. I had just heard the five chimes of the church bells and I knew that it was time to get up. I tried to stretch, but I was so cold that I could barely move. Wrapping the blanket around my shoulders, I scurried quickly into the bathroom. My teeth were chattering. and I turned the hot water on hoping that it wouldn't take the usual five minutes to warm up. Thank God, it seemed to be working better than most days. I held my hands under the flow, splashing some water against my face. I had started to wake up a little bit more and I quickly dressed, pulling on my heavy boots, two sweaters over my habit and my coat and scarf.

My stomach was starting to growl and I almost wished that I taken a few of those pieces of bread back up to my room, even though you weren't supposed to, it would've tasted pretty good about now. The massive wooden door creaked loudly, and I had to use all of my weight to push it open. The shovels were leaning up against the shed next to the building. and as I trudged through the piles of snow, I looked up into the night sky. You'd never know how near dawn was, the sky was like a cool sleek piece of black steel with a few lingering stars. The wind was icy and cut through my thin scarf, but I knew that I had to get the path completely shoveled before the early morning Mass.

Even though I was well into my thirties, I was one of the younger nuns, and our job was to make sure that the older nuns didn't slip and fall on the tortuous path from our residence to the chapel. I bent down, remembering the routine from my childhood in Buffalo, shovel down, scoop hard, throw behind you, then shovel down again, scoop hard, throw behind you. I was starting to get the rhythm. I was the only girl with three younger brothers and during the long winters, as far back as I could remember, we all shoveled snow. We used to take turns trying to figure out different ways to make it more interesting and it was my oldest brother who thought of the idea of putting it to music. He turned on the radio in the living room, opened the kitchen window, turning the radio up as loud as it would go. Then we'd try and shovel the snow to the beat of the music. It made the otherwise tedious task go a little faster, that is until my dad decided he didn't want that cold breeze filling up the house, and as he used to say, "wasting good money and raising the heating bill." So, he turned off the radio, slammed the window shut, mumbling the whole time as he grabbed a beer, sat down in the worn easy chair and put up his feet. But it didn't matter that much, we'd had the music just long enough to be able to hum the tunes to ourselves, so we'd do the little routine that we'd made up: shovel down, scoop hard, throw behind your back.

"That's a lot of snow to shovel, would you like some help?"

I looked up, startled to hear someone behind me. I couldn't imagine anybody else up at this hour, and as I whirled around putting the shovel in the ground, I came face-to-face with the assistant pastor. I think that I blushed in spite of myself and thank God the scarf covered my face, so he couldn't see my scarlet cheeks.

"I believe we met briefly in the Nursery…you're Sister…"

I could barely get the words out. "I'm…I'm Sister Sophie."

He held out his gloved hand, "I'm Father Grau, very nice to make your acquaintance, Sister Sophie."

I wasn't quite sure what to do. I almost felt like I should curtsy, but instead I just lowered my eyes, afraid that I'd say something stupid. He walked around looking at the drifts of snow. "That's an awful lot of snow for one person to shovel, are you sure that I can't help you?"

I blushed again. "Well, yes, that would be fine, thank you. I would like some help."

He smiled again, "Is there another shovel?"

"Oh yes, in the shed, I'll get it." I almost tripped over myself as I plowed through the snow, anxious to get the shovel before he thought better of his offer and changed his mind.

He smiled again as I handed him the shovel. "You seem to have quite a system. I'm impressed." He pointed to the path that I'd halfway cleared.

"I guess I'm used to it, I grew up in Buffalo and back home this kind of snow is nothing."

He dug his shovel in the snow, expertly picking up a large scoop. "I know, I grew up in Cleveland and we definitely have our share, too."

For a moment there was an awkward silence, then without stopping shoveling, he said, "So, Sister Sophie, how long have you been here?"

Feeling a little self-conscious, I answered quickly, "For a while, it's been my home for a long time now."

He smiled at me, and I relaxed, at least a little, maybe it was the way he leaned against his shovel or the way he shook the snow off his scarf, so nonchalantly, I felt a warmth and an ease with him. He leaned down, picking up another large scoop of snow, "Then you're an old-timer compared to me."

Not sure what else to say, I blurted out, "Do you like it here?"

Seeming not to notice me stumbling over my words, he replied without missing a beat, "I do. I like that it's calm and quiet. And the parishioners seem like good people. I feel as if I can make a difference here."

Intrigued, I asked, "Were you somewhere before here? I mean, of course you were somewhere, what I meant was were you at a different parsonage?"

Perhaps sensing that I was uncomfortable, he almost reflexively put his hand on my shoulder and again I sensed that electricity, something that I had never felt before. It had to be because he was a man of God, and so it must've been our Savior's presence flowing through him. Yes, that was it. I felt better now that I had figured it out on my own.

He continued, with no idea of my internal debate. "Yes, but before that I was in the War. I went overseas and now I'm back here."

"It must be very quiet compared to the War."

"Yes, I would say so." He continued to shovel as did I, neither of us saying much for the next 15 or 20 minutes. And when the bells chimed six, I couldn't believe that it had been almost an hour that we'd been there.

Glancing quickly at his watch, he said, "Well Sister Sophie, I have to go, but I hope that I've been able to be of some assistance to you, perhaps

I can help again sometime."

Smiling, trying not to blush, I responded quickly, "That would be nice. I'd...appreciate that. Thank you."

He turned to walk away and then quickly turned back. "I will see you at Mass, Sister Sophie."

I couldn't help but smile, "Yes, Father. I will see you at Mass."

CHAPTER

8

Very good job, Sister Sophie." I looked up and saw Mother Superior standing over me. She was a stern woman, very tall and thin with watery gray eyes. Her face was wrinkled and her hands seemed to be perpetually fidgeting with something whether it was a rosary or the giant cross that dangled from her neck. But she was not unkind at all and like now, she always made time for a few words of encouragement.

Smiling in spite of myself, really more because of the memory of that magical hour that I'd spent, but she, of course, wouldn't know that. "Thank you, Mother Superior."

"I understand that Sister Catherine wasn't feeling well and that you very generously shoveled the snow this morning in her place."

"Yes, Mother Superior." Something in her tone, the way that the words hung in the air as if expecting me to fill in the rest, made me wonder if she'd seen me speaking to Father Grau. But she continued, not so much directly to me, as her eyes wandered around the room.

"That type of selflessness is what we teach here, and I'm encouraged, Sister Sophie, that you are living it rather than just talking about it. So very good job."

I could barely mumble a weak thank you, relieved that my fears were unfounded. "It wasn't a problem for me Mother Superior. I didn't mind at all."

But she had already moved across the room as she often did, parachuting in on the unsuspecting Sisters who might have fallen behind on some chores or failed to complete an activity with the precision required by Mother Superior. As my eyes followed her, I thought that she doesn't even seem to walk, it's almost as if she glided across the floor with the long black habit trailing behind her and with the rosary twirled around her hands.

Breathing a sigh of relief, I picked up the rag that I'd been using to polish the large offering plate. Dipping my cloth into the pungent smelling soft silver polish, I rubbed it carefully around the ornate edges, flecking away the granules of soot that were burrowed in the crevices. Today was the day that I polished the silver. Every day was a different type of service either to the Parish or the community. But it was the quiet days like this when I could reflect on the words of our Savior and think how he had worked as a simple carpenter, but yet from those modest beginnings had changed the world. It made me think that there was truly a plan for all of us; no matter where we started, there was a path, a road that had been chosen for us by our God. It gave me a sense of purpose and that every job that I did mattered, regardless of how seemingly insignificant. I had learned that when I was a novitiate. They taught us to take pride in our work and to know that what we did was truly God's work, and that it was His will that we were here at this point in time.

It was in the early days that I learned the routine that had defined my life since I first made the choice to hear God's calling. So, I moved from the silver to the brass ornaments used for some of the many rituals, all of the holidays of the Holy Saints each having their own different types of symbols. I enjoyed turning the brass from a dull brown to a glistening bronze; it made me feel as if I was transforming something as God transforms us all. I smiled to myself, remembering back to my novitiate years—the first time that I'd entered the convent as a 14-year-old.

The quiet of the convent was such a change from my home that had been filled with constant noise, a byproduct of having three brothers. But me being the oldest, it seemed as if I was always changing a diaper or making a meal or sweeping and cleaning, with never a moment to myself. And then Mother and Dad started taking in the boarders, the men from Poland who didn't even speak English and came to work in the factory. The eyes that followed me down the small narrow hallway. I shuddered thinking about the hands that brushed a little too close and the day that I decided that I wanted another life for myself.

The clock was ticking in the kitchen, I pulled a wooden chair up to the square chipped red metal table. Mother was at the stove, where she always seemed to be stirring something, usually like today, a huge pot overflowing with potatoes and carrots and a few small pieces of tough, chewy beef swimming in the brown liquid.

I wasn't sure how to start, so I cleared my throat and then just blurted out, "I think I want to go to the Convent."

She didn't hear me, there was too much noise from my brothers shouting and shoving and grabbing toys from each other. So, I said it again, this time a little more forcefully. "I think I want to go to the Convent."

Mother turned around quickly, one brow arched. They said I looked like her, although I didn't really see it. Maybe before the children and the life of always scraping and scrimping, of never having quite enough, more than in Poland, but still not enough. Maybe before all of this she did look like me, but not now, her hair had turned gray, her skin was marked with deep lines, her right shoulder sagged a bit and her brown eyes drooped.

"What did you say again?" She held the wooden spoon up and a few droplets of juice dripped over the side falling on the stove, sizzling.

I knew that it was now or never, "I said that I want to be a nun."

"Why would you want to do that?" She leaned against the ice box eyeing me suspiciously as if I was hiding something. Ever since I was 12, Mother had told me that now that I was a "woman" as she put it, I had to be careful of the boys, careful to always act like a lady or end up like the young girls on the other side of town, the ones who came out at night with the sad eyes and empty smiles.

I didn't say, *"Because I want to escape this life. Because I don't want to end up like you. Because I wanted to do something other than raise my brothers, because I want to escape the lingering looks of old men with bad breath and hands that roamed a little too close to me."* But I didn't say any of that. Instead, I said, "Because I think that that's what God wants me to do."

My mother snorted, "How do you know what God wants you to do? You don't even know what you're giving, up, a husband, a family. You can't make that decision at 14!"

Very firmly, determined not to be swayed, I said calmly and in that way that mother knew that I would not budge. "I just know."

And now, more than 20 years later, I'm here polishing the brass ornaments smiling to myself, thinking of the relief when I closed the door behind me on that little crooked house on a narrow street with the parents who yelled too loudly and drank a little too much on the weekends, and the neighborhood where the boys went to war and mainly didn't come back. But that wasn't my life now. My world is serene and quiet, working in the nursery and doing my chores at the Convent. I felt like I had a purpose.

Knowing as I did then, that I'd made the right choice, that I wouldn't miss the things that I could no longer have. No, I wouldn't miss it. Any regrets that I may have had, I pushed away years ago. Then why am I feeling something different than the calm and peace that have defined my life for so long? All because a colored priest had come to the Parish. Maybe it was the novelty, never having seen many of them and only from afar. But I knew that it was more than that. I just didn't know what.

CHAPTER

9

Sister Catherine came behind me squeezing my shoulders and whispering, "Thanks, again, Sister Sophie. I'm feeling a lot better now."

I don't know why, but I felt a sudden sense of panic, my words tumbling out haphazardly, "I'm glad you're better, but..." And I wasn't sure yet what I'd say...I thought quickly. "I was thinking, you know, I *really* like shoveling snow, it uh...reminds me of when I was a child in Buffalo. And you know, really, I just love it."

Sister Catherine looked at me incredulously, "You're kidding, right?"

"No, I'm serious. I don't mind at all."

"I can't let you do that. It's not fair. I don't care what you say, Sister Sophie, you're just being too kind. I'd feel like I was taking advantage of you." She nodded her head firmly.

I knew that she wasn't changing her mind, so I don't know what made me say this, but I jumped in quickly, "I have an idea, why don't you do something for me that I just can't stand, like um...like um...mopping? I hate mopping. But I love shoveling snow." I was hoping that she wasn't sensing the desperation in my voice.

But instead she just hugged me and said, "Deal. I'll mop and you shovel."

The next morning when the bells chimed five, I almost jumped out of the bed, this time without any hesitation at all. The little voice in my head was telling me that I was foolish. *"I mean just because he offered to help again didn't mean that he was serious. I mean, after all, he was the assistant pastor; he had better things to do than shovel snow."* So I tried to calm the voices in my head, I tried to stop my heart from turning over and doing somersaults, but they all seemed to have a mind of their own. It was colder than the day before and my breath almost froze as I blew it out. The snow was packed hard from a late afternoon dusting and then there was black ice on top of it. It was so slippery that I had to walk carefully not to fall. I clutched the shovel, using it to steady myself, and then began slowly cracking the hard layer of ice in order to get below to the soft layer of snow. I couldn't help wondering if he'd come or if it was just my own foolishness. The hour passed, and a deep sense of disappointment had started to settle in. The excitement that I'd felt now dulled and the work seemed to be just back-breaking drudgery.

The clock chimed 5:30, then 5:45. I knew that I had to wrap up in five minutes; the older nuns would be coming out soon. I'd managed to clear the path and picked my way back through the drifts to the shed, leaning the shovel against the wall.

"Sorry I was late."

I almost stumbled, catching myself as I saw Father Grau coming up the path quickly. I smiled in spite of myself.

"I am a man of my word, Sister, and I said that I would help you with the shoveling. Will you be here tomorrow?"

I could barely get the words out, but yes, he was here standing in front of me with that smile that made his eyes crinkle up in the corners and I said, "Yes, yes Father, I will be here every day."

He smiled again, "Then know that you'll have my assistance. You have my word."

Buffalo, New York, Hospital; Present Time

The door opened and the nurse walked in briskly. "Well, Miss Legocki, you're looking well. The color has come back to your cheeks. I guess having a special visitor makes a difference."

I felt annoyed, like the nurse had stopped the flow, like when you're just getting to the good part of a movie and a commercial cuts in. But I restrained myself, saying only, "Yes, she does look a lot better."

"Well, they'll be bringing your dinner in about 15 minutes, so I just wanted to check up on you."

Sophie was beaming, it was almost as if remembering that other time was rejuvenating her and that as she was transported back to her much younger self.

As soon as the nurse closed the door, I quickly picked up the thread wanting Sophie to continue. "So, what happened, how long did he help you shovel snow?"

Settling back into the pillows, "Oh, every day that winter, just like he said he would. We learned a lot about each other during that time."

"Tell me about it, don't stop now!"

She laughed for the first time in a long time. "OK." Leaning forward and twirling a small piece of the blanket around her finger aimlessly, "We started really talking a lot about each other and who we were, where we'd been. And we went from shoveling snow to walks around the Rectory."

"Did anybody ever say anything? I mean, did people notice that you seemed to be spending time together?"

"Oh no, it wasn't that obvious, there was always a good reason. Father Grau wasn't like the other older Pastor, he made it a part of his routine to get feedback from all of the nuns on how things could be improved, things like what we thought the parishioners needed. So, he spent time with all of us, talking to everyone, always trying to make things better. Trying to make little improvements, he was very serious about his job and always wanted to do more. He was so different from everyone else, he really cared."

She closed her eyes as if seeing something else, a time past. "I remember this one day when he came by the nursery. It's when I really started to learn more about him as a person."

Flashback Through Sophie's Eyes
Queen Of All Saints Catholic Church, Parish Nursery; 1955

"Maria, sit down, no, not there, in your chair over there. C'mon." I took Maria's small hand in mine and guided her to the tiny red chair around the table.

"Yeth, Thister Thopie." She sat down obediently and picked up a doll and started combing her hair.

I sighed, thinking, *"Girls are so different than boys."* If I'd asked one of my brothers to sit down at that age, they probably would've taken the chair and tried to throw it across the room like a ball. As if God had somehow heard my thoughts, I felt something hit me on my shoulder; a headless raggedy Anne doll had clipped me. Whirling around, I heard a small voice snickering.

"Sorry! I was trying to get Johnny and missed him."

"Ok, Timmy, in the corner. Now."

"Aw, c'mon, Sister Sophie, it was an accident."

"I'm sure. Now, in the corner."

The door opened, and Father Grau walked in, he was immediately engulfed by the small children running to him. He smiled at the children and as he did, I couldn't help feeling this warm glow as if he was smiling at me also. In fact, his eyes met mine and for a moment lingered, then he turned away quickly as if suddenly afraid. One small child tugged at his long coat, "Will you help me? I broke my truck." The child handed him a sturdy yellow steel truck and the wheel that had broken off. Father Grau kneeled down so that he was facing the small boy at eye level. He turned the truck over in his hand looking carefully at the wheel. He picked up the pin that had fallen off the truck and then expertly screwed it back in the hole re-attaching the wheel. The boy beamed as he took the truck. He immediately dropped to the floor and pushed it around the room.

I stood over the boy, "Now what do you say to Father Grau?"

He jumped up obediently, running over to Father Grau, "Thank you, Father."

"You're very welcome, now be careful don't push it too hard, or it will break off again."

But the boy had whizzed off to the other side of the nursery spinning the truck around in circles on the floor.

As Father Grau turned to me, I felt suddenly tongue tied, "Thank you, Father. I'm afraid I'm not very good with putting things together, so when something breaks around here, it usually just stays broken." I laughed awkwardly, not quite sure what else to say.

For a moment, we stood there a few feet from each other, neither saying anything. Then he cleared his throat as if he was about to say something. He looked as if he was about to leave, so I said quickly, "Would you like some tea?"

Hesitating, and then glancing at his watch, he said suddenly in a very formal tone, "Yes, thank you, Sister." Smiling shyly, I quickly plugged in the hot plate that I kept high above in a top shelf, far from where the children could reach it and then grabbing the blue china tea pot, I filled it with water. Neither of us said anything, the only sound being the soft gurgling of the boiling liquid. I carefully poured the water into a cup, taking out a teabag and placing it in the cup, then offering it to him. "Would you like sugar?"

"Yes, thank you."

"One teaspoon?"

"Two, I have a bit of a sweet tooth." He smiled as he took a small sip. "Perfect. Just the way I like it."

"Thank you."

As I handed him the cup, he nodded thank you, but his eyes seemed to be somewhere else. He was looking at a small tin soldier lying on a pile of toys, then almost as if to himself, he said, "I had a soldier exactly like that." He smiled, continuing, "My father gave me one almost exactly like that. It's funny what you remember."

And then as he spoke, it was as if I saw his words come alive in front of me.

Flashback Through Father Grau's Eyes
Cleveland, Ohio, Downtown; Age 4, 1909

The sun is so bright and I'm holding Mama's hand really tight. It's summer and I just had my birthday, I'm four years old now. Mama said there's somebody who wants to meet me and give me a birthday present.

Mama was walking really fast, like we had to get someplace important. "C'mon now, Billy, hurry up, we're almost there."

I nodded to Mama and I was trying to keep up, but there was so much to see that I kept slowing down—horses that were pulling noisy carts filled with lots of big boxes, and ladies in long skirts holding them up just above their ankles, so I could see their shiny black shoes with buttons and the men with the push carts that had candy and lots of sweets to buy.

"Oh, Mama, can I have a piece of candy? See over there!" And I pointed to the cart that was overflowing with pink and yellow sticky candies, the kind Mama would sometimes buy for me when I'd been a good boy.

"Not today, Billy…c'mon we've got to hurry."

"Aw, Mama, pleeaaasseee!"

Mama just held my hand a little tighter and pushed through the crowds of people. Then she waved at someone and I saw who she was looking at. A man who had brown skin like me, and his eyes followed us across the street as Mama picked me up carrying me over a puddle of mud so I wouldn't jump in it, which was one of my most favorite things to do. We stopped in front of the man and Mama pushed me gently towards him. The man was taller than Mama, but maybe not as tall as Papa, and he had a round face and a mustache and black crinkly hair. She turned to the brown man and smiled, "This is Billy."

Then she leaned down so that she was looking me in the eye, "Billy, this is your other Papa."

I looked up at the man and then at Mama, not quite understanding, "My other Papa?"

Mama just nodded, and the brown man held out his hand to me.

"You certainly are a fine looking young man."

I held Mama's hand a little tighter and I didn't know what to say, except, "My other Papa?"

Mama said firmly, "Yes, Billy, God has given you two Papas, because you're such a special boy."

I looked the man up and down, noticing his shoes that had a little dirt in the corners and his kinda faded blue shirt, "Oh. And he's a brown man."

The man threw back his head and laughed, "Yes, I am. And I've brought you this for your birthday, Billy." He held out something funny looking wrapped in newspaper. "Go ahead, open it."

I tore open the newspaper and saw a tin soldier, just like the kind

I told Mama that I wanted for my birthday! I smiled and immediately dropped to the ground, standing it up for battle.

Mama pulled me up gently, "Now what do you say?"

Suddenly not feeling like I wanted to say anything, but I did 'cause I knew Mama wanted me to, "Thank you, Mr. Brown Man."

End Flashback
Queen Of All Saints Catholic Church, Parish Nursery; 1955

Father Grau stopped abruptly as if the memory had suddenly faded, and then without really looking at me, he continued, barely above a whisper, "That was my actual...father. I didn't understand it at the time, but years later when I asked my mother about it and why she had me meet him, she just said that she wanted me to know who he was. And I'm glad I did."

I played with the spoon in my cup, not quite sure what to say.

He ran his finger around the side of his saucer, looking out the window at the falling snow. "I only saw him one other time, for my birthday again, when I was 7, but then not anymore."

There was an awkward silence, then I blurted out awkwardly, "Did you have a big family?"

He seemed to shake himself back to the present. "Sort of. My mother never married my actual father. But she did marry my stepfather a few months before I was born. Even though I was obviously not his, he raised me as one of his own. He was a German immigrant who came here when he was a teenager. My mother was Irish, born in Cork."

For a moment there was an awkward silence between us, then he began again. "So, I never really felt like I was part of my family, although my stepdad did the best that he could. But sometimes it still felt like it was me and my mother and the rest of them."

As he continued speaking it was as if I, again, I could see his early life unfolding before me just as he had lived it so many years before.

CHAPTER

10

Flashback Through Father Grau's Eyes
Cleveland, Ohio; Age 10, 1915

hate him, I hate him." I was trying to wash the tears away, but they kept coming down. I lay my head on Mama's shoulder; I didn't want to cry. Big boys don't cry, but it hurts so much from where he'd socked me. Mama rocked me back and forth like I was a baby, not 10 years old. I wasn't a baby anymore, but sometimes I felt like one. The kids in the neighborhood would make fun of me and call me names and I got tired of it, so I decided I'd fight back, but then they ganged up on me. And one of the really big boys socked me and then pushed me down hard on the ground and I fell in the dirt, my face was still stinging, and I didn't want to cry. I really, really tried not to cry because big boys don't cry. But I couldn't help it, the dirt was stinging my eyes, and my face was sore and red, and everybody was laughing at me and I don't know what hurt more, the bruise on my face or the way they laughed at me.

So, I ran home to Mama and didn't even have to say anything. It's like she already knew, so she just rocked me back and forth saying, *"It's OK, Billy, it's OK, it won't happen no more."* And that night, boy, did I hear Mama yellin' at Papa. I could hear her through the bedroom door telling him, *"If you let any of those hoodlums touch one hair on my boy's head again, you'll have hell to pay, so you better tell 'em to leave him alone because if you don't, **I will**, and I know you don't want people thinking that you don't have the guts to tell 'em and that you gotta get a woman to do a man's job!!!"*

And then the door slammed, and I heard Mama coming downstairs. sitting in the rocking chair, rocking back and forth, back and forth like she always did when she was mad, and trying to calm herself down. Then a few minutes later I heard heavy footsteps...Papa's...couldn't really hear what he was saying other than whispering and I guess he was trying to make up with Mama 'cause after a little while the chair stopped rocking and I heard them both walking upstairs. But I slept good that night because I knew that Mama had taken care of it like she always did.

CHAPTER

11

Continued Flashback Through Father Grau's Eyes
Cleveland, Ohio; Age 17, 1922

I was thinking about that as I walked down the street, thinking back how I felt when I was 10 years old. Now I'm 17, all the other kids have plans to work in factories or other similar types of jobs, but not me. I don't know what I wanted, but I knew what I didn't want, and I didn't want that life. I didn't want to be like Papa and all his friends, working in a factory all week, getting drunk Friday nights, coming home sleeping it off, and then doing the same thing the next week and the next week after that until they were like the old men that sat on the stoop, their whole life over and nothing to show for it. I didn't want that life and Mama knew it wasn't for me. She knew I was different, not just 'cause I was colored and they were all white, but I was different because I wanted more. I wanted to live the life that I read about in those books in the library on the Saturday afternoons when the rest of the kids were out playing stickball. I was reading about places that I wanted to go to, places in Europe, places all over the world so far away from Cleveland.

Mama knew that probably more than anybody else in the world 'cause Mama knew me and knew what I needed and what I wanted. So, a couple of days ago, she asked me to sit down and she took my hand in hers, almost like she used to do when I was a kid, but I wasn't a kid anymore, I was 17. She looked at me and Mama had such loving eyes, they were pale blue and her hair that used to be bright red was streaked with gray, her pale skin had fine lines crisscrossing from the corners of her eyes to her cheeks, but to me, she was the most beautiful woman in the world. I always knew Mama loved me and even when I felt the most alone, I always knew she was there for me.

"Billy, I been thinking…"

"What you been thinking about, Mama?"

"Been thinking about your future and what might be best for you."

I didn't say anything. I just listened.

She continued, "And I was talking to Father Mulvaney over at the church and we was talking about how you like to read and how good you are in school and how I didn't really think you want a life like the rest of them and he said to me, well had you thought about the priesthood and I said no I don't know if he has, but I'd sure be mighty proud if my son was a priest."

The room got real quiet. All I could hear was the noise outside in the street. The day was bright and sunny, it was summer and the kids were outside running around, yelling back and forth at each other. I could hear all these street noises, but I wasn't thinking about any of that. I was thinking about what Mama had just said. I knew Father Mulvaney, he'd always been nice to me from back when I went to the Catholic elementary school. After I left that school and went to the Catholic high school, I'd see Father Mulvaney on most Sundays when Mama and me went to church and he'd give the sacraments. And I remember every time I walked in the church I felt this sense of peace and calm. Because my house was anything but peaceful and calm, with all my brothers and sisters and everybody always loud and arguing and yelling and screaming at each other. Sometimes I just wanted to get away someplace where it was quiet, and that's what the church was like for me. It was like a place I could escape to, from all the confusion in my house. And so, I got to looking forward to Sundays, to sitting there on the hard benches and smelling the incense and looking at the sunlight playing against the pretty colors in the stained glass windows and just having a chance to hear inside my own head without somebody yelling at me, or poking at me, or telling me to do something, or telling me to shut up.

I thought back on some of my days in the local Catholic school and remembered one time in particular that I know made me realize that maybe I could do something other than work in a factory like Papa. I think I was about 12…

Flashback Through Father Grau's Eyes
Cleveland, Ohio; Age 12, 1917

I was just about to get to the good part when I heard running behind me. Instinctively, I quickly shut the book that I'd been practically devouring, trying to shove it in my jacket away from the prying eyes.

"Will you look at 'em!! Always with ya nose in a book, yeah, that's cause he's a loser, whatcha readin' this time, huh, loser?!" Mack, whose pale face was covered with red freckles, tried to knock the book out of my hand, but I clutched it tightly, years of fighting with my brothers and their friends made me bold. I stood up in his face and then shoved him back hard. "Leave me alone!"

Another boy, Johnny McGill, snickered, "So the loser thinks he can fight, where'd you learn that move, in some damn book?!" The other boys laughed, pointing at me. "Go ahead, Mack, you gonna let'em push you like that?"

"Fight! Fight! Fight!" The three other boys surrounded us, and Mack, somewhat reluctantly, put up his fists swinging at me, I ducked and then landed a hard one right in his face. His nose started bleeding, and he was now swinging unsteadily, I was about to sock him again when I heard a deep voice behind me.

"William Grau. I can't believe what I'm seeing."

Father Mulvaney stood behind me disapprovingly.

I knew I'd really messed up now, and with Father Mulvaney, of all people, the one person who always seemed to be in my corner, I guess I'd lost my only friend at the school now.

Father Mulvaney shook his head sternly, "Come to my office, we need to talk, and the rest of you, to Confession. Now."

Sheepishly, I followed Father Mulvaney to his office. He sat behind his humongous wooden desk covered with papers, with a large picture window behind him. I always loved coming here because every inch of the room was covered with books—books on the bookshelves that lined the walls, books in stacks on the floor, each one holding secrets and a passageway to worlds that I could only imagine.

Father Mulvaney's deep Irish brogue interrupted my thoughts, "Now, William, you're not like the other boys, you're serious about your studies, you're the last person I'd expect to see in a fight."

I lowered my eyes, "Yes, Father Mulvaney, you're right. I'm sorry."

"So, what was it about, it's not like you."

"It's just that I get tired of them always making fun of me 'cause I like to read. There's nothing wrong with reading! It gets me away from…"

"That's why you were fighting him? Because he made fun of you reading?"

I nodded, half expecting Father Mulvaney to laugh at me the way the boys had, but instead, he leaned forward intensely, almost whispering, "Well, William Grau, I say the next time one of them makes fun of you 'cause you're reading, you give 'em an extra punch for me!" And then he laughed heartily, saying, "Anytime you want some peace and quiet, you let me know and you can come here. I got an extra chair over there, you can sit right there and read anytime you want to. And you just keep on reading, let the books inspire you, they inspired me to get out and do something with my life. Everybody in my family had been potato farmers and one thing I hated was potatoes, but I was like you. I loved to read, and the more I read, the more I knew that I could do something else. And so can you…so you just keep on reading." For a moment he was quiet, and all I could hear was the sound of the big clock in the corner. It was like he'd gone somewhere else, at least in his head. Then abruptly, he shook himself back to present time, saying, "Now go on, class is about to start."

I beamed, feeling almost like a co-conspirator, smiling as I left his office holding my book tightly.

End Flashback: Father Grau
Cleveland, Ohio; Age 17, 1922

I thought of that moment five years ago as Mama now put her arm around my shoulder, and I lay my head against hers. We were both quiet and then I said softly, taking her hand in mine, playing with her fingers, "Mama, what do you think that I should do?"

"I think that you do what your heart tells you."

"So how do I do it? Do I just go to Father Mulvaney and tell him?"

She thought for a moment. "I'm not really sure, but we can ask him, and he also mentioned a Bishop Mahoney from Sioux Falls, South Dakota. He's supposed to be a fine man. I think I'll write to him also, maybe he can help us."

CHAPTER

12

Buffalo, New York, Hospital; Present Time

Sophie sat up stiffly in the bed. I could tell that she was getting tired. And even though I knew what Father Grau had ultimately decided, I was riveted, I didn't want her to stop talking. But her hand was starting to shake slightly, this was taking a lot out of her. So, I smoothed the covers under her chin, saying, "I should probably go. I think you've talked enough today…"

"No, no, Joe. No don't. He wants me to tell you more."

I squeezed her hand gently, "Sophie, you've got to get well and you can't if you tire yourself out."

She slumped back against the pillows. "I guess you're right. I am feeling a little weary."

"Don't worry, I'll be back tomorrow."

That night, I called Glenn as I was leaving the hospital. "You're not going to believe what I'm learning, it's unbelievable, more than I could ever have imagined!" I could almost see Glenn smiling. I knew him well enough to know that he had that knowing look that said *I told you so, I told you this was the right thing to do.* So, before he could say anything, I said, "You were right, Glenn, this was definitely the right thing to do."

He chuckled, saying, "Good always happens when you do something good for someone else."

"I guess you're right about that. I came here thinking that I was going to have to sign a bunch of papers and hoping that she'd be OK because the way that doctor sounded on the phone, I wasn't sure if she'd make it." I leaned against my car door remembering everything that Sophie had told me.

Glenn interrupted my thoughts. "So how many more days do you think you'll be up there?"

"I don't know, she's definitely getting better, but I also feel like I'm learning so much that I guess maybe I just want to be a little selfish and not come back as quick as I should. I mean, it's not like I don't have enough work to do that's for sure…but I just don't want to leave yet."

"Look, Joe, you stay there as long as you need to, this is something that you've been wanting to do for a long time ever since you found out about Sophie. This is your chance." He paused a moment, saying reflectively, "You know, sometimes God gives us what we've been looking for, just maybe not the way we thought it would come. So, you go on and stay up there. I'll be fine."

"Thanks, Glenn, love you, man."

"Love you, too, Joe."

I felt restless, I didn't want to go back to my hotel room. I climbed into my car and was about to start it. I wasn't really tired, and then as if once again God heard my prayers, my phone rang. I looked down and couldn't believe it—it was my brother, Billy. Although we were close, I hadn't spoken to him in a while, and he was the last person that I was expecting to hear from.

"Hey, Billy!"

"Yo, little brother, what's up?"

"You're not gonna believe what's been going on..."

"Try me. I pretty much believe anything these days."

"Well, you remember me telling you about Sophie..."

"Yep."

"Well, she got really sick and had listed me as next of kin, so the doctor called to tell me that she was in intensive care at a hospital in Buffalo. He asked me if I would come because they weren't sure that she was going to make it. Turns out she did and, in fact, she's a lot better now. But the weird thing is that all of a sudden she started telling me everything about her and, in particular, about him."

"You mean your birth father?"

"Yeah...and what's weirder is that she keeps saying that he wants me to know."

"Damn, that's some deep shit...But hey, you got the right to know, and however it happens, if homegirl thinks he's talking through her...or whatever...just take notes." He laughed, but it was tinged with sadness, "You need to know, Joe, I've been telling you that for as long as I can remember, it's you. It's a part of you and who you are. So, she's right, or he's right, don't much matter, the end result's the same... you need to know!"

"I know...I just...Well..."

"Look, there's no reason to feel guilty because you want to know who you are, it doesn't mean that you didn't love Mama or Daddy, but there's a part of you that you need to know about and it's damn good that you're finally finding out."

I couldn't help but laugh. "Why did I know that was going to be your reaction?!"

"Boy! Because I been telling you to go out and find out for God knows how long."

"Well it's happening now."

"I'm happy for you, man...real happy."

"Thanks, Billy."

CHAPTER

13

You're back!" Sophie smiled brightly as I walked in the room. Her cheeks had more color than they had in days and she was starting to look more like her old self. "I told you I'd be coming back today." I handed her a small vase of daisies. "I brought you these, thought it would brighten things up here."

Sophie smiled, taking the vase of daisies and putting it on the table next to her bed, "Thank you. I love daisies!" She patted the bed, motioning for me to sit down next to her, whispering conspiratorially, "He's got a lot more that he wants me to tell you."

I smiled in spite of myself, feeling this little thrill that, layer by layer, I was uncovering a part of me that I had never known existed.

"So, where were we?" She leaned back as if she was about to thumb through an imaginary file.

"Well, I think it's where he'd decided to become a priest and study at the Seminary."

"Right, right. He told me how hard it was for him because of…well, because he was colored."

Flashback Through Sophie's Eyes
Queen Of All Saints Catholic Church, Parish Nursery; 1955

Anna, one of the infants, had awakened from her nap interrupting Father Grau as he told me about his childhood. I almost resented her plaintiff wail and then quickly chided myself, she has the right to wake up, but I didn't want Father Grau to stop talking, so I quickly picked her up, massaging her back gently until she fell back asleep. Some of the other children had also started to stir, but I managed to get them all back to sleep. Father Grau had been observing silently as I'd finally calmed the last of the little ones.

"You're good with the children. You seem to have a gift."

I blushed, not sure quite what to say. "I guess I had a lot of practice helping out with my younger brothers."

He cleared his throat as if preparing to leave.

The little voice in my head chided me again *"Sophie, you're so stupid, you couldn't think of anything else to say…He gave you a compliment! Do something…you don't want him to leave!"*

Glancing out the window and noticing the snow starting to fall again, I thought quickly. "Would you, um…like some more tea, Father? Now that the children are down you can actually enjoy it." *That didn't exactly come out like I'd planned, but it was all I could think of.*

He hesitated, then said somewhat formally, "Well, yes, Sister Sophie, a little more tea would be nice."

One of the children whimpered in his sleep, but other than that, the only noise was the sound of the snow falling on the trees.

He walked over to the window. "It's very nice here. It's serene. Sometimes on days like this I think about Italy, don't know why, it was very different, but I think it's the quiet, it has an almost sacred quality. Like there."

"What was it like…in Italy?"

"Depends on what part you're talking about. I studied at the Vatican, but then I was also there during the War and it was very different then."

"You studied at the Vatican?!"

"Yes, that's where I was ordained."

"Oh my Lord, how wonderful, what a blessing to have been there in that holy place. It must have been hard to get in. I mean, not just anybody can study at the Vatican!"

"You're right about that." He hesitated as if about to say something and then he stopped himself, changing his mind.

"You must really have had a vision to think about being there, so far from your home."

He laughed, almost bitterly. "Well to be honest, I didn't have much of a choice."

"What do you mean?"

He took another sip of his tea then setting the cup down on the table. "Let's just say that the Seminaries here weren't exactly rushing to accept me. I really have my mother to thank because there were times when I felt like I'd never realize my dream of being a priest. But she kept believing in me. She never gave up."

And suddenly his words seemed to come alive, with images playing out in front of me.

Flashback Through Father Grau's Eyes
Cleveland, Ohio; Age 24, 1929

I wondered if I'd spend the rest of my life looking out this window with the streak of dirt from the street car that sprayed mud across the glass on those cold damp spring days. The sky was the color of my lead pencil, and the dark gray matched my mood as I thought back over the last year, disappointment after disappointment. Every day hoping that I'd get a little good news, but instead just rejection after rejection. It seemed like forever that I'd been trying to get into a Seminary, any Seminary. I couldn't help remembering the brief time that I spent at the Our Lady of the Lake Seminary here in Cleveland until, barely a year later, they'd dismissed me, supposedly because they feared for my life because of *supposed conditions that made it inadvisable to adopt a colored student.* So here I was again, hoping that somebody would give me a chance, but every time I thought that maybe this time it would be different, it was just another NO. I'd passed all the examinations with no problem, and yet they rejected me again and again solely because of the color of my skin. Some of the Seminaries were bold enough to admit that it was because I was colored, others pretended that there were other reasons. I remembered thinking bitterly to myself, *"Sure, you're concerned about my safety. Right."* I got madder and madder just thinking about it, the hypocrisy of it all! Here we were all supposed to be God's children, if that was truly the case, then I should have been accepted a long time ago. God was colorblind, the Bible said that Jesus loved all of His children equally, so why not me? What had I done to be rejected like this other than be born a colored man in a white world?

"Billy."

I turned, seeing my mother leaning against the door. I had been so caught up in my own thoughts that I hadn't heard her walk in the room.

"Are you OK, Billy?"

I shrugged, looking down at the worn floor and my even more worn shoes. "Guess so. Just another day, huh?"

She put her arm around my shoulder, smiling hesitantly. "Well, maybe not..."

"Whatdya mean?"

She sat on the couch and motioned for me to sit next to her. "Remember the Bishop that I mentioned from Sioux Falls, South Dakota? Bishop Mahoney?"

"Yeah...so."?"

"Well, I finally heard from him and he said—" She stopped as if not quite sure how to say it. "He said that he was going to sponsor you to study....in Rome...at the Vatican."

I looked at her, not quite believing what I was hearing. "Rome? As in Italy?" She smiled. "That's the only Rome I know about."

For a moment I got really excited, then the impossibility of what she was suggesting started to sink in. "Oh, come on Mama, if they wouldn't let me study here in the States, I'll never get in there. I mean, the Vatican! Why would they want a colored man...nobody else does." And then I turned away, trying to fight back a tear, after all, I was grown and much too old to cry, but I was so tired of hearing no. I just couldn't stand one more rejection.

As if sensing my thoughts, Mama drew me closer to her tousling my hair and kissing me on my forehead like she did when I was a small child. "Now you listen to me, Billy, you don't go thinkin' that way. You're as good as any of 'em, you're smarter and better than any of 'em and they'll be lucky to have you. So, I don't want to hear no more of that talk from you." She turned her face to mine, "You're gonna get in, you're gonna be a priest and you're gonna do big things with your life. God has a plan for you, so you gotta help Him by believing. You hear me, you gotta just keep believin' and it's gonna happen for you."

"You really think so?" I felt a little ashamed that I'd let myself get so low, and just like always, Mama was able to lift my spirits.

"I know so, Billy. I know so."

Flashback Through Sophie's Eyes
Queen Of All Saints Catholic Church, Parish Nursery; Continued, 1955

One of the children yawned noisily. I rushed over to him trying to get him back to sleep, not wanting to interrupt Father Grau again. "Shh, Noah, back to sleep….still nap time."

Luckily Noah fell back into a fitful sleep and, once again, it was just the two of us.

I poured more tea in his cup.

He nodded. "Thank you, Sister."

I nodded leaning back in my chair.

"You have such an extraordinary life, Father. It's so humbling to hear what you've been through to be a messenger of our Lord. It is truly an honor for me to know these things."

Now it was his turn to blush. "Now Sister, I'm not a Saint, just a simple priest trying to serve our Father in the best way that I can."

"But you've done so much—studying at the Vatican. I can't even imagine what it must have been like. What was it like the first day when you got there?"

He put the cup down staring out the window. "It was probably one of the happiest days of my life. I almost didn't believe it was true."

And as he spoke, I saw his life again through his words.

Flashback Through Father Grau's Eyes
Rome, Italy, The Vatican; Age 25, 1930

The older priest looked at me curiously as if surprised to see me, a colored man explaining in halting Italian who I was and why I was there. I could feel my hand trembling as I reached into my satchel taking out the thick sheaf of letters that had been sent to me confirming my registration. The priest took the paperwork, carefully placing his reading glasses on his nose, but first rubbing the spectacles against a soft cloth that he took from his pocket, and then he meticulously pored over the documents. It seemed like an eternity before he folded the papers handing them back to me. My heart was beating so much, I thought it would jump out of my chest and I was just praying that it wasn't some sort of mistake and he was about to send me packing back to Cleveland. He took off his glasses, blew what seemed to be an imaginary speck of dust off of them, leaned back in his chair, looked me up and down critically, then saying in heavily accented English, "Well young man it looks as if you will be joining us. Congratulations."

I swear I think that my face was going to crack in two from my broad smile, thinking that everything had come full circle, remembering clearly the day when I got the letter.

****

Flashback Through Father Grau's Eyes
Cleveland, Ohio; A Few Months Earlier, 1930

"Mama! Mama, look!!!" I ran excitedly into Mama's bedroom. She hadn't been feeling well for a while, she was lying on her bed, eyes closed with a cool wash cloth across her forehead, but when she heard my voice she sat up knowing that it must be something special. "What is it son? Tell me!"

I sat on the edge of her bed, barely able to contain myself. "Mama, I'm going to Rome!!!"

She shrieked, "Rome!!! My boy's going to Rome!"

I nodded. "Yes! Can you believe it?! Even though nobody would let me study here, even though none of those racists would give me a chance, and Mama you know I love you, but you know they are racists!"

She nodded, "Yes, son, I know."

I continued, the words tumbling out triumphantly. "Even though nobody here, not **one** of the Catholic Parishes, would take me into study, none of the seminaries!!! But I, ME, Billy Grau, am going to the Vatican!!!! I'm going to study to be a priest at the Vatican!!"

Mama hugged me tightly; I could feel her tears against my face. "Son, I'm so proud of you. I'll miss you because you're my heart, but I'm so proud of you."

****

And now I was here at the Vatican, bursting with happiness, feeling like the possibilities were unlimited for me.

Flashback Through Sophie's Eyes
Queen Of All Saints Catholic Church, Parish Nursery; Continued, 1955

"Oh, Father, that is so extraordinary! I just…"

"Excuse me, Father. Sister Sophie. I hope that I'm not interrupting."

Sister Blanche, the one we called Mother Superior's "helper," had entered the room. Neither Father Grau nor I noticing, until she spoke, somewhat accusingly.

Father Grau turned to her smoothly, replying in a firm authoritative tone.

"Not at all, Sister Blanche. Sister Sophie was just completing her report on the children's progress. And I must say that she is doing a fine job with them. I'm sure you'll agree."

Looking as if she'd been check-mated, Sister Blanche nodded her head. "Of course, Father. Mother Superior has recently remarked on Sister Sophie's abilities with the children."

"Well, I would have to agree. And Sister Blanche, I'm glad that you're here, perhaps we can set a time for you and I to talk about the state of some of our buildings, in particular the Rectory. I understand from Mother Superior that your calling with the Order has been to ensure that we are aware of any pressing work that is required with our facilities so that we can make sure that we have the necessary funds to keep everything in good repair."

"Yes, of course, Father, whenever you would like to speak, I will be available."

"Thank you, Sister Blanche, your flexibility is appreciated. I have some other meetings this afternoon, but perhaps tomorrow morning?"

"Yes, Father."

He handed me his empty cup. "Thank you, Sister Sophie, for the excellent report and, of course, for the tea. It has warmed me on this rather cold day."

And with that, he draped his coat around his shoulders and headed out the door. Sister Blanche eyed me suspiciously and followed quickly behind him.

Buffalo, New York, Hospital; Present Time

Sophie had stopped talking for a moment. She reached for her glass and took a long sip of water from the straw that was dangling from the edge. The sun was lower in the sky now and I realized that she'd been talking for more than an hour. But she didn't seem like she wanted to stop. She continued, almost pensively. "I remember so well. I couldn't even imagine what it must have been like to go to Italy and, much less, study at the Vatican at the feet of the most holy men on earth." She leaned back against the pillow as if still not able to wrap her head around the thought of being there. "I mean, Joe, it was such an honor and I think it made me love him more because I felt as if he'd been there, where it all began, where our faith took hold, all of us Catholics. I felt so special and so honored that he was sharing his memories with *me!* Me! Sophie from Buffalo. The furthest away that I'd ever been was one time to New York City."

She smoothed the bedcovers, staring out at the sinking sun. "We talked a lot in those first months. And I began to know him so well."

1. Sister Sophie Legocki 1950's. 2. Father William Grau 1950's. 3. Joe Steele at Harvard in his 20's. 4. William Grau in his 20's. 5. Joe and his birth mother, Sophie Legocki, at their first meeting, 1991.

6. Father Grau (second row, third from left) standing next to his mother. **7.** William Grau's parents, Charles and Theresa Grau in 1945. **8.** Father William Grau meets Pope Pius XII as Army Chaplain to the "Buffalo Soldiers" 92nd Infantry in the European Theater in the1940's.

Received in audience by Pope Pius XII recently was Army Chaplain-William C Grau (above), colored priest of the Diocese of Buffalo. Father Grau, serving with the 92nd Division of colored troops, is one of two Negro Catholic chaplains on duty with the U S Army (NCWC)

CHAPTER

14

The door opened, and the doctor walked briskly into the room approaching Sophie's bed. "Well, Ms. Legocki, I have to say that you've come back from the brink." The doctor tapped his pen against the clipboard as if not quite believing what he was reading. "Your bloodwork looks excellent and most of your vitals have stabilized."

"So, I have to go home?" Sophie looked crushed as if the doctor had said that she was about to die of some incurable disease.

"No, not that quickly, we still need to watch you. I want you to stay here at least another week until we're sure that you're breathing regularly throughout the night. I assume that there's no one at home who's trained to care for you?"

"No, no one, my nephew calls when he can, but he's got his own family and doesn't live that close."

The doctor scribbled some notes on the clipboard paper, "That's what I thought, so we'll keep you here a little longer, although I think that we can probably move you out of intensive care, I'll have the nurse check you into another room."

Sophie seemed to breathe a sigh of relief as she settled back on her pillows. "Yes, doctor, thank you. I definitely would like to stay longer… to…uh…make sure that I'm completely well. I wouldn't want to relapse."

The doctor turned to me, one eyebrow arched. "I don't know what you're talking about in here, but I have to say I've never seen a recovery quite like this before…so whatever it is you're doing, keep up the good work and we'll have your mother home in no time."

Now it was my turn to feel panicked. I felt that for the first time since Sophie and I had met several years ago, that we were finally really connecting. I didn't want it to end it that quickly. I think that Sophie must have been thinking the same thing because after the doctor left, she whispered, "I really don't want to go home, there's still so much to tell you."

I squeezed her hand. "Well, then let's not stop."

She smiled. "Now, where were we? Oh yes! After that afternoon in the nursery, I think we both started feeling a little awkward. Once the snow melted, we didn't really have much of an excuse to spend much time together. He'd come back to the nursery for his regular weekly visits, but he never spent more than a few minutes, so we didn't have a chance to really connect again until months later. It was early June—a beautiful day, the first really warm day in months. I remember that afternoon in the garden."

Flashback Through Sophie's Eyes
Queen Of All Saints Catholic Church, Parish Garden; 1955

The sun felt good. I stretched my legs and wiggled my toes as best as I could in my heavy shoes. My eyes lingered on a white butterfly hovering over a flower. I loved summer, everything was so alive. I stretched my arms out trying not to seem too uncouth, but I felt like jumping up and running around and drinking in every bit of light and warmth that the sun radiated. This was my first real break in days, we'd had visitors at the Convent the past week and they'd just left, a delegation from the Archdiocese, I wasn't really sure why they'd picked our obscure Parish, but something about a report on how well we were doing in growing the Parish and bringing in more of the local colored and Spanish speaking parishioners who had started to move into the area looking for jobs. I didn't know all the details, only that Mother Superior had said that everything had to be shining and bright and that I, in particular, had to make sure that all of the children were well-behaved. It was a lot of pressure on me because although I loved the children, some of them were quite difficult, particularly the older ones. But I must have done OK because Mother Superior told me that the delegation had been pleased with what they saw. I smiled to myself, thinking that God had truly chosen the right path for me. I turned my face upwards to the sun, scrunching my eyes closed tightly as I used to do as a young girl so that I could see what appeared to be a kaleidoscope of lights dancing in front of my closed eyes.

"Well hello."

I popped my eyes open, sitting up immediately. I knew that voice and felt suddenly embarrassed at the way that I was lounging on the bench. "Hello, Father."

Father Grau was smiling broadly and he clutched a stack of books under his arm. Sitting down on the chair facing me, "I've been looking for you. I wanted to give you these." He handed me the books.

They were children's books, some of them classics. Before I could say anything, he continued, "The delegation from the Archdiocese brought several boxes of children's books with them. I had written a few months ago letting them know how much we needed books for the children. So, when they came this week, they brought these and others."

"Oh, Father, thank you, how thoughtful of you! You must have noticed that the children had begun to tire of hearing me read the same stories over and over again." I turned the books over excitedly reading the titles of some of the most cherished works.

"What I noticed, Sister Sophie, is someone who was doing her very best with extremely limited resources, and as your Pastor, it was my duty to provide you with the tools to do your job."

I blushed, because as his eyes met mine, I felt that same thrill that I always did when I was near him.

He ran his hand across the front cover of one of the books, smiled as if satisfied, and then handed it back to me. "They're not new, but they're new to us and that's what counts."

I think that I sensed something more, as if by this gesture he was giving me part of himself. How silly, I had to stop those ideas; it sounded like one of those romance novels that the teen girls read. But I couldn't help myself. I felt him drawing nearer to me as he pointed to the book on the top of the stack.

"I loved Robinson Crusoe, I must have read it ten times. Something about the adventure of setting out to sea and ending up on a desert island always appealed to me."

I turned the books over picking out one of my favorites. "The Secret Garden—that was one of my all-time favorites."

"You have good taste, Sister, one of the most popular classics."

I almost giggled thinking back on my childhood. "This book in particular, the idea that you could bring something alive that had been neglected and overgrown, made me think that there was hope in every situation." I thought back on those days saying, almost to myself, "I could never talk about books or any of these things with my family, they weren't much into school or reading."

He leaned forward, "Tell me about yourself, Sister. I feel as if I've talked on and on, but haven't heard that much about you. What was your family like?"

"Oh, Father, there's nothing much to tell. Mother and Dad emigrated from Poland as teenagers. The funny thing was that they were from the same village in Poland, but didn't meet until they came here. They married and had four children, three boys and me, I'm the oldest. Dad has a regular job and Mama mainly stayed home to take care of all of us. Dad got sick a couple of years ago, and so Mama has pretty much had her hands full taking care of him. I'm only close to one of my brothers, but the rest I don't see much of. We just lived a simple life in Buffalo, nothing very exciting."

"When did you get the call…to become a nun?"

I smiled wryly. "Honestly I don't know if it was as much a call as a way to get out of the house. I was very young, only 14, but I knew enough to know that I didn't want to end up like my mother, raising a bunch of kids without much else in life. I think that I felt that by becoming a nun I could at least help someone and have a chance at a life for myself."

"And has it been what you expected?"

I hesitated, not quite sure how to respond. "Yes, I think so. I don't really know much else at this point." I couldn't believe what I was saying, I didn't want to sound ungrateful for all that the Church had given me. So, I jumped in quickly, "What I meant was, that it's a fulfilling life in many ways."

There was an awkward silence, and not wanting him to leave, I blurted out, "You've been gone for several weeks, that is before the Archdiocese delegation came."

"I was traveling to some of the other Parishes in the area. They asked if I would help out during Easter and the Lenten season. Because I speak Italian, I'm in great demand for confession." He laughed, "Although it is amusing sometimes to see the parishioners' reaction when they see who they've been speaking in Italian to. I don't think that I'm quite what they expected."

Now it was my turn to smile, thinking about some of the Italian families that had grown up near me, and their reaction at seeing a colored priest speaking fluent Italian. "Yes, I can imagine."

He cleared his throat. "Speaking of Confession, it's almost time for Mass, so…" His voice trailed off as if he wanted to say something else and for a moment our eyes met. And now I knew that it was not my imagination. I felt an electricity that I hadn't before and his eyes seemed to swallow mine, and I felt myself wanting to move closer and become a part of the energy that was emanating from him. He leaned forward in his chair, his hand inching towards mine, but then he stopped himself. "So, I hope that the children enjoy the books."

Pulling myself back on the bench, lowering my eyes, afraid to meet his again. "Yes, Father."

He got up quickly then stopped, and again I felt that energy drawing me to him. "Will you be at Mass, Sister?"

I nodded, afraid that I'd reveal what I was feeling. "Yes, Father. I'll be there."

CHAPTER

15

I realized that I was sitting at the edge of my seat. I hadn't moved since Sophie had begun speaking and now she sunk back on the pillows, her face pale and drained. Seeing that remembering all of this was exhausting her, I lay my hand gently on hers, saying, "That's OK Sophie, you can stop."

She shook her head weakly. "No, I'm fine, I'm fine. He wants you to know everything, everything that I wrote down for him, everything he put in that notebook, I was typing it up for him, you know. That's why I know everything, because he would write it down and he had such beautiful handwriting. It was so flowery it looked almost like calligraphy, perfect just like everything about him, perfect so he gave me the notebook. He wanted me to have it so that I could transcribe everything. He was writing a book, you know."

"A book?? You mean that there's a notebook, there are notes that I can read?!" Suddenly excited realizing that I might actually have a chance to have something written in his hand. In my wildest dreams, I'd never thought that there could be something that would be such a direct and tangible link to him.

"Do you have the notebook, Sophie, so that could I see it?"

She closed her eyes again. "He was very private. You know, even though he wanted to write his book, there are some things that I think he only really wanted me to know and when he died, well I guess until today, I haven't really thought much about all of that because it was almost as if what he wrote was for me and now for you. But who knows really."

She sank deeper into the pillows, the edges of the soft white mass blending with the translucent white of her skin. I wanted to ask more. I wanted to ask about the notebook again, but she turned over mumbling almost to herself, "It's hard when someone you know and love dies. One minute they're there and the next minute they're just gone and you don't know why. And you wonder why were you chosen to be there when they took their last breath, when the good Lord our Savior brought them home again. And sometimes you wonder why did they leave me behind? Have you ever had that feeling, Joe, have you ever been there when someone you love dies?"

I don't know why, but suddenly I wanted to be able to share some of my life with her because even though we'd known each other a few years at this point, I still felt as if she didn't really have an idea of who *I* was. And in fact, almost every time that I tried to say something, to give her an insight into my life and my family, it was like she dismissed it, as if she didn't really want to know. But these past days I felt as if we'd gotten closer than we'd ever been and that this might be the time that I could open up to her about me. I swallowed, remembering, pulling back the pages of my life, going back further and further, until I was five years old again.

"Yes, I know exactly what you mean. I was there when my father died. I was five years old."

Flashback Through Joe's Eyes
Cincinnati, Ohio; Age 5, 1962

It's night time. The TVs going in the background. *Bonanza*, Billy and Daddy's favorite show. Mama's out playing Bingo. Billy's on the phone; he talks a lot on the phone, probably to that girl he likes, but then again, I think Billy likes a lot of girls or maybe it's that a lot of girls like Billy. I don't know. I'm playing with some of my toys. Daddy's sitting in his chair, he looks tired. Billy's talking loud on the phone, and then Daddy starts coughing, he can't get his breath. Billy throws the phone down; he's trying to help Daddy get his breath, he picks up the phone and he's yelling into the phone hangup, hangup!! But they won't hang up I don't know what to do. Billy runs out the house…Daddy's closing his eyes; he can't breathe. Now Billy's running back in the house, he's with one of Daddy's friends, a man, and they're trying to help Daddy. And now some other men are running in and they're still trying to help Daddy, but he won't wake up.

Daddy's eyes are closed now. There's lots of people around and now Mama is coming in the house. And I hear them telling her that Daddy's gone and she's just standing there. Mama doesn't cry, she just stands there, and they grab my hand and take me upstairs. And now I remember a few days later, maybe it's the next day. I don't know, everything seems just blurry, but we're in a big place and Daddy's there lying in a big box that's open and his eyes are closed and there's lots and lots of people lined up all the way down the block and nobody's really saying much and a lot of people are crying and Mama's just standing there. She's not crying. She's just standing there, and all the people come by and they look at Daddy and some people cry, and some people touch his forehead and then walk by sadly and there's just lots and lots of people. And I remember being so tired, and I don't understand everything. I just know that Daddy's gone.

The house is empty without Daddy. It's just me and Mama and Billy. Mama and Billy argue a lot, but it's odd because even though they argue, it's like Billy's become the man of the house, not for me, he hasn't become Daddy for me, but there's times when Mama seems to rely on him like he was Daddy. Like the time that man came to the house and he was trying to get Mama to buy something. I don't remember what it was but it was something that she didn't want to buy and the man just kept trying to get her to buy it and so she called Billy and Billy came downstairs and he yelled at that man and told him to go away and the man wouldn't go away, he said that Billy was just a kid. And then Billy went back up to his room and he came down and he had a gun and he told the man he'd kill him if he didn't leave Mama alone, and that man gathered up his stuff and left so fast. And I remember thinking Billy must really love Mama a lot even though they argue all the time. It just seemed like Billy was mad at Mama a lot and I didn't know why.

But then one day when I was about 10, I heard Billy yelling at Mama saying, "If you don't tell him then I will, Joe has a right to know." I didn't want to ask what he was talking about, but I remember other conversations and I thought that what he was talking about was that I was adopted but that Mama and Daddy never told me. But I was afraid to say anything or ask any questions. I didn't want to seem ungrateful. I think Billy had found out that he was adopted when he found some papers, I think a newspaper with an article about Mama and Daddy adopting him, and he was so mad he felt like they had lied to him. But I guess I felt differently. I loved Mama and I loved Daddy and I loved Billy and I guess I wasn't mad. I guess I was happy that they were my family.

CHAPTER

16

Buffalo, New York, Hospital; Present Time

Time to take your temperature, Ms. Legocki." The nurse pushed the door open with her free hand, the other one clutching a thermometer as if she were brandishing a tiny glass sword. She had cut me off completely, and for a moment I felt disorientated, my mind was still back there in Cincinnati in our living room all those years ago, but my body hadn't moved. I was in Sophie's hospital room looking out at the treeless landscape below her window. Tapping her foot impatiently, the nurse shoved the thermometer into Sophie's mouth, "Let's see what we've got."

Sophie frowned, and I could tell that she was as annoyed as I was at the nurse's untimely interruption. "Don't stop." Her words were mumbled, blocked by the thermometer.

But I felt as if these were things that I only wanted to share with her, not with the prying eyes and ears of the nurse who seemed to be particularly curious about what I was saying. I think that the doctor's last words about *"...what we were talking about in there that seemed to be having such a miraculous effect on Sophie's health..."* had traveled through the noisy corridors, and we seemed to always have someone popping in, supposedly for a legitimate reason, but always lingering longer than necessary. So, I shook my head no, making eye contact with Sophie, hoping that she'd understand my hesitancy with our "company." She winked conspiratorially. "Right, OK." And then turned to the nurse sweetly, "I'm beginning to be a little weary, will this be the last interruption tonight, nurse? I'd like to get a little rest."

"Well, then I guess you better tell your visitor to leave, he's been here all day, no wonder you're tired."

Now I was not only annoyed, but also a little angry, who was she to suggest that I needed to leave? I was about to say something, but Sophie, as if sensing my feelings, interjected quickly. "Oh, no. I actually sleep better when he's in the room, he has such a calming presence with all of the constant commotion in the hallway. But I know that you and the other nurses are just doing your jobs, even if it means that the rest of us can't sleep."

I almost laughed. Sophie would not be "one-upped" by anyone! Getting the obvious hint, the nurse scowled, shaking the thermometer, reading it in a perfunctory manner, and then heading towards the door, "You don't have a temperature. But I'd suggest you get some rest. Alone."

Sophie giggled like a little girl who had just put one over on her parents, then leaning towards me eagerly, "So after your father died, what happened, how did your mother handle it?"

"Mama was a strong woman, she never let anything get her down, even in the lowest moments, I never remember her as anything less than stoic. She taught me how to face life head on." I paused, thinking back on those days. "But you know, they say there's a reason for everything and I think that if my dad hadn't passed away so prematurely I might never have had the relationship with Pops. He kinda stepped in and become a dad for me starting when I was about eight years old."

Flashback Through Joe's Eyes
Cincinnati, Ohio; Age 8

"Joe," Mama stuck her head in my door.

I was in my room pretending to be Batman. I had on my cape and was jumping off my bed onto the floor chasing the imaginary bad guys.

"I want you to change your clothes and come on downstairs, there's somebody I want you to meet."

"Do they have candy?" I sat up eagerly remembering the last one of Mama's friends who came over, she was one of the ladies from the church and she had a whole purse full of candy bars, all my favorites, so I was hoping she might be back again. But seems like I was out of luck this time because Mama just eyed me sternly and then pulled out a pair of pants and a shirt from my closet, handing them to me, "Just put these on quickly, he wants to take you on a little outing, and he's a busy man, so hurry up."

"Who is he?"

"A friend of Sis,' but you'll see, he's heard all about you and what a good boy you are and he's a fine man and he said he'd like to come meet you and maybe take you to dinner."

I was kinda hungry, it was almost seven and I hadn't eaten since lunch. It was Saturday so I'd had a late breakfast and then had gone outside to play with my friends. I was thinking all that as I pulled the shirt over my head and buttoned up my pants. I knew when Mama had that look, there was no use arguing, better to just get dressed quick and get downstairs.

I wanted to slide down the stairs the way I sometimes did when Mama wasn't home, when it was just me and Grandma, who almost never got mad at me, so I could get away with a lot more when it was just her and me. Sis' friend was sitting in the living room next to Mama, when he stood up he smiled at me. He looked kinda like me with the same light tan colored skin and wavy black hair. His eyes were nice and his whole face seemed to smile, not like some people who were just pretending to smile, but you knew that inside they were frowning.

"Joe, this is Otis."

He held out his hand and I shook it the way Mama had taught me to do.

"Well, it's certainly nice to meet you, Joe, I've heard all kinds of great things about you and now I know that they're all true!"

"What do you say, Joe?" Mama prodded me and I quickly remembered.

"Uh, nice to meet you, too?" I said it uncertainly, looking at Mama for approval. She smiled and nodded. I heaved a sigh of relief, I didn't want Mama to be mad at me 'cause I forgot what she told me about being polite when you're introduced to someone.

But Otis didn't seem to notice, he just kept smiling and the whole room seemed to light up, more than it had in a long time.

"Your Mama said that you hadn't had dinner yet, so I was thinking that maybe you'd like to go out for a bite, we can go to Frisch's, how does that sound?"

"Real good. I like Frisch's!"

"Then let's get goin', my favorite waitress starts at seven." He winked at me like we shared a secret, and I knew from that moment on that there was something special about Otis, like a place inside of me that had felt empty since Daddy died was being filled up.

End Flashback
Buffalo, New York, Hospital; Present Time

"Was Otis related to you?" Sophie interrupted my thoughts as I smiled to myself remembering Frisch's and our many dinners there.

"No, not technically, he'd dated my cousin, Sis, for a while before they both married other people, so he was almost like family and he was close with my parents. When he'd moved to Cincinnati from Kentucky they kind of took him under their wing, but he was more than that—he was probably the person other than Mama who had the biggest influence on me growing up. It all started when I was eight, and what began as a once a week outing ended up with us getting together every weekend until I left for Harvard."

"He must have been quite something."

"He was. I remember one of our many evenings at Frisch's, but this one in particular because he brought my cousin, Tony, and I'd gotten used to having Uncle Odie all to myself."

"Uncle Odie?"

"Sorry, that's what I started calling Otis after not too long, like I said, he wasn't technically a relative, but he felt like a part of the family and since he and Sis had dated, people just always called him Uncle Odie."

I lay my head back in the stiff metal chair and remembered, the thoughts overwhelming me and taking me back to a brown leather banquette with my eyes fixed on a bright red plastic cup sitting on the table in front of me.

Flashback Through Joe's Eyes
Cincinnati, Ohio; Age 8

"It's mine! I always get the red cup!" I shoved the blue plastic cup across the table at Tony. Tony wasn't much older than me, he was sitting next to Uncle Odie, kind of snuggled up to him the way I always was when Uncle Odie and me would go to Frisch's the way we did every Sunday. But not today, 'cause today Uncle Odie had brought Tony, and I was mad. I mean, really mad, and it started the minute I ran out my front door expecting to slide into the front seat of Uncle Odie's shiny black Cadillac. Uncle Odie worked as the head of the whole used car Service Department at Thomson-MacConnell Cadillac dealership and he had to drive all the cars to make sure that they were ready to sell, so almost every week he came in a different Cadillac. And boy did the neighbors look! But not just the neighbors, but also all the kids at school, it made me feel like I was one of the rich kids even though where we lived wasn't a rich neighborhood, but, just riding around in those big cars with the soft leather seats and the wood grain finishes made me feel important.

And my place was always in the front seat next to Uncle Odie. But not today, 'cause today Tony was sitting there, in my seat, next to my Uncle Odie. So, when I got to the car, Uncle Odie turned around saying, "Just hop in the back seat, Joe." What could I say, I couldn't get mad at Uncle Odie, and it was pretty obvious that Tony wasn't budging from my seat up front. So, I gave Tony a dirty look which he didn't seem to notice, and I got in the back seat.

I was thinking all that as I pushed the blue cup over to Tony and tried to grab the red one, but he wasn't letting go. "I got the red cup, the waitress gave it to me." He pushed the blue cup back across the table and then turned to Uncle Odie. "Isn't that right, Daddy?"

Now I was really mad, how come he could call Uncle Odie 'Daddy', he wasn't his daddy, Uncle Herschel was, but he always called him that. I could feel tears starting to well up in my eyes, "Uncle Odie, I want the red cup! I always get the red cup and I'm taking it now!" I tried to grab the cup, but Uncle Odie gently put his hand on mine, saying firmly, "Joe, I want you to stop acting up. Tony's got the red cup today and you got the blue one, it's just as good, next time you can get the red cup."

"I don't care about next time, I want the red cup now!" And I kicked my foot against the table leg hard. For the first time that I could remember, Uncle Odie wasn't smiling at me. Without saying another word, he took out his wallet put some money on top of the check and said, "Let's go, boys. Time to go home."

"I don't wanna go home! I wanna stay here! I didn't get desert! I wanted a milkshake in my red cup!!"

Ignoring me, Uncle Odie got up, followed closely by Tony. I had no choice but to trail behind, and by now the tears were really coming down and I was so mad, I wanted to kick Tony and grab that red cup. But I knew I better not, so instead I hurled myself on the back seat and started crying as hard as I could. Uncle Odie couldn't ignore me, he'd have to take Tony home and then it would just be the two of us and maybe we'd go back to Frisch's and he'd get me another red cup. But instead, he pulled up in front of my house. I'd been crying so hard I hadn't noticed that he wasn't going in the right direction to get to Tony's.

"All right, Joe, you're home, you can get out now."

Now I really started crying, barely getting the words out, "But Uncle

Odie, it's his fault all he had to do was to give me the red cup, he knows it's mine, he knows it! He's just a big fat liar if he says he doesn't."

Uncle Odie's voice was calm, but I could tell he wasn't pleased. "That's enough, Joe. I want you to get out of this car and go upstairs and think about your behavior tonight."

I could tell he wasn't going to change his mind, so in between sobs I got out and ran to my front door.

CHAPTER

17

When I got inside, Mama was waiting at the front door, she looked out and waved goodbye to Uncle Odie as he pulled away. Concerned, seeing the tears streaming down my face, she turned to me, "Now what happened to you? Why are you crying?"

Mama wasn't the type to hold me in her arms and comfort me the way some of the other mothers did, but she did pull me closer to her, asking again seriously, "C'mon, Joe, did Uncle Odie say something that hurt your feelings?"

Now I really started crying, except I started hiccupping in between the tears, so I could barely get it out. "Nooooooooo!!! It was Tony, I hate him! He stole my red cup!"

"Your red cup? What are you talking about?"

I threw myself on the couch, burying my head in the pillows. "E....e.v eery...time we go to F...F...Frisch's...." I hiccupped, "I get the red cup, but this time Tony got it and I had to take the stupid blue one and Uncle Odie didn't make him give it back, and then he called Uncle Odie 'Daddy' and he's not even his daddy!!!" Just remembering that made me even madder. "He has his own daddy, why does he have to pretend that Uncle Odie is his daddy?!"

Mama sat next to me, "Sit up, Joe."

Reluctantly, I sat halfway up, clutching a pillow and still hiccupping.

"Now I know that your Uncle Odie loves you, but that doesn't mean that he doesn't love Tony, too, but if you act like this, Uncle Odie may decide that the doesn't want to come over and take you out because you're crying in public and embarrassing him. Now he's a fine man and he's been awfully good to you. Now you don't want Uncle Odie to stop coming over, do you?"

"Nooooo."

Mama wiped the tears from my face with a soft tissue. "I didn't think so. So now what are you going to do?

The thought of losing Uncle Odie made me want to cry again. I was quiet for a minute and then said, "Do you think Uncle Odie would mind if I called him 'Pops?'"

Mama smiled and gently stroked my hair. "No, Joe. I think he'd be proud."

I smiled, just a little because I still wasn't sure I'd finished crying. "So that's what I'll do."

"And what else are you gonna do, Joe? I think an apology might make sense."

"Not to Tony, I won't!"

"Now, Joe."

I grabbed the pillow harder burying my face into it, barely forcing the words out. "Ok…maybe."

End Flashback
Buffalo, New York, Hospital; Present Time

"So, from that point on, I called Uncle Odie 'Pops,' and in every sense of the word, he was a dad to me. I remember in high school when I started going to some of the school dances, he'd come and pick me and my friends up in one of the new Cadillacs. Everybody thought we were rich," I smiled remembering. "Especially the Jack and Jill crowd."

Sophie raised an eyebrow curiously. "Jack and Jill?"

"It's a black social group, the children of black professionals, back then it was all the kids of the doctors and lawyers and successful business people. It's all over the country; they have parties and trips and things for all of the age groups. We weren't in Jack and Jill, but everybody just assumed we could've been when Pops would drive up in a different Cadillac each time."

Sophie seemed a little uncomfortable at the thought of a world that she knew nothing about and was so different from her idea of 'colored people,' so she quickly steered the conversation back.

"So, tell me more about Pops."

The thought of Pops made me remember the good times and everything that he did for me, and what a void there would've been in my life without him. "He's really the one who taught me about a being a proud black man, about being a man of your word, how important things like good grooming and being on time were. He was never late to pick me up, if he said 7 p.m., he was there at seven on the dot. I used to stay with him and his wife, Aunt Callie, on the weekends and we'd watch *60 Minutes* together. I learned a lot about the world from him. And then when I was around 11, we started visiting some of his other friends."

Flashback Through Joe's Eyes
Cincinnati, Ohio; 11 Years Old

I massaged my temples; my head was beginning to hurt from so much reading. I'd just finished English and was starting my geography homework. I loved school but sometimes I wished the teachers wouldn't give so much homework, especially on the weekends. I glanced at my watch, I only had a half hour more, Pops was coming to get me at eight. I thumbed through the maps in the book, thinking, someday I'll go to some of these places. I thought of my best friend, Chris. I'd hang out with him on the weekends in his crazy attic room. Chris' mom was from Japan, his dad was black and Chris and me were always talking about taking a trip to Japan. We even went so far as to plan the trip and call the airline to find out how much tickets would be, way more than either of us had, but it was nice to dream. I was thinking about all that as I shut my books quickly and bounded down the stairs to the living room.

Mama looked up from the sofa, the television blaring in the background. "It's almost eight. Your Pops will be here in a minute."

"I'm ready." I grabbed an apple and before I could finish it, the doorbell rang. Slinging my jacket over my shoulder, I waved at Mama. "See you later."

I slid into the front seat of the car. "Hey, Pops."

"Hey there, Joe." The steering wheel glided through his fingers as he expertly did a U-turn.

"We're not going to your house?"

"Want to introduce you to someone, we're going over her place."

He winked at me. I loved it when Pops shared his secrets with me. I'd met some of his other "friends" before. Mostly nice women, some white, but mainly black. and I never mentioned it to anyone, not Mama, and definitely not Pop's wife, Aunt Callie. I liked that Pops trusted me.

"Here we are." He parked in the driveway like it was the most natural thing to do. Knocking twice and the door swung open. "Joe, this is Verna. Verna, Joe."

"Nice to meet you, Joe."

"You, too."

Verna was a striking black woman, in fact, just a couple of inches taller than Pops. She had smooth nut-brown skin and a curvy figure and the way she stood made her almost seem like one of those fictional Amazon women from the comic books except that instead of their fierce scowl, Verna was all smiles. In fact, the whole room seemed to glow with her warmth and I could see why Pops was attracted to her. She seemed at least ten or maybe fifteen years younger than Pops, but the way that she looked at him and he looked at her, I could almost sense the deep feeling of love between them. Pops' eyes followed her as she walked ahead of us swinging her hips easily and tossing her hair back as if she knew that he was fixated on her.

Pops had a different kind of relationship with Aunt Callie, it's not that he didn't love her 'cause I knew he did. I knew from the times that I'd curled up at his feet in their cramped living room filled with overstuffed furniture and lots of the kinds of tchotchkes that Aunt Callie collected. But the feeling between them was more like they'd decided that their relationship would be one way and that it would be solid and permanent but without a lot of silly hugging and kissing and the kinds of things he did with Verna. By now I had perfected the "cool" nonchalance of not having any reaction to any of Pops' special friends and so I just followed him into Verna's house.

Pops looped his arm around Verna's waist and kissed her lightly on the lips, then meandered over to the liquor cabinet and poured himself a glass of Wild Turkey bourbon and settled on the couch, turning on the TV.

Verna walked into the kitchen, sliding a roast from the oven, it was pretty clear that she'd been expecting Pops. The smell of savory pot roast and baked potatoes curled through the room. My stomach started to grumble, so when Verna said, "You hungry, Joe?" It was all I could do not to grab a plate. "Yep."

"You know how to set a table?"

"Yeah, sure."

"Well, the silverware and the plates and glasses are over there." She motioned with the gravy spoon to a cabinet on the other side of the kitchen. "We can sit in the dining room since it's Sunday."

And so just as if this was the most natural thing in the world to do, I set the table and the three of us sat down. Pops held out one hand to Verna and the other to me as he bowed his head. "Lord, we thank you for this food that we are about to receive and for the hands that made it." He gave Verna a peck on the cheek, "Now let's eat."

And from that day on, I alternated my weekends with Pops at his and Aunt Callie's place or Pops with him and Verna, either way, I was happy, I just liked being with Pops.

CHAPTER

18

End Flashback
Buffalo, New York, Hospital; Present Time

Sophie sat up in the bed smiling broadly. "That Pops sounds like quite a guy, did his wife ever find out, I'm assuming your Aunt Callie was his wife?

"Yep, she was, but in reality, so was Verna, they were together for years and it was Verna who was with him until the end."

"Did your Aunt Callie ever find out about Verna?"

"I think that she must've known Pops always had women on the side, but Verna was more than that...way more."

"And nobody ever said anything? I mean, it seemed like he was a well-known man from what you're telling me, and it's kind of surprising. You know people do talk, especially in small communities."

I shrugged, "Maybe they did. I was just a kid, so I don't really know what the adults were saying, all I know is that Pops was a big deal. He was a 32nd degree Mason, and at Thomson MacConnell's he was responsible for a lot of their business. Their dealership was located in the black community and I know it was in large part because of Pops and the respect that people had for him that they patronized the dealership, even if Mr. MacConnell never really appreciated it." Even now, I got a little bitter at the thought of the way they treated Pops, especially at the end. But I didn't want to think about that now; I just wanted to remember the good times. So, I continued, "In fact, when the riots broke out in '68, they didn't have hardly any damage 'cause Pops made sure that people respected their property. And Pops was so proud when I got into the same school as Mr. MacConnell's younger son. I liked his son, we were friends, but I was smarter than him and always got better grades. I think that Pops liked to rub that in a little at the dealership, especially when I'd come over there and hang out with him on the weekends."

Flashback Through Joe's Eyes
Cincinnati, Ohio, Thomson MacConnell Dealership; Age 12

Pops pointed to a shiny new black Cadillac that had just arrived at the dealership. I was there when they drove it into the showroom and Pops had let me get behind the wheel.

"Wow!" It was about all I could say. All the cars were special, but this latest model was something else. Mr. MacConnell came up behind me. "Hello, Joe. Like the new model?"

"Sure do."

"We think it's gonna be quite a good seller." Then, turning his back to me and facing Pops, "You better get back over to the service department, it looks like we may have a situation with one of the customers, she's claiming the work wasn't done right…but you know how to handle it."

Unconcerned, Pops glanced over in the direction of the service area. "I'm sure that it's nothing that we can't make good and…oh, did you hear, Mr. MacConnell? Joe made honor roll again. He's quite a student, bet he'll end up at one of those fancy Ivy leagues someday."

Pops was beaming. I could tell he was getting a special satisfaction from telling this to Mr. MacConnell, barely forcing out a smile as he hurried past me. "Good work, Joe, keep it up."

Pops winked at me, whispering, "That's right, Joe, you just keep it up."

CHAPTER

19

End Flashback
Buffalo, New York, Hospital; Present Time

We were both very quiet. Outside the window I could hear sirens and then the sound of shouting and scuffling feet. I assumed that someone was being brought into the hospital and I felt thankful that Sophie seemed to be steadily improving and was now out of intensive care. She seemed pensive suddenly, "When did they tell you that you were adopted?"

"Well, it's interesting, we never really had the conversation. I mean, when Daddy died I was only five, and well, Mama never said anything about it."

Sophie propped herself up on an elbow, looking at me inquisitively. "You mean she never told you?"

I shook my head no. "Never directly. I pieced it together and I figured it out, but I never really had that direct conversation with Mama. I knew she loved me and I loved her, and I loved Daddy and Billy and so I guess it just didn't bother me that much."

Sophie's questions made me think of something that I hadn't in so long. Mama has been dead now for many years. And so, I wonder why I never asked her about the adoption, and I know deep down because on one level it didn't really matter. What I needed in a mother Mama gave me and much more. Mama wasn't the hugging and kissing type. I don't remember being curled up in her lap and smothered with kisses, but what I do remember was unconditional love. And what I do remember was an acceptance of me for who I was and for what I wanted to be. And I guess that's what I really needed.

I turned back to Sophie, saying, "Mama, my mother," I could see Sophie cringe when I spoke of Mama in such a loving way because although she, that is Sophie, was my mother by birth, I think she knew that she could never be for me what Mama was.

Sophie sat up tentatively, "Tell me about her, what was she like? What was your life like with that family?"

I smiled in spite of myself, so many memories, a patchwork of images floating before me.

Flashback Through Joe's Eyes
Cincinnati, Ohio

Now I'm eight, maybe I'm nine; it's all a little fuzzy now. What I see is a big gymnasium, a little stuffy, filled with women of all ages most of them Mama's age in their fifties and sixties, some older, the same age as Grandma, all black women playing bingo, socializing, laughing. The gymnasium is stuffy, sometimes the ventilation is so bad, I feel like I can hardly breathe.

"Joe, come on over here and play another round of bingo." Mama waved me over and patted the chair next to her for me to sit down. "Come on now, boy, sit down, you can't win every game."

I pouted, digging my hands in my pant pockets, "I know, but I like to win, I don't like losin'!"

My Grandmother laughed, drawing me closer to her and hugging me tightly, whispering, "Now don't you worry 'bout that, Joe, you are a winner, you can do it, now sit on down and play bingo with us." I love my Grandma, she was the center of my universe. As I looked into her eyes, pale skin, shiny silver hair/piled in braids on top of her head, probably most people would never think that she was black and sometimes I wondered if she even thought of herself that way, but she was. Like most of the folks in Mama's family, my Grandma, Aunt Boo, Mama's younger sister and her husband, they were all very light-skinned like me.

I had straight black hair and olive skin, white folks probably thought we were Italians or maybe Mexicans, most of them never thought that we were black, except that we lived in a black neighborhood.

I think our neighborhood's a nice neighborhood. The houses are small, but the people are good, they're hard-working like Mama and like Daddy was, but sometimes I wonder if our neighborhood is changing. Sometimes there's gangs of kids fighting when they're leaving junior high and it makes me think that maybe my neighborhood's not as good as I thought, especially when I'm on the bus with Mama and we pass Hyde Park and some of the white neighborhoods. I see the big brick houses and think maybe someday I'll live someplace like that, but then I think Mama wouldn't be there and Billy's not there either, so I guess I'm right where I'm supposed to be.

I think those thoughts sometimes when I'm with Mama even though sometimes she doesn't hug me or hold me or kiss me the way I might like, but then there's others who do. Grandma always has something nice to say to me, sometimes I wish she was as nice to Billy as she was to me, but she seems not to like him so much. But me, I feel like with Grandma I could sit in her lap and lean against her shoulder and talk for hours and watch TV with her always, she's kind of like my best friend except that she's not my age.

I don't know why I'm thinking all this stuff, maybe to take my mind off the fact that I'm in this big hot gymnasium with Mama, and Grandma and Aunt Boo, and all those other ladies playing bingo, and what I really want to do is to go outside and play or maybe to spend time with some of my friends. That's when I got the idea that maybe I'd sell soda pop to the ladies playing bingo, I mean gosh, who couldn't use a cold pop in this hot place? So, I gathered my little bits of money together and I bought some pop and then I'd go over to different groups of them. I always chose the ones who were a little heavy, the one's that had little beads of sweat on their foreheads, and the one's with the big church fans fanning their faces and saying, "Lawdie, it's hot in here."

The ones who had the nice smiles and wouldn't shoo me away; the one's who'd pinch my cheeks and say, "You're Miz Steele's boy, aren't you?"

I'd smile and nod, "Yes ma'am."

"Well I think that I will take one of those cold pops from you, how much would that be?"

I told her and then she'd fish in her big black purse overflowing with all sorts of papers and change and bring out some money and maybe sometimes she'd give me a little extra, saying, "Miz Steele, you got you a good boy there, nice boy, handsome boy—you're lucky."

Mama wouldn't say anything, but she'd smile and I could tell by her smile that she agreed. But I guess all the pop in the world still wasn't enough for me to want to hang around that gymnasium, just too hot, too darn hot and stuffy.

"Time to go." I turned and saw Mama and Grandma. Grandma had a broad smile so she must've won, sure enough, she put her arm around me saying, "We won!"

I could also tell that Mama hadn't won, although typical of Mama she didn't say anything and just had the same calm look whether she'd won the big jackpot or lost every game. Mama was always the same, no big ups or low downs, she was somebody I could count on and the only time I ever saw her really angry was if somebody messed with me or Billy.

Mama eased me towards the door, "You hungry?" I nodded, sitting in a hot stuffy gymnasium definitely got my appetite going. "Well, we're going over to Mama Lan's, seems she's going to be frying up some chicken and I know how you love her chicken." I jumped up. "Yah!!!!" 'Cause I loved Mama Lan's fried chicken. It was like the best and most delicious crispy chicken ever. Then I remembered what came before the fried chicken and I asked tentatively, "Are the chickens already dead?"

Mama shrugged. "Don't know, guess we'll find out when we get there."

I gulped, much as I loved Mama Lan and REALLY loved her fried chicken, I can't say I loved the part where she'd cut off the poor chicken's head and rest of its body would be flapping around spurting out blood. The first time I saw it, it was hard to get my appetite back. I was used to it now, but I still didn't like that part. But I guess you had to make some sacrifices to get that crispy delicious golden brown fried chicken, like Mama would always tell me, nothin' in life is free, you always have to sacrifice if you want something really good, and Mama Lan's fried chicken was REALLY good. So, as we left the gymnasium, I told myself that seeing the poor chicken without its head was just a sacrifice I had to make.

Besides, I loved Mama Lan and looked forward to seeing her and feeling the love that always seemed to surround her. She wasn't really a relative, but I felt closer to her sometimes than to Aunt Boo or Mama's other family. Mama Lan didn't look anything like Mama's relatives; like I said they were all light-skinned like me with straight hair and most of them tall and thin. Mama Lan was a deep chocolate brown with warm cushy arms that would surround me with love and the fragrance of fresh soap and spices. Mama Lan was almost like another mother to me, she would stroke my head and give me lots of hugs and kisses. Mama didn't mind, she seemed happy that I was part of this warm comfortable embrace that was Mama Lan.

****

I was remembering back further, now I'm about six and it was after Daddy had died. I'm on the bus with Mama holding her hand tightly.

"Well hello there, Miz Steele," the bus driver tipped his hat smiling at Mama, he always seemed to smile at Mama in the same way, like he expected her to smile back at him.

But Mama just answered the same way every time. "Fine, I'm just fine, thank you."

And every time I'd hear the bus driver saying really softly to himself kinda whispering, but loud enough for Mama and me to hear, "You sure *are*..."

And Mama would act like she didn't hear a thing and would keep on walking down the middle of the aisle holding my hand. Once we got to our seats, usually in the middle of the bus far enough away from the bus driver, but not in the back with the loud big kids, she'd put me on the inside and she'd sit on the outside. I'd look out the window thinking about Daddy. It hadn't been that long since Daddy had died and sometimes I'd wondered if Daddy was still here if we'd be driving instead of taking the bus. I remembered our car, a nice big black shiny car and then I remember, not a long time ago, Mama and Billy yelling at each other like they seemed to do a lot, Billy running in the house shaking, telling Mama he crashed the car. I could tell that Mama was happy that Billy was OK, but mad that he'd messed up the car. So, then we didn't have a car anymore.

Mama rang the cord for the bus to stop. "Come on, Joe, give me your hand."

"OK, Mama," and I'd slip my little hand into hers.

Now, I'm walking to school with Mama. It's in a church, in a big basement full of a lot of kids like me. Some are brown, others look more like me. On the first day that I went to that school, Mama pointed out a big kid, a nice-looking boy, who went to the school for the big kids. She said that he was going to walk me home. I was in the afternoon kindergarten so she said that he'd come and pick me up every day and walk me home, since Mama was working she wouldn't be able to get me, but Grandma would be home when I got there.

I remember Mama saying, "Joe, he's going to walk you home after school. He's going to come every day to walk you home."

And I remember saying, "Yes, Mama." And smiling at the nice boy. But on this day, I'm outside the school and the cars are going *whoosh, whoosh* past me and I'm waiting for the boy to come and walk me home. It's really hot and the sun is shining in my face, so I can barely see, but I can hear groups of big kids walking by. They're loud, chewing gum, some of them yelling at each other. I'm just sitting and waiting and waiting for that boy to come and I'm kicking my feet against the sidewalk thinking, "*Where is he?*" The lights change to green and then back to red, then back to yellow. The cars keep going past me and everybody seems to have someone to come take them home, everybody but me. And I know that Mama is working, so I know she can't come, so I'm waiting and waiting and then I think, "*Well, I know my way. I'll just go by myself.*"

So, I pick up my little book bag and start walking. After a while, my legs are getting kind of tired as I think, "*It's a longer walk than I thought.*" Mama taught me when you cross the street you stop and you look both ways and only when you don't see any cars, you cross the street. There was a big street with lots of cars and lots of people running so fast and walking fast. Everybody seems to be walking faster and faster not noticing me, so I stopped and I look both ways and cross the street. It seems like I'm walking and walking and getting so tired and I'm getting so thirsty, so I stop on a bench and rest for a minute and then start walking again, and then finally, finally I see the house. When Mama got home, I told her what happened, and she got really mad, not at me; she just hugged me and said, "Are you OK?" a lot of times and then hugged me some more.

I don't really know what happened except that I changed to the morning kindergarten and I didn't see that boy anymore, but now I could walk home with my friends who were in the morning kindergarten with me.

End Flashback
Buffalo, New York, Hospital; Present Time

Sophie interrupted me. "How old were you then?"

"Five, I was in kindergarten…when I think about now, I bet that's where I got some of my independence and self-reliance—from Mama. Because after my father died she was really on her own, but she never complained. I think back all these years later and I know how hard it must've been for her, particularly with her and my brother Billy not really getting along, and Billy and my Grandma not getting along either. I remember one time in particular when it really came to a head, that is between Billy and Grandma. I guess I was about maybe eight or nine…" Thinking back to the thoughts that I had then…

Flashback Through Joe's Eyes
Cincinnati, Ohio; Age 8

Billy was my big brother and I really loved him, and I love Grandma, but Grandma and Billy just didn't get along. She would say mean things to him, things about his color. I was light-colored with straight hair and Billy had wavy hair, but he was brown. Grandma had very light skin and straight gray hair that she put into braids on top of her head. She seemed to care a lot about the color of people's skin, especially black people. She didn't seem to like black people who were too dark and I think maybe Billy was too dark for her. I remember this day we were sitting watching TV, seems like things always seemed to happen when I'm watching TV. This day I wanted to watch what I wanted to watch, and Billy wanted to watch something else, so I got in front of the TV and I wouldn't let him watch it, so he got mad at me. And then Grandma came in the room, she hadn't seen the whole thing, all she saw was Billy yelling at me and being mean to me, so she started yelling at Billy.

"You let Joe watch what he wants to!!!"

"Why should I?! I was watching my show and then he got in front of me, you're always on his side!!!" And Billy stood in front of the TV.

"Boy, I said get from in front of that TV and get out from in front of it now!"

Before Billy could say anything, Grandma grabbed a heavy beveled glass ashtray and threw it at him, barely missing his head. Now I felt kind of bad because I really had started the whole thing. When Mama came home, she and Grandma really got into it and I think she finally understood that Grandma had never really been nice to Billy, and she'd always said mean things because I think of his dark skin. So that day, Mama told Grandma not to come back and to leave her house. I cried because I really loved Grandma and I wanted her to stay. I didn't want her to leave and I felt bad because I really had started the whole thing. The house was empty without Grandma, nobody to stroke my hair and hug me and give me kisses and tell me what a great boy I was. Then one day she came back, and I was so happy because my Grandma was back.

End Flashback
Buffalo, New York, Hospital; Present Time

Sophie coughed, interrupting me. "Did you have your grandmother with you for a long time?"

"Not long enough, she died when I was 10. Then it was just Mama and me."

"What about your brother, Billy, that was his name, right?"

I nodded. "Yeah, he left to join the Navy around the same time, so it was really just Mama and me in the house."

"Was that during the Vietnam War? So many people protested, it's surprising that he'd go...I mean...on his own without being drafted."

I was quiet for a moment, thinking back on the pictures of the war on TV, and how I'd always think about Billy and when I'd say my prayers every night I'd ask God to keep him safe. I couldn't help but feel a little guilty about what might have made him leave.

As if reading my thoughts, Sophie prodded me gently. "Was he that unhappy at home?"

"I don't know if it was unhappiness as much as just feeling confused and angry. He'd found out as a teenager that he was adopted and in hindsight I think that he almost felt betrayed...not that he didn't love Mama and Daddy 'cause he did and he took Daddy's death really hard. But I think there was just a lot going on in his head at that time and running away to the War seemed like an escape from the things he couldn't face."

"Did you and Billy look alike? I mean, even though you weren't biological brothers it seems like you looked a lot like your Mom's family from the way you described them."

"You know, it's funny. Billy did look like us except that he was light brown skinned and had wavy black hair instead of olive skin with straight hair like me and Mama. But since Daddy was a darker brown, Billy looked like he really could've been Mama and Daddy's biological son."

Sophie looked like she wanted to say something, but she stopped, letting me continue.

"I guess the real issue that nobody talked about directly was how everybody on Mama's side was so what we used to say, 'color struck.'"

"Color struck?"

Thinking back, it all seems so pointless now. "Yeah, back then light skin and straight hair was like some kind of badge of courage, so much so that one of my mother's brothers passed for white. He married a white woman and moved to California and pretty much turned his back on the family. We never heard anything else about him until he was dying and then his wife reached out to Mama, but at that point, she didn't want to have anything to do with him. I remember her saying he'd died to her a long time ago." I got up out of my chair, needing to stretch my legs a bit, then without turning back to Sophie, continued. "But you know the funny thing is that by the time I was a teenager, things were the exact opposite, everybody was bending over backwards to show their blackness, big afros and 'black love.'" And me, well I felt like the odd man out. People didn't know what I was, and truth be told, I wasn't sure myself sometimes. I wanted to fit in, so for a while I told the kids at school that I was Spanish, but then I did like a one-eighty and decided I wanted to do something with my hair to proclaim my blackness. But you see this?" I pointed to my hair. "Dead straight and wouldn't take a curl no matter how hard I tried. So, I decided that what I had to do was to get what they called a "Grecian Curl." Now I really chuckled thinking back on that day.

CHAPTER

20

Flashback Through Joe's Eyes
Cincinnati, Ohio; About 16 Years Old

I took a deep breath, shoving my hand in my pocket to make sure I had all my money. I'd done extra chores around the house and had also helped Pops with some things he needed. I was determined to have enough money, but I didn't want to tell anyone what it was for. So, when Mama eyed me suspiciously when I told her that I really wanted to do that extra yard work and could she pay me a little something for it, she raised her eyebrow, but didn't ask what the money was for, just counting it out carefully after I'd raked every single leaf and mopped the basement floor where the dogs had done their business, holding my nose but knowing that it would be worth it. And so now as I re-counted for probably the third time, the dollar bills stuffed in my hand, I pushed the heavy glass door and walked into the barber shop. There were a bunch of middle-aged men, mostly black, and all seated in barber chairs or against the wall waiting for an open spot.

But the thing that caught my attention, and in fact the reason I was there, was a large poster that swung lazily over the door catching the mid-summer breeze. A young man about my age was on the poster and his hair was covered in lustrous curls. I could almost feel my fingers running through curls just like that, which I knew that by the time I got out of the barber chair that I was being motioned towards, I'd have on my head.

The barber took out a towel, tucking it expertly under my neck. "So, young man, here for a cut?"

He grabbed his scissors out of the Barbicide, but before he could go any further, I stopped him. "No. I want one of those," and I pointed to the poster.

"You mean a Grecian Curl?"

I nodded enthusiastically. "Yep, exactly like that, can you make it look *exactly* like that?"

He looked me up and down, taking a tuft of my hair in his fingers, then releasing it. "Yeah, I think we can do that."

I got this little thrill as I envisioned myself looking like the guy in the poster on the wall. Flyaway collar, confident smile and those amazing Grecian curls just skirting his shoulder. I couldn't wait to see the reaction at school—nobody would be asking me what I was, black, white, Spanish—nobody seemed to really know with my olive skin and straight hair that just wouldn't seem to do anything but lie flat on my head—with the Grecian curls, they wouldn't have to ask 'cause they'd know without me saying a word that I was just COOL and THAT just about said it all!

I was thinking what a statement I'd make at school with my new hair-style, as the barber started to layer some really foul-smelling gel on my head. He combed through it and I had to stop myself from gagging. It had a weird chemical scent mixed with a kind of rotten egg stench, but I didn't care 'cause if this is what it took to get my Grecian curls, then so be it. Like Mama had always said, whatever was worth having was worth working for, and this was definitely going to be worth whatever I had to go through to get that suave, sophisticated, totally COOL Grecian curl look.

"Close your eyes, boy…tight now, don't want none of this dripping in them eyes." The barber then stretched what looked like a plastic shower cap over my head, tucking it around the sides and then brushing another layer of the gel around the sides of the cap like he was sealing it on my head.

I nodded, afraid to open my mouth too much and be filled up with that strong acid smell of the Grecian Curl gel. After about 20 minutes, I started to feel a little uncomfortable, there was a stinging at the back of my neck where the gel was starting to drip down my collar through the sides of the shower cap and my cheeks had also started to burn where the gel was plastered directly on my skin. I didn't want to say anything, but it had really started to hurt, so I asked tentatively, "Uh…sir…is it supposed to…sting?"

I could hear one of the older gentlemen in the back chuckle, "Clyde, what you done giving that boy a curl, you know his hair ain't made for that…"

The barber glared at him, "Look, Al, jus' lemme do my job, the boy say he want a curl, so I'm givin' him a curl."

The other man just shook his head, turning back to his game of checkers, "Your move."

By now, I felt like the back of my neck was on fire and I couldn't hold it in anymore trying not to sound alarmed, I barely squeaked out, "Um, can we, um, wash this out? It's really burning now."

Seemingly unconcerned, the barber glanced at the crooked wall clock, "Well we got another ten minutes…but I guess we can wash it out now." He carefully lifted the shower cap off and then guided me to the sink.

"Keep them eyes closed."

I could feel the cold water rushing over my hair, but instead of cooling the burning sensation which by now had covered my entire head, it seemed to make it even worse and I felt like I wanted to jump out of the chair and stick my head in a bucket of ice cubes, anything to make the burning stop.

"Now don't worry, it's gonna sting a little, that's the gel workin', I's just gonna put this on." He squeezed a glob of some equally foul-smelling paste into his hand and then started massaging it in my scalp. "This'll take the sting away—it's the finishin' cream."

Sure enough, the stinging was starting to subside and I was beginning to breathe a little more normally. He covered my head with a towel and then motioned for me to follow him back to the chair. Turning my chair away from the mirror so that I couldn't see anything, he took the towel and roughly dried my hair. He then took out some type of pomade from his drawer and dabbed a bit of it on several large tufts of my hair. Finally, he ran his fingers through my scalp and then, with a flourish, twirled my chair back to the mirror. "We done."

Expecting to see the soft sexy Grecian curls trailing down my neck, I looked at the mirror and almost screamed. I was so shocked I couldn't even speak, my eyes darted from the poster on the wall to my face in the mirror and then back again. My hair was a mixture of grotesque spikes that by now were as hard as cardboard with a few limp curls. I looked as if I'd stuck my finger in a light socket and half of my head had been electrocuted and the other half looked like a bad Orphan Annie clone. I could feel tears stinging my eyes, especially as I heard a few barely suppressed grunts of laughter from the back of the shop.

"Clyde, what you done to that boy?!"

"Whoo, wait till his Mama see him, she gonna come after you!" They slapped each other high five.

By now, I had regained my voice, but just barely. "I said I wanted that!!!!!" And I pointed desperately to the poster, all hopes of my beautiful Grecian curls now fading with each moment.

"Look, boy. I done the curl, it don't always take. Now that'll be twenty dollars."

"Ooh, and you gonna make him pay for that! Clyde, you got no shame!"

"Al, I had just 'bout enough of your shit..."

By now, I was just totally speechless, all I could think was that I'd be the laughing stock at school. Instead of being cool, I'd be a bigger outcast than ever. I didn't want to cry. I couldn't, but I knew I had to do something and there was only one person in the entire world that I trusted to get me out of this mess. Quickly, I threw the crumpled bills on the table and ran out of the barber shop, hearing someone bursting into laughter as I slammed the door behind me.

CHAPTER

21

"Oh, my Gawd! What happened to you?" Chris, probably my best friend in the world since we met in elementary school, was admiring himself from different angles from his three-sided floor length mirror in his long attic room. There was fabric strewn in every corner and fashion magazines stacked on the coffee tables. His bed was covered in a large soft comforter with brightly colored Asian print silk pillows propped up against the wall, with posters of Japan, where his mother was from, on one wall. Chris' father was black and his mother was Japanese, and Chris had that classic Afro-Asian look—wavy black hair, light skin and decidedly handsome. Chris was almost like a male Auntie Mame; he was one of the most uninhibited, over-the-top people that I knew. Chris also had an incredible fashion sense and his dream was to go to New York to work in the fashion industry, so if there was anybody who could fix this mess I had gotten into, it was Chris.

By now, the reality of what I'd done had sunk in and my tears had turned to depression. "I tried to get a Grecian Curl." I plopped on his bed, head in my hands. I didn't even want to touch my hair and I purposely averted my eyes when I passed his mirrors, not wanting to see the horror that was on my head.

"A Grecian Curl?! Joe, don't you know that's for black people with that kinky black hair? You don't have that, you got the good stuff, *blow hair*, like my sister would say."

"Right. Look, can you help me? I gotta do something. I can't go to school like this! I'll never live this down."

"Calm down, calm down. We'll have to reverse it. The chemical in the curl is supposed to make kinky hair get wavy and then the finisher is supposed to lock the curls in—but obviously none of that happened here!"

"It's not funny."

"Ok, sorry, look, I think I've got some reverse cream here, that guy, you know the cute one, the hairdresser's assistant I met, he sent me a bunch of samples, I think they're over here." He opened a large trunk and started tossing things out dramatically, "Not this…no…not this… this is where that was. I've been looking for this, I wonder how that would go with my black jacket…hmmm."

"Chris!"

"What do you think about this shirt?" He held up a Kelly green shirt that he'd fished out of the bottom of the trunk.

"CHRIS!!!! MY HAIR!"

"Right, right…hold on, you can't rush genius."

I rolled my eyes. I loved Chris, but his penchant for drama, usually at the most inopportune times, was maddening.

"OK. This is what I was looking for." He held up a small pink jar with a flourish. "This should do the trick."

"It better, or I don't know what I'm going to do."

The next hour was a blur, I was afraid to open my eyes as Chris carefully parted my hair, wet it and then started combing the entire contents of the pink jar through my scalp. The previous two hours kept playing in a loop in my brain, the sense of sheer horror as I saw what my hair had become. The laughter, and the guy in the poster seeming to smirk at me as he tossed his hair back with the Grecian curls glowing in the sunshine.

"OK, we're done, I think I got it all out."

"Are you sure??" By now I was so traumatized I couldn't even

open my eyes, so I pleaded, "Chris, tell me I'm back to normal."
"Just open your eyes, don't be afraid."

"Easy for you to say!!!"

"Joe, have I ever let you down? Now just have some faith." He shoved a small hand mirror in front of me. I refused to open my eyes.

But Chris wasn't having it. "Joseph Edward Steele, open your eyes, you know I know how to work it!" And with that, he turned on the record player and started to dance along with the song, *I Can Work It*.

"Chris, please!"

"Look, until you open your eyes, I'm not stopping." And he continued, "Baby, I know how to work it." He was bumping and grinding with an invisible male partner.

I couldn't stand it anymore. I had to see what he'd done. Slowly, I opened one eye, but still couldn't bring myself to look in the mirror, then slowly I forced the other eye open. And I couldn't believe what I was seeing…my hair…my own straight dark brown hair plastered to my head was BACK! All traces of the aborted Grecian curls were gone.

"Chris!"

He waved me off as if it was nothing as he continued pulling things out of the trunk. "When I say I'm a genius, what do you say?"

I smiled in spite of the trauma I'd just been through. "You're a genius."

"Thank you, Ma'am." Now I'm starving, let's see what Mom's got for lunch."

CHAPTER

22

End Flashback
Buffalo, New York, Hospital; Present Time

Sophie was sitting up in her bed and for the first time since I'd been coming to the hospital, she was really laughing. So much so that the nosey nurse couldn't help poking her head in the door.

"Ms. Legocki, are you all right?"

In between chuckles, she waved her off, "I'm fine, just fine, great to get a good laugh in."

The nurse snorted in disapproval. "I suppose." Both Sophie and I ignored her as we continued thinking about my poor teenage self, trying to fit in and instead almost making things worse.

Sophie wiped a tear away from her face from laughing so hard "Thank you, nurse, but I'm fine, no need to waste your time here."

The nurse eyed us both suspiciously as if she thought that she was the cause of our mirth, but finally, I guess satisfying herself that it was not the case, she stomped out of the room.

"Oh, Joe, I wish I could've seen you!"

I shook my head, remembering again. "I'm glad no one did!"

"So, your friend Chris, are you still in touch with him?"

Suddenly hit by a wave of sadness, "Chris died… a while ago…much too young, like too many others that I've known."

For a moment there was an awkward silence.

"Was it AIDS?"

"Yeah…it was…he was one of the early cases, before they had the medicines they do now. So, he didn't have much of a chance. But he was brave to the end. Never lost his flair…his love for life. I just wish I could have been there for him."

I couldn't help remembering when I found out that Chris had passed.

I was living in Brazil and felt so helpless, like a small part of me had died with him.

Sophie interrupted my thoughts, "So, that was never an issue for her?" Back to present time, now Sophie prodding me.

Shaking my head, "You mean that I'm gay? No, never. Never." And then I smiled remembering back. "Mama was one of the most tolerant people that I knew."

"How so?"

"Well, she never had a problem with me or any of my friends. I'd come home to visit with my lovers and she'd give up her room and her bed for us. There were times that we'd travel together or meet in some of the places where I was living, and I even remember one time when we went on a trip and shared a hotel room. I was there with my boyfriend at the time, we were in the same bed and Mama was in the same room in the next bed. She never had a problem." I smiled to myself, remembering that trip and others that Mama and I had taken together.

Sophie leaned back on her pillow not saying anything, then hesitantly, "When did you first know…or did you always know that you were…that…way?"

Thinking back, musing, "I think I knew I was gay early on, I remember being seven or eight and kind of fooling around in my room upstairs, with some of the boys who were like me, especially Chris."

"Were you close to her growing up?"

I hesitated for a moment thinking back about Mama because on one hand we were very close. "We traveled together all over the world," I told Sophie. "We went to Brazil, we went to Paris and our last trip to Martha's Vineyard was one of the most special times for us, but could I say we that we were close? I don't know. The one thing I know is that Mama never judged me, she just loved me."

And I thought back on the time that Mama had come to visit me in LA. I remember it like it was yesterday.

Flashback Through Joe's Eyes
Los Angeles, California; Early 20'S

We were in Ralphs supermarket walking down the aisles. I was pushing the cart and Mama was next to me.

"Mama, what do you want for dinner tonight?"

"Oh, I don't know, Joe, whatever you're in the mood for. I'm not particular." She stopped in front of the refrigerator aisle, opening the door, "But I do think that I'd like some orange juice for breakfast."

She pulled out a carton of orange juice and put it in the shopping cart and was about to walk down another aisle when I said, "Mama, we can't buy that kind of orange juice."

Puzzled, she looked at me, "Why not? It's the kind we always buy."

"That's the orange juice that I'm boycotting because of the things that Anita Bryant said about..." and I hesitated, "gay people..." And then I knew that I had to tell her. I had to tell her the truth. I hesitated again, "Because, Mama...I'm gay."

Mama didn't say anything, she just smiled as if to say, 'And you think I didn't know that?' But she took the orange juice, put it back and got another brand. Mama never judged me. In fact, a couple of times Mama almost caught me in bed with some of my friends, but she never said anything, she never judged.

End Flashback
Buffalo, New York, Hospital; Present Time

Sophie absentmindedly twisted the bedspread around her finger. "I guess she must've been proud of all your accomplishments. I mean, Harvard and everything."

"She was really proud, and to think, I almost didn't go to Harvard."

"What happened?"

I chuckled remembering back to a happier time before sickness had ravaged the community and decimated my core of close friends. It was 1975.

Flashback Through Joe's Eyes
New York City; Spring 1975, 18 Years Old

New York was like this constant drum beat of noise and people and cars and bright sunlight and the smell of sweaty bodies and movement everywhere. Nothing and no one was ever still. I felt a little overwhelmed but energized at the same time. It was the first warm day of spring and a long way from Cincinnati. Chris and I had been hanging out all over the city for the past three days, mainly around Seventh Avenue and the fashion district. Chris had met a big designer, this up-and-coming "boy genius" or at least that's what everybody said. He was in his mid-twenties, but already his collections were being shown around town. He had taken quite a liking to Chris and I suppose that the feeling was mutual, but with Chris you never knew.

He'd flash his smile at anyone who he thought was worth his while and he had a way of attracting just about anybody that he put his mind to. And this guy was someone who Chris wanted. He had the access to the world that Chris saw himself in, so he was more than happy to tool around with him and soak up the atmosphere of what he'd been dreaming of for so long. And me, well, I guess I was kind of along for the ride. It was senior year of high school, spring break, I'd heard back from all the colleges and I'd gotten accepted everywhere I applied. All the Ivies, including my first choice, Columbia. I couldn't wait to hang out with Chris and his new pal and really start living the high life away from the quiet boredom of Cincinnati.

"Penny for your thoughts?" Chris jolted me back to reality. His friend had some business to attend to for the afternoon, so it was just me and Chris at his friend's studio—this fabulous loft with high ceilings, really hip furniture, fashion stuff all over the place, basically everything you'd expect from a designer.

"Are you ready to party tonight? We got tickets to see Nancy Wilson and she is just so FAB, we got backstage passes, thanks to Hector, so we're gonna be hanging tuff! God, Joe, I can't wait until you're here in the fall, we are going to turn this town out!! Watch out, New York, you ain't seen nothing yet." And he started absentmindedly humming to himself, then hanging out the window and yelling to no one in particular. "New York, New York! Watch out 'cause Chris is in the HOUSE!"

Someone across the street yelled back. "Aw, shut up…like we cares!" "Oh pleasssse! You're gonna know who I am, all you people!" And he stuck his head out even further. "You are going to know my name!"

I hated when Chris got on these rampages, so I knew it was time to dial him down before he got even more boisterous.

"OK, Chris. I think everyone hears you."

He popped his head back in the window briefly. "You think?"

"Definitely."

"OK, then I guess I can stop." He pulled out a joint from his pocket. "Want some? We got a couple of hours to kill before the show."

I grinned. "Sure, why not?"

****

I groggily opened one eye realizing that several hours must have passed since I took the toke on the joint. Chris was in a tizzy fussing with his shirt and picking his hair out. "C'mon, sleepy head, you've been knocked out for hours. We don't want to miss the show."

"Right, I'd almost forgotten."

"Gawd, Joe! How could you forget Nancy, how could anyone forget Nancy?!"

The next couple of hours were a blur, I was so exhausted. I think the travel, all the late nights studying for midterms before spring break, and just the general soul-sapping energy of NYC in full bloom had finally caught up with me. I really wanted nothing more than to crawl into a warm bed and sleep for about ten hours, but Chris, who never seemed to need any sleep at all, would have none of that. So, I found myself shoved into a taxi and then crammed into a concert hall full of die-hard Nancy Wilson fans. I had to admit that about half way through her show I started to wake up and really enjoy the music, and just as I was finally relaxed, Chris was revved up again.

"Ok, Joe, we've got backstage passes to see Nancy. *We cannot* miss this." I was more awake but still dragging.

"Come on, Joe! Oh, my God, let's go!" Impatiently, he sprinted in front of me heading for backstage. Officiously, like he was the star, he sashayed past the guards, flashing his signature smile and marched straight to her dressing room. He knocked firmly on the door, "Miss Wilson, it's Chris, you know my friend, Hector."

From the other side of the door, I heard her deep throaty voice with just the hint of a southern drawl, "C'mon in."

She was still wearing her gold lamé gown from the last number and looking every bit the diva. "So, you're friends of Hector's?"

Chris never missed a beat, "Very close. We're very close friends."

She smiled, "Well any friend of Hector's is a friend of mine. Sit down." She motioned to me. "And you, what's your name, young man?"

Suddenly shy and feeling on the spot, I barely forced out, "Joe, Joe Steele."

"Well, Joe, a pleasure to meet you, too. So how old are you young men? You don't look too much older than my son, Kacy."

"Eighteen, ma'am."

She smiled to herself, "Well, I remember 18, yes I do. So, are you headed to college?"

I nodded eagerly, "Yes, Ma'am. I am."

"And where are you going?"

"I've pretty much decided on Columbia. I got in everywhere I applied, and I was originally thinking that Harvard was my first choice, but now I think I really want to be here in New York."

She slowly raised one eyebrow and then patted the sofa next to her. "Sit down, Joe. Right here next to me."

"OK," I lowered myself on the couch hesitantly, I wasn't quite sure what I'd done, I hoped I hadn't offended her in some way.

"Now, Joe. I'm not your mama, but I'm sure she'd want me to say this. You **cannot** turn down Harvard. If you got into Harvard, then you go to Harvard because if you don't, you'll regret it for the rest of your life. Trust me. Besides, New York is not going anywhere, you can always live in New York. But you only get one chance to go to Harvard. So, don't blow it. Now you remember I told you that."

I nodded, "Yes, ma'am. I'll remember. I promise."

End Flashback
Buffalo, New York, Hospital; Present Time

I smiled, thinking back on that day, "So, to answer your question, that's how I got to Harvard." I couldn't help gratefully remembering Nancy Wilson and the advice that literally changed the trajectory of my life.

"Well, that is something. And did you ever wish that you'd gone to Columbia instead?"

"Not for a moment. For one thing, I might never have graduated hanging out with Chris."

Sophie smiled. "I can definitely see that."

"And the people that I met at Harvard are still some of my closest friends today." Closing my eyes, remembering graduation like a snapshot in my mind that will never fade…

Flashback Through Joe's Eyes
Cambridge, Massachusetts, Harvard Yard; June 1979

A blisteringly blue sky, the first Thursday in June—always the first Thursday in June for Harvard's graduation. Everyone walking proudly in their caps and gowns, Harvard Yard dressed up for the visiting alums… close friends that I'd made over the past four years, over all-nighters and laughter and growing up, some had become more like family than just friends…snatches of conversation coming back in fragments. "Hey Joe, congrats! Ready for the real world?!"

"Hear you're headed to HBS…"

"Yeah, in a couple of years, gonna work first."

"I hear you."

"Joe, Joe." Mama, walking towards me, smiling, followed by Pops, Aunt Callie and Billy. Mama was older than the other moms, she'd been in her late fifties when she and Daddy adopted me, so she was definitely probably close to 20 years older than most of my friends' mothers. I remember being in elementary school and people asking me if she was my grandmother, not really understanding until I was old enough to do the math and figure out that there was no way that she could've been my biological mother. But it didn't matter, Mama still looked good, even though her hair was gray, her skin was fine and not lined at all, still soft very light and she looked at me with love the way she always had, only on this day she was brimming over with more pride and love than I ever remembered.

She walked over to me and I gave her a big hug, saying, "Mama, I want you to meet some of my friends, you've heard all about them, now you can finally meet in person." And so I started rattling off the names of the people that I'd spent the last four years of my life with, and as I looked up into the blue sky, I realized that college was over and I was about to start a new CHAPTER as an adult. I was excited, but at the same time just not quite sure what lay before me.

Mama clasped my hand and though she wasn't normally the hugging type, that day she hugged me tightly, saying, "Joe, I'm proud of you. I'm real proud of you."

End Flashback
Buffalo, New York, Hospital; Present Time

"She never remarried after your father died?"

I was catapulted back to present day with Sophie's question. And once more I was in the sterile hospital room with monitors blinking and me starting to get uncomfortable on the hard guest chair, suddenly feeling very far away from that idyllic day in June so many years ago.

I reflected back, much further now to childhood and my teen years, mulling Sophie's question over in my head. "No, Mama never did marry again, not that she didn't have the chance to. She was attractive, and she had men interested in her, in fact I remember one of the gentleman had a nice car and a nice house and I used to wish that Mama would decide to marry him, but she never did."

Sophie settled back on her pillow, her turn this time to be reflective, "I understand...I do...because when you've really loved someone and then they die, nobody can ever really take their place." She hesitated, as if searching for the right words. "No. Nobody can ever really take their place."

"Mama told me once, when I asked her later why she never married again, and I remember her saying, 'You know, your father was a good man, he never ever took a hand to me and I just don't know if there would be anybody else like that, so I decided that I was just fine the way I was.'"

"She sounds like a real independent woman..."

I almost sensed a tinge of jealousy, and then remembering that after Father Grau died Sophie moved back with her parents. "So unlike Mama," I thought to myself, but of course didn't say. But thinking back about that time again to my childhood, and although I don't remember a lot because I was so young, I somehow always knew that Mama was very independent and that she never asked anybody for anything, even her own family. Now that I'm grown, I understand how difficult it must've been for her to ask Grandma to come live with us since she never really got along that well with her or even with her own sister. I always felt like Mama really didn't have Aunt Boo or her husband, or any of them, really, to depend on. Sometimes, I'd wish that we could have been closer to them, they always seemed to have parties and fun things to do and I remember one day wanting to go to one of their parties and begging Mama to let us go. "Mama, why can't I go there??? Why don't we ever get to go to their parties? They're our cousins, why can't we go???"

She didn't get angry or even raise her voice, she just said in a matter of fact tone, "Joe, if they'd wanted you to come, they would've invited you, and if somebody doesn't invite you, then you don't go asking if you can go, do you hear me?" I scuffed my foot against the door, not really wanting to say much except that I really wanted to go to that party.

"Now, Joe," Mama took my chin and tilted it up to her, "You hear

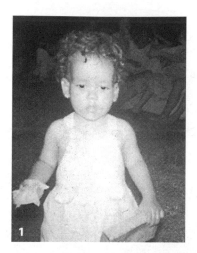

1. First photo of Joe with his newly adoptive family the Steeles. **2.** Joe at age 8. **3.** Joe (right) with high school best friend, Chris Vaughn (left). **4.** Florence Steele, "Mama", with Joe.

5

7

5. William Steele, Joe's adoptive father in the 1940's. **6.** Florence Steele, Joe's adoptive mother in the 1940's. **7.** Joe at 3 years old with his brother William "Billy" Steele. **8.** Cousin Tony (left) and Uncle Dal (center) with Joe at 7 years old.

what I'm saying, we don't go asking anybody or begging anybody to include us, we don't need that, we're just fine, if somebody doesn't ask us, then it's just not that important, do you hear me? You remember that."

"Yes, Mama." I said yes, but I still really wanted to go to that party.

That was just one of the many lessons that Mama taught me about independence and self-reliance, not judging and standing on your own two feet. When I think of Mama, I can't imagine what my life would have been without her. She was my lifeline. She made me the man that I am and for that I will always be truly grateful.

CHAPTER

23

The morning sun was coming in weakly through the white metal blinds. I'd come back early that day and noticed immediately that Sophie seemed to be getting stronger. The nurse took her temperature and nodded approvingly, noting that it hadn't spiked overnight as it had previously. I had brought a cup of coffee with me from the cafeteria and set it down on the small table.

Sophie smiled broadly, "So many parallels, so many things that are alike between you and him."

"You mean Father Grau?" By now I'd come to understand that when she spoke of "him," it was always Father Grau, my birth father, the man who seemed to be the invisible hand that had brought us together and was now orchestrating what seemed to be an unfolding of his life so that I could better understand where it fit within my own.

Sophie nodded her head. "Yes, just like *him* raised in a different family that was not your own, at least not by birth, but it sounds like there was a lot of love in your home. For him, it seemed like other than his mother, well it was hard for him, being colored and all in that family. Maybe that's why we connected so much, both of us had it kind of hard growing up, for different reasons, me because I was the only girl. When I first met him, I felt like he was so different from anyone I'd ever seen, but then the more I got to know him, the more I realized how much alike we really were."

Flashback Through Sophie's Eyes
Lackawanna, New York, Queen Of All Saints Parish; 1955

Sister Blanche stuck her head in my door. "Are you coming to Mass? You better hurry or you'll be late."

"I'm coming, don't wait for me. I'll catch up with you."

"OK, but you better make it quick, you know how Mother Superior is when you're not in your seat exactly on time."

I nodded as she dashed down the stairs. I heard her footsteps fade in the distance and I leaned back on my bed. Truth was, I felt torn, I knew I had to go to Mass, but ever since Father Grau and I had spent that time in the garden, I'd felt even more awkward around him. I wondered what he thought about me. Was I just some silly nun acting like a teenager? I even found myself looking in the mirror wondering if I was attractive. Those thoughts were not only silly, but really dangerous. I was sure that I was only imagining that he felt anything at all towards me. After all, he was the Parish priest and above those types of worldly thoughts. Not like me. I felt so confused. I heard the chime and I knew I'd have to run all the way to get in just before Mother Superior sat down or it would be extra chores for me.

I managed to slip in just before the heavy doors were closed and the first rolling tones of the opening music began. I heaved a sigh of relief, just in the nick of time. Sister Blanche had saved me a seat next to her and she smiled as I settled in. My eyes wandered around the small church, the light filtering in through the simple stained-glass windows, not the elaborate frescos of larger churches, but still capturing the serenity of our

Savior. I focused on his peaceful gaze, wishing that I could feel the same. But instead, it was like I was churning inside, not an unpleasant feeling, to the contrary, it was like I was tingly all over, something I'd never felt before. I tried to think of other things, the children, the chores that I had to do after Mass, anything but him. And just as I thought I was able to tame my runaway thoughts, I saw Father Grau walking solemnly up the aisle followed by the two altar boys. He carried the large gold urn and was waiving the aromatic incense, filling the small sanctuary with a billowing smoke and a fragrant smell that curled around me. I think those smells, the sunshine forcing its way through the minute cracks in the heavy sanctuary door, the silence, I felt almost hypnotized, so much so that when Sister Blanche prodded me gently whispering, "Time for Communion," I almost didn't know where I was for a moment. Was I in the garden seeing his perfectly formed hands turning the pages of the book or was I on a cold snowy black morning with stars beginning to fade, and hearing footsteps behind me, and turning and seeing his scarf blowing in the icy wind?

Sister Blanche whispered more loudly, "Are you OK?"

"Fine, I'm fine."

"Then c'mon, it's our turn."

I think that with every step I could feel some energy pulling me forward, I didn't know what or from where, but it was like I was being pushed by an invisible force. When I reached the altar, I opened my mouth to receive the body of the Christ, and for the first time looked into his eyes, and what I saw was as if I was coming home, like the eyes were for me and me alone. As he gently placed the small wafer on my tongue. As he handed me the chalice to drink the Communion, his fingers lingered and then *squeezed* mine. And at that moment, I knew that I was not imagining it. His feelings were wrapping around my soul and I felt a warmth and a joy that filled me completely. I wanted to stay there and not move and just exist in that moment. But then his hand dropped to his side and I knew that I must turn before someone saw how I looked at him, and he at me.

I don't know how I made it back to my seat, my heart was literally jumping out of my chest and there were small beads of sweat forming on my forehead. I felt light-headed, but at the same time incredibly energized. As soon as I got to my seat, I immediately kneeled in prayer, realizing in horror that the thoughts and feelings that I had were contrary to every vow that I had taken. Had my life been a lie? Everything that I'd done for more than twenty years from the time that I came as an awkward 14-year-old to now, a woman of 35, I felt consumed with this sudden pang of guilt. But as I looked upward at our Savior, instead I saw Father Grau walking from the altar. I wanted to turn away, afraid of the feelings. But I couldn't. I couldn't stop looking at him. I couldn't stop feeling like I could gaze at his face forever.

That night, I couldn't sleep. I turned over in my hard, narrow bed picking up the Bible from my bedside, thinking that reading some scripture would re-focus me on what really mattered. My life here at the Parish, my duties, the sacred vows that I'd made, and above all, the love of our Savior, the only true love that any of us would ever know, far surpassing the transitory feelings of those of our temporary journey in the flesh. I was starting to feel better, but still wide awake. Now that summer had finally come to the frozen yards and hard walkways of the Parish, I felt restless as if the life in full bloom around me was also calling me like the proverbial siren song. "That must be it," I told myself. "It's just because it's summer. The magic of the summer solstice was just a few days away."

Then why do I get up dressing silently so as to not wake any of the other Sisters? Why do I walk out of the Convent wandering down a pathway leading to the Rectory where a dim light burned? Why do I try and shield myself from view behind a large gnarly oak, and why do I wait expectantly for a figure to walk before the window, hoping that he'll open the drapes and look out, hoping that he will hear the summer song as I have, hoping that what I felt was not the imagination of a nun who had acknowledged and actually encouraged feelings that could only lead to unhappiness and betrayal of everything that I'd worked for? I felt like I was on a precipice and I knew the path back, but I wasn't sure, so I just stood there, waiting, for what, I didn't know. Just waiting.

CHAPTER

24

Sister Gerta stuck her head in my open bedroom doorway. Her face seemed to be getting rounder every day and now it was also flushed pink as if something had rattled her. "Where were you?" Confused, I got up from my chair, "What do you mean?"

She threw her plump hands into the air in exasperation. "At the meeting! Mother Superior's special meeting! To talk about the new rules! Did you forget!"

Suddenly remembering, "Oh Lord! I forgot all about it, did she say anything about me?"

Nodding, "Sort of, but without saying your name, but she did mention that these new rules were going to be particularly important for *some* of our Sisters who unfortunately were not here with us today. So, she didn't exactly point the finger at you, but since you were the *only* one not there..."

Her words hung accusingly in the air. Ever since taking Holy Communion last Sunday, when Father Grau's fingers had brushed lightly against my tongue as he placed the wafer there and his hand had squeezed mine as he gave me the chalice to drink from, I'd been torn between euphoric ecstasy and an unspeakable guilt. Forgetting Mother Superior's meeting was just the latest in a string of mishaps. While daydreaming about Father Grau's warm smile, I'd dropped a heavy brass ornament that I was polishing causing some of the other Sisters to run out in alarm thinking something had broken. While feeling again in my mind, the way his hands had touched mine, while mopping the floor, I'd knocked over the pail of soapy water, when I leaned on the mop too hard, and the worse was the way my heart beat so quickly when I saw him at daily Mass, so much so that I almost tripped on my long habit while leaving the Church, barely catching myself. Mother Superior had rushed over, whispering accusingly, "What is wrong with you, Sister Sophie?"

I could barely respond. "Nothing, Mother Superior. Mother, I just... um...tripped."

****

Interrupting my thoughts, Sister Gerta blurted out, "So, what's going on with you, Sister Sophie? You seem so….um distracted, people are starting to talk. You've never been like this before!"

Thinking quickly, I answered, "It's my father. He's not well. I'm worried about him."

Sister Gerta's demeanor changed immediately and she ran over hugging me tightly, "Oh, I'm so sorry, Sister Sophie. I know how you feel, my father died two years ago and it's been really hard for me." She sniffled, taking a hanky out of her pocket, dabbing her eyes.

On the one hand I felt guilty for not exactly telling the truth because although my father had been ill, and I was worried about him, I knew that this was not the cause of my sudden change in behavior. The flutter that I felt in my heart, accompanied by the pain shooting through my stomach that happened each time that I thought of Father Grau, and the seemingly never-ending desire that I had to be near to him.

Sister Gerta finally let me go from her enormous bear hug, saying, "Now I understand, but take my advice, tell Mother Superior so she'll know why you've been acting this way." She sniffled again, "Oh, I almost forgot, the reason I came was because Mother Superior asked me to tell you that the new rule is that we each have to go to Confession every week. She said she wants us Sisters to set an example for the parishioners. She told me to tell you since you missed the meeting." Then she headed out the door, saying, "You better go soon. She's really not pleased."

As Sister Gerta closed the door behind her, I walked over to my bed, despondent. A sense of panic was crawling over me, what should I do? Ever since last Sunday, I had been purposely trying to avoid Confession. How could I confess my feelings to the very person who was causing them? But I knew I had no choice, I was already in trouble with Mother Superior for missing the meeting and I didn't want to give her anymore excuses to start questioning me.

CHAPTER

25

The sanctuary was dimly lit with the flickering offering candles providing tiny pin points of light, and the ever-present aroma of incense hung in the air. Usually, walking into here, would be like a balm for whatever cares or concerns that I might be carrying from the day. I would light a candle and pray for peace and then, as if God had immediately heard me, peace would come. But today, my mind was churning, my stomach was in knots, and as I walked hesitantly toward the confessional booth, I felt anything but peaceful. I kneeled at the confessional then opened the heavy burgundy velvet curtains and sat on the hard bench. I closed my eyes, praying silently that Father Grau wouldn't recognize my voice. He couldn't see me, of course, and you never gave your name, but we had spoken enough that I'm sure that he would know that it was me.

I heard the confessional window slide open and I said, almost mechanically, "Forgive me Father, for I have sinned. It has been more than a month since my last confession." I hesitated and then swallowed, "And I accuse myself of the following sins." I continued barely above a whisper, hoping that he might not hear me too well, "I accuse myself of the sin of adultery in my thoughts. As a bride of Christ, I am forbidden to think of another and I have thought of…someone else."

My palms were sweating as I continued. "I accuse myself of the sin of coveting the attention of someone other than our Father in Heaven." My stomach was doing somersaults and my legs felt heavy, "I accuse myself of the sin of desire of the flesh." *And as I mouthed the words, in my mind's eye, I saw his face. I saw the curve of his smile, I saw the deep brown of his eyes.* And much as I tried, I couldn't wrest the image of him from my thoughts, I wrung my hands together, forcing out the words, "I accuse myself of desiring to know the touch of someone and I am forbidden to have such thoughts."

I remembered the feel of his hand on mine as he laid the books in my lap that day in the garden. And I said with increasing difficulty, now breathing faster and faster, but feeling like no matter how much I tried to gasp for air, there wasn't enough. "I accuse myself of the sin of wanting to know a man other than our Savior." *Thinking of how he'd curled his fingers around the cup of tea that day in the nursery and seeing again his lips lightly brushing against the rim of the cup.* I interjected quickly, "What I meant to say was that I accuse myself of wanting to know a man...But in my thoughts only... But as a bride of Christ, I am forbidden to have such thoughts."

Suddenly I was overwhelmed with the memory of those early winter mornings that we shoveled snow together and my eyes lingered on him as he firmly held the shovel and his scarf billowed behind him in the chill breeze. I said, "And I accuse myself of wanting that which I am forbidden to have."

I stopped. I couldn't go on, I was mentally drained and feeling physically ill from confessing the magnitude of my sins. But I had to finish with the final confession, so I somehow choked out, "I am sorry for these sins and for the sins of my whole life, and I ask for forgiveness."

There was silence. I heard Father Grau clear his throat, "My child, I pray for you." His voice cracked for a moment, "I offer you penance and forgiveness of the Holy Father." He stopped and I could hear him shifting his weight in his chair, "I...I...offer you His forgiveness." And then, as if forcing himself to continue, he said, "When you have these thoughts that as a bride of Christ you are forbidden from having, pray for the Holy Father to clear your mind and fill it only with thoughts of Him." He hesitated before continuing, "Light a candle for forgiveness."

And then I heard him say, very softly, below a whisper, "That is what I do."

And I knew that he knew that it was me confessing *my* feelings to him. And I knew that he, too, was wracked by the same guilt and consumed with the same thoughts. Those thoughts that we both knew we could not have— yet, we did.

"Thank you, Father." I quickly got out of my seat and it was all that I could do to not run out of the sanctuary. Tears were filling my eyes and I had never felt such pain and guilt in my entire life.

****

I couldn't go to the evening meal, I had completely lost my appetite. I was mired in guilt, guilt for confessing my thoughts and desires to the very one who had caused those feelings in me and even more guilt and fear over the possible consequences for both of us. I couldn't bear the thought of seeing him again, but then I couldn't bear the thought of not seeing him. It was almost 7:30 p.m. and the final Mass for the evening at five would have been long finished. I knew I needed to pray, but away from the other Sisters, all of whom I feared knew my secret. Did they? Did Mother Superior? Or was it just my imagination out of control, propelled by the knowledge of the mortal sins that I had committed. I decided to go to the Sanctuary and throw myself at the mercy of Our Father and Mother Mary and ask for their forgiveness and guidance.

So that is how I ended up here now, in the sanctuary kneeling in front of the cool ceramic statue of Mother Mary, her hands extended in supplication. I felt that perhaps as a mother and a woman, she might understand what I was going through. She might be able to help me tame my emotions for good. After a while, I don't know how long, I started to feel some calm and my breathing slowed. I opened my eyes and inhaled deeply. I remembered Father Grau's words to light a candle for forgiveness and I thought that I would. The row of large offering votives was in the back of the church, so I pulled myself up from my knees and walked to the table where the candles were bathed in small halos of light. I looked under the row for a lighting stick, but they seemed to be all used. I picked up one of the charred ones in order to poke a little further in the back of the shelf. I finally felt one and gingerly pulled it out. It wasn't very long, and I didn't want to burn my fingers, so I carefully touched the end on the flame of one of the candles. I think that I was so intent on making sure that the flame didn't eat up the stick too quickly and singe my fingers that I didn't hear the footsteps which had been muffled by the thick red carpet.

"Can I help you with that?"

Startled, I turned and saw Father Grau standing before me. Speechless, and with my heart racing, I could only nod and hand him the lighting stick.

He blew it out and then expertly placed it near one of the candles until it burst into light, then he lit another offering candle with that flame. Our eyes locked together and neither of us wavered, neither of us looked away. And in that moment, we saw each other as we were: a white nun and a colored priest in God's house with something happening between us that neither could ever have imagined or explained. But it just was. Neither of us spoke, but in that moment, I felt a closeness to him that I'd never felt for any other human being. And in that moment, my heart opened like a flower that had lain dormant only to be reawakened by the spring sunshine.

Finally, he said softly, "It's...very peaceful here. I come often and light candles. It helps me."

I could only nod in agreement; no words would come out. We stood there looking into the small flame, our bodies near, but not touching. But with each flicker, we drew closer to each other. So close that I could feel the light wispy sensation of his robe brushing against the skirt of my habit.

I didn't know how long we'd been standing there when we heard the footsteps. We turned, almost in unison, and saw Sister Gerta marching up the aisle towards us, her face red and eyes fixed on us. I wondered how long she'd been there watching us and my stomach doubled over in pain at the thought.

"Good evening, Father." She stopped, standing deliberately between us.

He nodded to her solemnly, "Good evening, Sister."

She whirled around, facing me accusingly, "You missed the evening meal. We were worried about you." She stopped and then almost spit out the words, "But I guess we didn't need to. I'll let Mother Superior know that you're OK." Then continuing, "Well, are you coming?"

I was afraid to look at Father Grau, and my hands were shaking so much I had to thrust them quickly into the folds of my habit so that she couldn't see them, as I responded, trying to sound as if nothing had happened, "Yes, I'm coming now."

When we got out the door, she turned facing me, tersely hissing, "Be glad that I'm your friend." And with that she walked away.

CHAPTER

26

I was miserable. I hadn't seen Father Grau for three days. Ever since Sister Gerta had walked up on us in the Sanctuary, I had feigned sickness, staying in the bed since that day. But I knew I'd have to get up and inevitably face my feelings and the reality of what was starting to well up in me. I knew I needed to get away for a few days; that's it, I would go home. I would tell Mother Superior that my mother needed me to help with my father.

Mother Superior eyed me suspiciously as she put down her reading glasses. The grandfather clock behind her seemed to mock me with its incessant ticking. "So, there's no one else who can help your mother? After all, you've been sick for the past several days and I've been told that the children are clamoring for you, and then of course there's all of the reorganization that we need to do here at the Convent based on the Archdiocese's report. In short, Sister Sophie, I don't know that we can spare you even for a few days."

I had to think fast, I needed to get away. "Mother Superior, my father is so ill and my mother is so exhausted from caring for him, I feel as if it is my duty to assist her. After all, that is what we were taught—to selflessly give of ourselves. It would be a great sacrifice for me to leave the Convent knowing how much I'm needed right now, but I feel as if...well, as if ...I um...am being called to do this for my family."

Still not pleased, she firmly shut her book saying, "All right, but just the weekend, I need you back here on Monday."

"Thank you, Mother Superior." I lowered my eyes, afraid to meet her gaze directly.

"And Sister Sophie..."

There was something about her tone that made me apprehensive.

"Remember that the love of God should be your only comfort. The solace of our Savior is what binds us in this special marriage to our Christ, and nothing and no one should ever come between you and your sacred duty of piety and faithfulness to our Lord."

Something in the way that she said that made my stomach turn over and a dull throb began in my temples. *Did she suspect something? Did Sister Gerta speak to her about what she'd seen in the Sanctuary? My life was the Church, was I about to lose everything for foolish schoolgirl fancies?* I felt panicked and could say nothing but avoid her accusing stare and walk quickly out of her office, trying to calm myself while I prayed for forgiveness.

The rest of the day I stayed in the Convent, helping with some of the work that I knew I'd have to finish when I got back on Monday. I realized that I needed to check the bus schedule, so I ran down to the Parish office remembering some bus schedules stacked up on the desk. It was the middle of the afternoon and I figured that I probably wouldn't see Father Grau, since he was usually in meetings most afternoons, so I could barely catch my breath when I heard someone calling my name.

"Sister Sophie…do you have a moment?"

I turned around slowly, trying to get myself together, hoping that my cheeks weren't as flushed as they felt.

"Of…of course, Father, is there something that I can do for you?" That didn't exactly come out the way I had intended. I couldn't believe my thoughts. So inappropriate. So unlike me.

And then it seemed for a moment as if he was the one who seemed awkward and unsure. "No, not at all, it's just that Mother Superior mentioned that you were going to your parents' home for the weekend, and I need to uh… drive right past there on some Parish business, so I'd be happy to drop you off."

His voice trailed off and before he could say anything else…I blurted out. "That would be lovely. Yes. I would like that."

He smiled broadly, "Good, that way you don't have to take the bus. I'd planned on leaving around ten tomorrow morning."

I couldn't believe what I was hearing, and the only thing that I could say was, "That's perfect."

His eyes lingered for a moment, "Then I'll see you in the morning."

My heart was beating so furiously that I could barely reply, "Yes Father, I'll see you in the morning."

CHAPTER

27

I couldn't believe that I was sitting in his car, my hands folded primly in my lap, trying to seem more virtuous then I felt. He expertly glided the steering wheel through his fingers as he turned the car onto the road. Even in my most undisciplined thoughts, I had never imagined that I would ever be alone with him away from the Parish and of all things driving with him to my parents' home. He'd taken off his priest's collar and was wearing a simple black shirt and pants. I suddenly felt awkward in my habit, wishing that I, too, had worn "street clothes" as we called it. Although Mother Superior had made it clear that we were to wear our habit at all times, it had been tacitly accepted that if you were traveling for personal reasons you could dress in something else as long as it maintained the appearance of modesty and devotion.

"How long has your father been ill?"

He interrupted my thoughts and I fumbled with my words, "Um, for a long time, he started getting ill a few years ago and it just kept getting worse and worse, and now he just can't do much of anything, he's pretty much bedridden."

"That must be awfully difficult for your mother."

"It is."

"And I remember you said that you have younger brothers, are any of them able to help?"

"Not that much, that's why she still really relies on me most of the time."

"Well, I admire you Sister, with all of your duties at the Parish and then to still be able to support your mother like this."

I lowered my eyes, not wanting to say the real reason that I was here was because of the feelings that I'd never had before, that I needed to get away to clear my head and that now, instead of being alone, I was here next to him, the very person that I thought that I was running from. But I didn't say that, I just said softly, hoping that it sounded more sincere than I felt, "It's important for me to be here for my mother."

His voice became wistful, "I often wish that I could have been there for my mother, she passed away when I got back from the War."

"That must have been hard for you." I felt this wave of sympathy for him and I wanted to stroke his cheek. I wanted to hold him and comfort him. I felt his pain so keenly because even though he didn't say it, I could sense that her death had left an emptiness that had still not been filled.

For a few minutes, we rode in silence, he turned on the radio and a song about a man pining away for a love that was no more played in the background. I looked out the window at the gray day, with a few slivers of sunlight playing hide and seek with the heavy clouds, seemingly pregnant and ready to burst with a fleeting summer shower. But instead of feeling drops pelting down, sunshine suddenly poured out and everything the light touched was encircled in a hazy rose color—the trees, the road before us, even the street signs. It felt almost magical, as if our path was being illuminated by something greater than us.

"I'm glad that we could drive together today." He turned and smiled almost hesitantly, as if not sure if he should be saying anything, and I felt that energy again, the same force that had drawn me to him from the first time that I saw him walking down the aisle in church. And now I knew for sure that it wasn't just me because when I smiled back, he took my hand and laid his on top of mine, squeezing it as he had in church. And without thinking, as if it was the most natural thing in the world to do, I encircled my fingers through his.

"I don't quite know what is happening...Sister...Sophie..."

"I...don't um...either..."

I didn't notice, but he had turned the car into a small overlook by the side of the road. It was no more than a rough circular drive bordered by a white fence with the paint peeling and a sign stuck into the dirt that said: *Scenic Overlook*," but when I leaned out the window of the car, I saw a view that swept across the horizon, the powder blue low hills, moss green trees pressed against the side of the road, and picturesque houses scattered across the vista.

He opened his car door. "Do you want to get out and stretch your legs?"

I sensed that same hesitancy on his part, as if not sure of my reaction and if somehow, he was being presumptuous.

But all I could think was that something was pushing me down a path that was good and right, even though in the eyes of others it might not be. So, I nodded and opened my door, again feeling self-conscious in my nun's habit and sensible shoes, a dress that had been so natural and so much a part of me for more than half my life, but now seemed stifling.

He leaned against the rail, looking out, "It's beautiful, isn't it?"

"Yes, it is..."

"Sometimes I come here and just gaze out and wonder at the marvels of our Creator. This is the first time that I've been able to share this with someone." And he paused, "I'm glad that it's you."

I wanted to edge closer to him, to touch his hand again, but I was rooted in place. I couldn't move, I was so overwhelmed. And I think he knew what I was feeling even though I couldn't get the words out. So, neither of us moved, it was like the few feet between us was a wall that neither could traverse, at least not yet. We remained there in silence for a few minutes letting the serenity bathe us in feelings that we knew existed but couldn't form words around.

He cleared his throat and gently led me towards the car. "I think we should get going."

I knew that I should say yes, but again the words wouldn't come out, so instead I followed him to the car and slid into my seat, my heart thumping loudly. He took out the car key and put it in the ignition, then before turning it he said softly, almost so softly that I could barely hear him, "Sister Sophie, can I kiss you?"

I drew closer to him, barely whispering, "Yes, but, please call me Sophie."

He gently placed his face against mine, whispering, "If you'll call me Billy." He turned my chin upwards to him, his lips first lightly brushed against mine. I felt his mouth open and his tongue flickering across my lips, then in my mouth, and I felt breathless and filled with such a joy that I'd never felt, and I pressed my lips harder against his, feeling his breath in me and when I thought that I could live in his presence forever, never wanting this feeling to end, he pulled away, almost awkwardly.

"It's…um…getting late, and I think it's going to rain."

Finally, my words came out, uncertainly, "Yes. I guess we should go."

CHAPTER

28

I don't remember much of the rest of the ride to my parents' home, only that I told him to pull up enough away from my house to avoid the prying eyes from the neighbors who had nothing better to do but to talk about people whose lives were more interesting than theirs. He squeezed my hand, "I would get your door, but…" And he looked around at the white children playing in the street, a working class white world where the only colored people they saw was when one of the braver ones ventured to the other side of town, as brown as this was white.

"No, you don't have to, but thank you."

He looked at me, then very slowly brushed his fingers across my hand, and with every touch I felt electricity surging up and down my spine, and then feeling like I was inhabiting someone else's body, someone else's life, I mechanically opened the car door and walked out. He lingered for a moment, nodded his head and smiled, and then drove away slowly.

Before I could knock, the door to my parent's home flung open, and my mother, with her eyes narrowed, blurted out, "Who was that colored man?"

Trying to sound nonchalant, "He's the priest at my Parish, Father Grau."

She snorted as if not believing me, "A colored priest, I never seen one a them."

Again, trying to control my feelings, which were all a jumble in my head, but knowing that I couldn't let on anything, "Well you haven't seen everything, it's a new world, there's colored priests, it's not so unusual now."

She closed the door hard behind me, turning her back to me, "Just remember who you are and what you are."

"I don't know what you mean, but I don't see anything wrong in accepting a ride from the priest who runs my Parish, it's certainly a lot better than being on the bus with a bunch of old men and drunks hanging out in the bus station."

I was a little angry, angry at her and at myself for allowing myself to feel defensive because I knew that I had started something today that I had to accept, or not, but either way it was my choice, my decision and not her or anybody else was going to live my life for me.

"I'm tired, it was a long drive, I'll be in my room, I'll come down and help with dinner after I unpack."

"You do that now." And I could see the bitterness in my mother that I had escaped, that I had found another life. I could sense her seething anger that she was trapped in this one, dependent on the whim and goodwill of others to throw her a lifeline that would never really rescue her. And I knew as I had when I was fourteen years old that I had to get out, that there was something more for me. But I never ever thought it would be with a colored priest in a Catholic Parish. And maybe this was just a fleeting kiss that would be forgotten in the dark corners of our minds—but maybe not.

CHAPTER

29

took the bus back to the Parish that Monday. Father Grau was still away, he would be gone for a few more days. The first night that I was home I hadn't slept well, in fact I hadn't slept well any of those nights, and when I did, I dreamed of him, but always as if he was far away in a place where I couldn't quite reach him, like a gauzy film was between us that was translucent but impenetrable at the same time. On the last night that I was home, I dreamt that we were in a boat, just the two of us. It was a dark moonless night with no stars. Only black waves hurling the boat violently up and down like a cruel roller coaster. The boat was starting to fill with water, and we were both desperately trying to bail the water out with our hands. I could feel every joint in my body aching as I tried to empty the boat of the waves that were choking us. Then suddenly, the sea became calm and the boat was bobbing up and down gently and the moon came out and a cone of light unfurled in front of us and something pushed us on that path of light. And I woke up.

I was thinking of those dreams as I mopped the floor in the nun's dining room. Mother Superior was still miffed at me for leaving over the weekend, so she'd assigned the task that I hated most. But I didn't care because all I could think of was what would I do when he came back, how would he act, how should I act? My thoughts were racing, should I pretend that nothing had happened and be nonchalant and go about my chores? Should I try and speak with him discretely? Maybe we should agree that the path that we were treading was far too dangerous for both of us. I didn't know. I just didn't know what to do.

And then suddenly the decision was made for me. "Sister Sophie, you have a call."

I wondered who would be calling me, I half hoped, but dared not, that it was him, maybe calling to say what was unsaid when we left, that something had changed in both of us from the moment that we each admitted that there was something there, that maybe he had the answer to the question of what was next. But instead when I picked up the phone, I heard another familiar voice.

"Your father's had a bad fall."

"Is he OK?????" I knew that my father was really ill, but I hadn't yet accepted the fact that someday he just wouldn't be here anymore.

My mother blurted out, "Yes, thank God, he's OK."

I felt a wave of relief wash over me.

"But I need help. I can't do it myself any more. I need you to try and come more often, maybe weekends. I don't know what to do, but it's too much, it's just too much for me now."

And for the first time, I heard a sob in my mother's throat, for much as we disagreed at times, I'd never seen my mother weak, no matter what life had thrown her, she'd met it straight on. And then I knew what I had to do, God told me, He said as clear as if he was speaking in my ear.

"Go home."

"Go home??" Was it as obvious as all that? And I knew the answer to my own question. I would go home, for the moment at least, and leave my life here that had become so complicated until I could understand what God wanted for me next.

****

A Few Days Later

And now, less than a week later, I closed the suitcase in my room, wrapping the Bible in some clothes, looking around at the only home that I'd known for most of my life. I knew that I'd be back, but this time it would be a different Sophie.

Mother Superior's rigid frown couldn't change my words or tapping fingers impatiently and disapprovingly. "You're sure this is what you want to do, after devoting most of your life to God, you suddenly leave…like that…

Sophie, what are you thinking, what has come over you? Leaving the order."

Firmly, but without hesitation, "I'm not leaving the Order for good, I'm taking a leave of absence. My mother needs my help, she can't go on without me."

"And God, and your Sisters here and your duties here?"

"I'm sorry, Mother Superior, but I've made my decision. I'll be leaving next week."

****

And now I'm in Billy's car again, but this time we know that we're traveling down a different road, we've pulled up to a different overlook. We'd gotten out of the car and were standing next to a small dirt path that led down the side of the steep hill.

"C'mon. I want to show you something, down here." He took my hand and led me down the narrow path between some short stubby trees and soft moss. "Watch out, it's a little slippery here." He took my hand more tightly and carefully guided me down the hill. I was glad that I'd decided not to wear my habit and instead, like him, I wore "traveling clothes," a loose dark brown tweed skirt, a roomy modest white blouse and sturdy shoes. But for that clothing, I'd never been able to navigate this incline. It was a steep climb down, but now it seemed to be getting flatter. He put his arm around my waist and pulled me down gently. The feeling of his arms around my waist, even through the bulky clothes, sent little electric shocks through my spine. And then suddenly he turned me around, pointing ahead, "It's Lake Erie, isn't it beautiful?"

"Oh, my Lord, I don't think I've ever seen it like this! It's breathtaking!" The massive lake before me was like a cool plane of deep aqua blue, the light breeze that broke the water causing foamy white peaks. Birds dipped and soared overhead and as far as I could see were undulating waves of blue. I turned back to him still in awe, "It's positively majestic."

He took my hands in his, raising them to his lips, "I was hoping that you'd appreciate this. It's a special place that I go to when I need to be truly alone with God. And I wanted to share it with you."

"Billy." I couldn't say anything else. I could feel tears coming to my eyes.

He drew me nearer to him, engulfing me in a hug. "Don't cry, Sophie.. It's ok, we're safe here and we're alone." And he dried my face with a white cloth that he took from his pocket.

I smiled through my tears, "I feel so good, but so confused at the same time. I can't believe that I'm taking this leave of absence and going home, but everything is just so jumbled up inside of me. Billy, do you think they know? About us, I mean?"

He looked at me in surprise, "Why do you think that?"

I turned away, remembering my earlier conversation with Mother Superior, "It's just that after Sister Gerta saw us together in the Sanctuary, I'm afraid that she might have said something to Mother Superior because when I left the last time to go home, Mother Superior kept talking about faithfulness to God and my sacred duty…and I don't know, Billy. I'm probably just paranoid. But do you think that they suspect something?"

He paused for a long moment, looking out at the lake, pondering my words, then he took me in his arms, saying firmly. "I don't believe that she knows anything. But…" He held my hands in his firmly. "What I do know is that the Church can keep its secrets. We won't be foolish, but God has given us something that neither of us were seeking, something that is bigger than either of us."

I held his hands even more tightly. "Billy, I'm just so overwhelmed and so happy even though I know that I don't have the right to be happy and to have these feelings."

He pulled me closer to him. "No more than I do. But we do." He brushed my hair away from my face and then his lips touched mine and I allowed myself to slowly drop to the ground and lie on the flat surface. His hands roamed over my back with his fingers running through my hair, my modest bun unraveled. All of the desires and the feelings that I'd denied were bubbling up in me, and I met his lips hungrily, my hands which were at first tentative and unsure, now traced around the curves of his face, his lips, his nose, his soft wavy hair, so different from mine.

I felt as if my emotions would burst wide open into the most inexplicable feeling of joy that I'd ever experienced as he whispered, "I want to see you while you're with your parents."

I couldn't contain the happiness rising up inside of me. "And I want to see you, too, so much."

He sat up on one elbow, drawing me closer. "I've been thinking that if you want to, I can come on Tuesdays. I have business at a Parish in Buffalo, so I have a reason to go there and..." He stopped, hesitating. "I don't want this to sound...well...presumptuous, but we can go to a motel on the Canadian side. We can be alone there. The Canadians aren't like the Americans, a colored man and a white woman won't create the problems that they do here...and well...that's what I was thinking. But, if you're not comfortable, I completely understand. And I..."

I kissed him on his cheek, whispering, "I want to do it, I want to see you on Tuesdays in Canada, or wherever you want."

He smiled, hugging me tightly. "Then that's what we'll do, every Tuesday I'll pick you up somewhere in Buffalo, far from your house, and then we'll drive up to Canada."

I nodded, refusing to let anything—not the guilt, or the voices in my head, or the memory of Mother Superior's accusing look, mar the euphoria that I was feeling in that moment. So, I hugged him back, whispering, "I'm so very happy."

He kissed me with a passion that I hadn't felt before, "So am I...my Sophie."

CHAPTER

30

Canadian Side Of The Falls, Small Motel
About One Month Later, 1956

A s I lay next to Billy, my eyes traced every detail of the room, the small desk in the corner, the flowered wallpaper, and the window that looked out over the road that led to Niagara Falls. We couldn't see the Falls from here, but we could hear the crashing of the water at night and see the lines of cars of tourists that passed on the road in front of us. The bed was small and lumpy, and I felt a little uncomfortable in my blouse and heavy woolen skirt and stockings. I brushed against him. Billy was also fully dressed, except that he'd taken off his shirt and had on his undershirt and long pants. We'd been lying there for about an hour as we had every Tuesday during that month, kissing and feeling his mouth travel over every part of my face, my arms, my fingers and I kissed every curve of his chin and let his tongue roll over mine, darting back and forth. We laughed, and we kissed, and we ate, usually Chinese food, the half empty cartons littering the desk. But that's all we did. I wouldn't take off any of my clothes and since I wouldn't, he didn't either. I remember the first time he started to lift my shirt over my head and I jerked up, clutching my blouse to my chest.

"No…no. I'm not ready for this." And although I realized my own hypocrisy, he didn't press me.

Just kissed me on my forehead, saying, "That's OK, when you're ready."

And so, I'm lying here thinking, *Am I ready? Will I ever be ready?* I'd told my mother that Mother Superior had asked me to help out at a Canadian Parish every Tuesday since I was on leave, and so I would be gone for at least two days each week. Mother had not been happy. It was amazing how alike my real mother and Mother Superior were, each wanting to own me, each expecting that I had nothing else in my life but to serve them, each wanting to control my time. But it was my time. It was mine and only I controlled ME. I was thinking that as I heard his gentle breathing next to me. As I snuggled closer, I could feel his strong arms encircle my waist and I pushed myself closer to him. And suddenly I felt myself kissing his chest, every ripple, every muscle, and I felt myself lifting his shirt and my lips covering his waist in kisses.

And now he sat up, and said, "I don't want to force you to do anything."

And I couldn't say anything, I just lay on my back and unbuttoned the first button of my blouse. Then I stopped. I unbuttoned the second button. And stopped. Then his hands replaced mine and he unbuttoned the third and fourth buttons 'till there were no more buttons to unbutton. And he slipped the blouse off of me. I turned over, suddenly shy, not wanting him to see me. "It's OK." He got up and closed the shades so the room was bathed in shadows.

Then he kissed my throat and he kissed below my throat and he continued down and un-clasped my bra, and I felt so embarrassed by it all, but at the same time so unbelievably good like I'd never felt before. His hands seemed to have a mind of their own and they caressed my back and continued down and then slid my skirt down to my knees then tossed it off the bed and I wanted to say no, but I really didn't. I wanted to say, *"I'm not sure,"* and maybe his mind heard mine because he stopped and sat up on one elbow and said, "I can stop, if you want me to."

And for a moment I turned away from him, thinking back over everything, I'd never been with a man before and didn't really know what to expect, but I wanted to know, I wanted to feel what it was like to be with not just a man—but with him. And so, I finished taking off the bra myself and hugged him tightly and he kissed me like he'd never kissed me before. And he slipped off my panties and then my skin was next to his and my skin was his and his was mine, and gently, oh so gently, we became one.

CHAPTER

31

ow I was speechless, you almost don't know what to think when you hear words that express how the two people who were responsible for *you* became one. The room was very quiet, even the constant chatter of the nurses in the hallway had seemed to subside. Sophie had stopped talking and in her eyes I could see the slight glistening of tears that she hastily wiped away. I can only imagine the feelings that remembering must have stirred in her. She turned over, perhaps not wanting me to see her like that. I felt awkward, almost as if I had intruded on memories that were only meant for her. Clearing my throat, I said softly, "I think I should leave."

Silence. Her eyes closed and she slumped against her pillows.

Gently, I lay my hand on her shoulder, noticing how thin and frail she suddenly seemed. "Sophie, I think I'm gonna go."

She just nodded, but still said nothing. I picked up my coat and started for the door.

Then she called out softly, "Don't leave."

Turning back, I could see that she was now sitting up and as if a wave had passed over her, she seemed suddenly tranquil, almost at peace. Surprised by the sudden transformation, I hesitated in the doorway. "Are you sure? It is almost six and I've been here all day."

"I'm sure. I guess that....uh…" She paused, choosing her words carefully. "I guess that it's been so long that I've not thought of that day…well, for many years." She shook her head slowly. "Even after all this time, I still can't believe that he's gone. I know that it doesn't make sense, here you are a grown man, and Billy's been gone more than 40 years, but sometimes the memories are so fresh." She smiled brightly, "We had such good times then, and I learned so much about him. He had lived such a life, from Cleveland to the Vatican and then Italy in the War. I guess I never stopped being amazed and truly in awe of him.

"Did he tell you much about the War? 'Cause it's ironic, that's how the journey started for me. I'd been thinking about him and saw this newspaper article about the Regiment that he served in, in Italy, the Buffalo Soldiers, the all black regiment. They had a reunion in the city not far from where I live, and I went there. I don't know what I was really looking for, maybe some connection to him. I didn't meet anybody who knew him personally, but one of the men said that they'd heard of him."

"What did he say?"

"I didn't have a chance to talk much to him, but the one thing he said that stuck with me was that he wasn't like what you'd expect a Priest to be, he said that the men really respected him. He was a fair man and one thing I do remember was that they talked about a Christmas Eve Mass that he'd done right in the middle of all the fighting and welcomed everyone.

Sophie was very quiet and then spoke softly. "He told me about that… it was a time when the men were very discouraged, he said they'd been trying to take a mountain from the Germans, but they kept getting beaten back because our own commanders wouldn't send enough air cover. He mentioned how so many men had been killed." Her voice started drifting off and then suddenly it was as if I was seeing through his eyes, my father…it was as if he was speaking to me directly, like his mind and mine were the same, like I was seeing what he'd experienced. And I felt that same sensation that I had so many months before when I had the vision or dream, I wasn't sure which, and I was in Italy hearing bombs going off around me and bodies flying through the air. Now he was speaking to me, opening up his memories to me, allowing me to see what had been, so many years ago.

Flashback Through Father Grau's Eyes
Northern Italy; World War II

"So, Father, is there a Heaven, really? I mean, all I see is hell…one living hell."

The young colored soldier looked tired and defeated. A few days before, a group of men had been killed trying to advance up the mountain that they'd been trying to re-take from the Germans. There wasn't enough air cover from our white pilots and this young man had been in the group. He was the only one who'd survived. He walked away without a scratch, but every night since then, he'd awakened screaming, not able to excise the horror of what he'd seen from his head. It was times like this that I silently prayed to our Savior to bring me the words that would comfort, but like so many other times, I seemed at a loss.

"Son, we don't know the ways of the Father, but only that there is a reason. We just may not be able to see it, but with faith…"

He whirled around angrily. "Don't talk to me about faith, faith can't bring them back," choking on his tears and running out of the room.

I felt despondent and powerless, and asked myself as I did so often, *Why, Father? Why?* When they brought in the broken bodies of the young Negro men who were giving up their lives for a country that used them to fight their wars but denied them equality at home. All the hopes of a generation dying in my arms and all I could do was to numbly give the last rites and move on to the next one. It was cold and rainy, that bone chilling cold that made you ache in every part of your body. I slumped down wearily on a hard bench. I felt an arm lightly touching mine and I looked up.

"Hey Father, don't take it so hard, it ain't your fault, he's just mad, he'll get over it, like we all do. And if he don't, well, then…nothin' you can do." He offered me a cigarette, I shook my head no. In the background I heard the faint echoes of "Silent Night" on the radio and I realized that in all of the chaos of the past several days, I'd almost forgotten that it was Christmas Eve.

I looked around the small room, a group of soldiers was huddled together talking, another small group was playing cards, and yet a few others were nodding out, wrapping thin blankets around their shoulders. All of these men had willingly come to a land so far away, some were in college, the best and the brightest of the Negro race, others straight from the farm, barely able to read and write. I thought bitterly of the young man from the tiny hamlet in South Carolina who wanted more than anything to be able to read the letters from back home. I worked with him for months, teaching him to read and write, and then the same day that he finally learned and proudly read aloud a letter that a few months earlier had been meaningless scribbles to him, he was killed running to an air raid shelter. And then the UCLA student who wanted to be an engineer, not a profession where there were many opportunities for Negroes, but yet he persevered, but when he got the call, he came, and now his life like so many others could be no more in an instant.

I thought of my advice to the young soldier who'd survived physically, but mentally was broken in two because he'd lost all hope. Then it came to me. Hope. The one thing that I could give them, the one thing that would carry us all through. That intangible quality of such unimaginable power. It was the beacon that I could carry and instill as best as I could in the men. And tonight, on the eve of our Savior's birth, was the time.

I stood in the middle of the small shelter, raising my voice above the radio and saying, "I want to wish everyone a Merry Christmas. It's Christmas Eve."

A few mumbled "Merry Christmas" and then a return to whatever they were doing before. Determined not to be discouraged, I continued, "Since it's Christmas Eve, I'm going to give Mass and I want to invite everyone to take Mass with me, Catholic or not, it doesn't matter, we're all one in our Father's eyes." I picked up a candle stub from the table and lit it and then passed it to a soldier sitting next to me. "Everyone, please join me. Let's celebrate the birth of Christ together. There are some candles around the room, everyone, take one and light it. The light of the world can shine right here, it doesn't matter what's going on outside, inside. Here, there's love and there's hope."

I could see that my words were starting to have an effect, and slowly one, then two, then more men began to gather around, the candles that were on most of the makeshift tables for the many black outs that we had, were suddenly being lit and passed from man to man. A young soldier with a rich baritone voice began singing "Oh Holy Night" and others joined in. Soon the room was washed in light and was reverberating with the many voices singing the Christmas carols that we'd all known in happier times. I noticed that men from other shelters had started to come in, attracted by the singing and the warm glow of the candle light. And one of those young men was the one who'd run out earlier, and now he, too, took a candle and raised his voice with the others.

End Flashback
Buffalo, New York, Hospital; Present Time

And then as quickly as it had come, my father's words in my head faded away and I was back in Sophie's room and she was looking at me, as if not sure where I'd gone in those few minutes when the presence of Father Grau had overwhelmed me.

"Joe! Are you ok? You just stopped talking and you were staring out like you were seeing something in front of you, but when I asked you what you were looking at, it was almost as if you didn't even hear me."

I shook myself back to present day, not sure what I'd just experienced and even more unsure of what to tell Sophie. "I'm fine, Sophie, sorry, I guess I was just thinking about what the men had said about Father Grau. That's all. But it's late, I think I should go. I'll be back tomorrow."

CHAPTER

32

ophie, are you awake?" It was almost 2:30 in the afternoon, usually I'd come much earlier than this, but I'd had some international calls that lasted longer than they should've. I felt badly because I knew that Sophie had come to expect my visits. I walked slowly over to her bed. She was slumped down in the pillows. The shades were drawn in the room and she looked thin and small against the covers. She stirred slightly.

"Joe, is that you?"

"Yes, I'm sorry I couldn't get here earlier. I had some conference calls that lasted forever...I'm sorry."

"I understand, it's OK...really. I think I just dozed off. All of this remembering, you know, things that you haven't thought of for so many years, and then when you do, it's like the remembering doesn't stop. In fact..." She propped up on one elbow, "I was thinking about the day that changed all of our lives."

"What do you mean?"

"The day that I found out that I was having you." Her voice started to trail off and then suddenly got stronger, and once again I felt as if I was living through her eyes.

Flashback Through Sophie's Eyes
Canadian Side Of The Falls, Small Motel; 1956

I choked over the toilet, my stomach had been churning all day. And now I finally threw up, what, I don't know since I hadn't eaten much that week, but it seemed that no matter what it was that I had, didn't agree with me. I wondered if it was some type of stomach virus, whatever it was, it seemed to come in waves, I'd be OK and then suddenly I'd be hit with this nausea. Billy massaged my back, concerned. "Do you feel a little better now?"

I nodded and leaned against his shoulder as he gently walked me back to the room and helped me lie down. "OK, let me take off your shoes…get under the covers."

He sat next to me on the bed, massaging my fingers. "I think that you should go to the doctor."

"I'm fine, it's probably just a virus, some kind of flu, I used to get them all the time when I was a child. I'm sure it's nothing more than that."

"Maybe, but I want you to promise me that you'll go to the doctor this week." He gently tilted my chin up. "C'mon now, Sophie, promise me."

Reluctantly, "OK, I will."

CHAPTER

33

I felt conspicuous in the doctor's waiting room, although I wasn't wearing my habit, I still subconsciously felt as if I had it on and felt as if I was being judged by the other people sitting there. *"Did they know?"* I wondered, maybe it was my own guilt, but I felt as if everyone knew that I had broken my vows so many times now that I couldn't even count. The nurse's officious manner made me feel even more scared and self-conscious,

She briskly ushered me into a small waiting room. "The doctor will be in, in a moment."

I nodded and barely forced out the words meekly, "Thank you." I was just hoping that he could give me a shot or some pills to get rid of this nausea and then I could just get on with my life.

The busy and sterile doctor's waiting room started to recede into the background. I leaned back against the hard couch and thought back over what had become our life together, Billy and me. The sounds around me of the nurses, the constant chatter of the typewriters, and the flipping of pages from patients absentmindedly shuffling through the assortment of magazines on the tables in front of them, melted away into the memories that I clung to tenaciously, trying to block out my uneasiness and wish to be anywhere but here.

Instead, I focused on Billy and me, and our routine. He would pick me up on Tuesdays and we'd meet downtown in the colored area of town and then we'd drive to a small motel in Niagara Falls on the Canadian side. Once we got over the border, we both were able to breathe a sigh of relief that the prying eyes in Buffalo were far away.

We decided to meet in the colored area of town because there were always a few white people scattered around, but for the most part everyone pretty much kept to themselves. Usually it went off without a hitch. I'd stand under a doorway trying not to look too conspicuous, but for some reason on this day, I seemed to stick out like I was wearing a neon sign.

Flashback Through Sophie's Eyes
Buffalo, New York, The Colored Area Of Town; 1956

There was music from a radio coming from the open door to a shop that sold odds and ends, everything from pots and pans to children's dresses, something like a Woolworths, only all the customers were colored. Seems as if Woolworths wouldn't serve colored customers. But here, everyone was colored, all the patrons and the checkout girls, and I guess it was probably owned by a colored man. I believed it was this small round man with medium brown skin and just a few tufts of hair on the side of his head who always seemed to be bustling around in a crisp white rolled up shirt sleeves and dark pants. I could see him sometimes in the window arranging the displays, seeming to take such pride in his small store.

This day he was putting up the new display, he carefully took out the hodge-podge of women's clothing, kitchen odds and ends, and children's toys, and brought out a new mix of equally eclectic items, but this time all summer themed with beach pails and beach balls and bathing suits. I guess that I got so absorbed in watching him that I didn't notice a group of three young colored women walking towards me.

One of them I recognized, she had always seemed to eye me suspiciously when I got off the bus every Tuesday walking quickly, looking down, trying not to make eye contact with anyone until I got to my spot on a bench next to the store. I'd then reach into my large purse and take out a book and start reading, trying to focus on the words in front of me until Billy got there to pick me up. Usually he was right on time, but sometimes the bus was late and then he'd circle the block a few times, so as not to look too suspicious. We had our routine and it usually worked well.

Nervously, I looked down the street hoping to see Billy's familiar car, but nothing, just the three colored women who by now had crossed the street and were just a few feet from me.

"Hey there, white girl, what you doin' over here?"

I caught my breath, the colored woman that I'd noticed before was looking directly at me, she was probably not more than 18 or 19, and almost reminded me of some of the young mothers who brought their children to the Parish nursery. But those women were grateful to have a place to leave their children as they headed off sometimes as much as an hour away to the jobs that paid little but just enough to keep them and their families going.

This woman had a cockiness and defiance to her that showed in the way she strutted towards me, pointing her finger at me accusingly as if my very being offended her.

"Yeah, YOU, bitch, don't pretend like you don't know I'm talkin' to you!"

"Aw Retha, leave her 'lone, she ain't doin' nothing, just some white ho' waiting for her man ain't that right, white girl?"

I was so seized with fear that I couldn't move, I couldn't speak as I clutched the book to my chest. I wanted to disappear into the bench, hoping that they would go away. The third just looked at me dismissively as if I was no more than a piece of trash on the street.

Hissing angrily, "Yeah, I seen her man, he come pick her up in his car, they lookin' at each other like they think nobody see what they be doin.' Jus' another white girl, trying to take a colored man."

"Ain't that the truth." The first woman got directly in front of me, leaning so close that I could smell her breath in my face. "Ain't that what you doin', white girl, tryin to steal our colored men? All white girls want that black dick, don't they--mmmmh. How is it, white girl? Is it good? Does he fuck you good?" She laughed coarsely.

I was so petrified, I couldn't speak, I couldn't breathe, I knew that the next moment she'd probably pull out a knife and slash my throat. I'd never felt hatred that was so real and so palpable, all I could do was to pray, *"Dear God, help me, protect me! Dear God, please help me!!!!"*

"Whatcha gotta say? You think you too good to talk to us?"

I couldn't make the words come out, barely whispering, "No."

"What we gonna do wit' this white bitch?"

By now, a small crowd had gathered, a couple of young colored men catcalled, "Whoooo they gonna kick that white girl's ass. She gonna wish she stayed on her side of town."

I was starting to feel nauseous, I felt like I was going to throw up, but I knew that if I did, that would be it, so I tried to swallow the foul-tasting stench that was rising in my throat.

Suddenly, I felt a hand around my collar pulling me up from the bench and then slamming me down again hard. The first colored woman was shaking me like a rag doll. I was powerless. I wanted to fight back, I wanted to do something, but I was paralyzed with fear.

I heard the door to the store swing open and heard a loud voice bellowing over the crowd. "Retha, let her go, she ain't done nothin' to you." And I saw the older colored man from the store coming out brandishing a frying pan, waiving it in the air like a weapon.

Before Retha could answer, I heard footsteps running towards me and I saw Billy, panting, his face covered in sweat, with a rage I'd never seen before in him, "Get the hell outta my way!!!!!!" He brusquely shoved the crowd aside, grabbing my hand and pulling me across the street to the car, I could barely move I felt like my feet were stuck in clay. I was so numb.

Billy gunned the engine aggressively, leaving the crowd behind. I barely remembered hearing words being hurled at me like bricks. "Don't come back here no more, white girl!!!! Keep yo' honky ass away from here, next time yo' white ass ain't gonna be so lucky!!!!!!" I barely remembered slumping forward, and then the nausea rising in my throat again, barely choking out the words, "I feel sick."

The car screeched to a halt and Billy bolted to my side, gently helping me out as I leaned over retching again and trying to erase the memory from my mind. When I finally had emptied everything that was in me, I sat on the ground and large tears started to course down my face, angry tears, hot tears that turned my cheeks flaming red. Billy, tried to gather me in his arms but I shrugged him away, suddenly angry that he hadn't been there, angry at what had almost had happened, barely spitting out the words, "Where were you?????" Why weren't you there…they almost…those vile, hateful colored women…they almost…" And now as I remembered back, I felt like I was starting to hyperventilate.

Ignoring my attempts to push him away, Billy just held me tighter and I could feel tears on his cheeks. "I'm so, so sorry. I got there early, and I was parked down the street, there was nothing in front and I figured I'd pull up right on time when the bus got there. But then I heard someone calling my name and I looked up and it was Father McManus—he works in the Parish in that area—asking me what I was doing there, I couldn't ignore him, so I had to make something up and the whole time, I was trying to get away, but he just kept talking and then I don't know what, but something in me said, *'Get going now!'* I couldn't see the store from where I was parked, but I turned on the motor, told Father McManus for the hundredth time that I had to go, and turned the corner and then saw the crowd."

He stopped, his voice choking in this throat, "I didn't know what was happening, all I could think was that if anything had happened to you…I don't know what I would've done to them!" He was now shaking with the same anger that I'd seen in front of the store, and suddenly I felt ashamed that I'd lashed out at him, and so we just sat there and held each other until our arms were stiff from squeezing each other so tightly.

He tilted my chin up to his face, kissing me fiercely and whispering, "I love you so much, Sophie. I don't know what I'd do if I lost you."

And I buried my face in his chest and cried out all the anger and shame that I felt.

CHAPTER

34

Buffalo, New York, Hospital; Present Time

I was literally sitting on the edge of my seat, "Oh my God, Sophie, I can't believe you went through that!" She didn't say anything, I think still back in that faraway time.

I got up from the chair for the first time since she'd begun speaking, pacing back and forth, "You know, we always think about racist whites who'd lynch a black man for being with a white woman or just for being what they'd call "uppity," but I guess we forget that racism goes both ways, and there were just as many blacks who weren't happy about interracial couples as whites. I guess the bottom line is that things have changed at least enough so that we forget that back then in some states in the South it was a crime to be in an interracial relationship. And even though this was the North, you still had the same ignorant people and narrow thinking in all races."

She spoke slowly, "It was dangerous what we were doing. Our love had risks—not just at the church—but everywhere."

Sophie lay back against her pillows and her eyes clouded over as she continued to speak.

Flashback Through Sophie's Eyes
New York State Near The Canadian Border; 1956

"Oh damn." Billy shook his head in disgust, slamming his palm against the steering wheel.

"What's wrong?" I sat up anxiously. I'd been listening to the up-beat music on the radio, I was trying to relax but I could never really BREATHE until we crossed over into Canada. And since that incident with those colored women, we had changed our pick-up place to the bus station. In a way, it was riskier because you never knew who might be coming on the bus, that's why we'd chosen the other location to begin with, but we'd decided even with that possibility it was still safer than being on the street. We had a new routine now. I'd sit in the bus station and he'd pull the car slowly in front but wouldn't park. When I saw his car, I'd come out, casually walk down the street to where he'd parked around the corner. That way I was at least safe in the bus station and didn't come out until I knew that he was there.

So far, it was working fine, and slowly, I was starting to not be haunted by the memories of that day. But even now, months later, I still wake up in a cold sweat, seeing the faces of those vile colored women bearing down on me. In one dream, I touched my face and it was covered in blood and I could hear their brittle laughter, then footsteps running towards me, Billy trying to shove his way through the crowd. But they'd locked arms and he couldn't get through, and those angry colored women kept punching me over and over again until my eyes were closed with blood and pus. I saw the glint of a switch blade coming towards my face. I screamed. Then I woke up.

I was beginning to understand the veterans who came back from Korea with the shakes, mumbling about bombs and people being killed. While I'd always tried to be kind to them, I don't think that I'd fully understood what this type of trauma could do to you, when you literally saw your life flash in front of you. And now I did. And I prayed to God every night that I'd never know that fear again.

I was thinking that as I looked over at Billy.

He was drumming his fingers against the steering wheel nervously. "The tank's almost empty, we're gonna need to stop for gas. I'd hoped we'd be able to make it to Canada without stopping, but I guess not now. Damn."

I massaged his neck, "Isn't there a gas station not too far down the road?"

"Yes, but I'd just prefer…if, well…"

He didn't say anymore, just turning the wheel sharply and heading down a narrow road. There weren't any street lights and it was beginning to get dark. It was early September and the days were already noticeably shorter, with that first biting chill in the air in between the last few breaths of summer warmth.

Billy pulled the car up to the tank. An older wizened man in coveralls, his back bent with age, walked slowly out the station, "Can I help you folks?"

Billy dug in his pocket, taking out two dollars and handing it to the man. "Yeah, fill it up. Thank you."

"Sure thing." He slowly and painfully lifted the handle to the gas tank and then, in what seemed like an eternity, slowly unscrewed the gas tank and put the nozzle in the tank. He whistled aimlessly while the gas flowed into the tank.

Billy seemed tense, lowering his voice. "I wish he would hurry up."

Behind me I heard another car pulling up. I had gotten used to not looking up when cars passed us or came too close so as not to feel the sometimes curious, other times angry, stares as people saw a colored man in the car with a white woman sitting next to him.

"Now what we got here?"

My breath came in short stiff puffs and I lowered my eyes, but out of the corner of my left eye I could see two white teenage boys. One jumped out of the car and walked slowly and defiantly over to our car, leaning over to my window which was partially opened.

"What's he doin' to you? Did he kidnap you? Is he trying to take you away? You just tell us and we'll kick the shit outta that Niggah!"

The old man shook his head. "Now listen here, fellas, just go on home. I don't want no trouble here."

"Shut up, granddad, we're just tryin' to look after our women." The other one ran over to Billy's side of the car. "Get out 'fore we pull you out!!!"

I didn't dare say anything. Billy carefully and without looking down slowly put the key in the ignition, luckily the car doors were locked; we'd always gotten in that habit.

"What's wrong, you scared, Niggah?" You wasn't too scared to try and kidnap a white woman, was you?"

I could feel Billy putting his gas on the ignition, and as we heard the click of the gas pump signaling the full tank, Billy floored the pedal and backed up, nearly running down the white teenager. Billy yelled to me as he raced the car out of the station, "Get down, get on the floor, he might have a gun."

I dove to the floor, shaking. "What about you?!!!!!!"

"Just get down, we're only a couple of miles to the border."

Stunned, the white boys had barely scrambled in their car and gunned the motor, enraged screaming. "Why you Niggah son of a bitch!!!!!!"

Steely faced, Billy revved up the motor even more. I couldn't see out because I was still on the floor. I could hear the yelling getting fainter and fainter as Billy outran them, and when our car slowed down, I knew that we'd reached the border, but my heart was still feeling like it was jumping out of my chest and my hands were trembling as we drove into Canada.

That night, we just lay there next to each other, both still numb from what had almost happened. I put my head on Billy's chest and he stroked my hair, but neither of us spoke. We both knew without saying anything that we'd agreed to this when we declared our love for each other. My head was spinning, thoughts of the Church and what would happen to me, and especially to Billy, if anyone found out. Excommunication, disgrace, but this—this constant fear that some enraged white man or colored woman would suddenly take it in their head that they had the right to hurt us just because we dared love someone different from ourselves. I felt angry but knew that my anger didn't matter. I'd made a choice and I wasn't looking back, Nobody was going to make me look back.

****

"Hey there, sleepyhead." I looked up at Billy's smiling face. It was one of those picture-perfect fall days. I had been dreaming listlessly and wasn't even aware of how long I'd slept.

"What time is it?"

"Almost one."

"You're kidding?! I slept that long!!!"

"You woke up a couple of times, but I think we both needed to de-compress after yesterday."

Suddenly remembering the teenage boys, the gas station and our narrow escape, I slumped back onto the pillows. "I think I was hoping it was all just a bad dream."

Billy sat up on one elbow and kissed my face and then my lips. "It's real. Sophie, racism is real. But we're more real. You and I together, we can face anything. God is with us always. So, I'm not afraid. We'll be fine."

"I love you, Billy."

"I love you, too."

For a long moment neither of us said anything, just looking at each other and knowing how far we'd come to get to this place, and knowing that this was just the beginning, that there were many more roads for us to travel together.

Billy brushed my hair away from my face and then kissed me on the lips, whispering, "Now come on, get dressed, I've made a decision and we need to get started."

I looked at him quizzically, suddenly alarmed. "What do you mean?" But then he smiled that smile that I remembered from that first day when he came up and offered to help me with the shoveling, that smile that radiated from the corners of his eyes to his perfect lips to his dark warm eyes, taking it all in and realizing that I had nothing to fear. As if reading my mind, he gently drew me to him, "Don't worry, it'll be fun."

CHAPTER
35

Ok, we're here." Billy parked the car. "Where's here?" It was an abandoned parking lot; no other cars, and the only building was a broken down structure that had probably been some sort of small office building. But now there was nothing here and whatever workers had been there seemed to have been long gone.

"How did you find this place?" I hopped out of the car, noticing the scrubby trees and pock marked black top as if no one had been here for a while.

"A couple of months ago when I went out for the paper early one morning, I took a wrong turn and stumbled on this area. I didn't think anything of it at the time, I was just glad that I was able to find my way back to the hotel, but the more I thought of it, the more I realized how perfect this would be."

"I guess I'm missing something," I walked in front of him teasingly, "Perfect for what????"

He grabbed my hand and opened the driver's side of the car motioning for me to sit behind the wheel, "Perfect for teaching you how to drive."

I looked up at him, barely containing my broad smile, "You're kidding, right?"

"Nope, I've been thinking about this for a while. You need to know how to drive and especially after yesterday." His voice trailed off for a moment, then he quickly shrugged off the memory. "You need to be able to take the wheel. So, it's decided, today will be your first official driving lesson."

I hugged him. "I've always wanted to learn to drive, but when I joined the Order I knew I'd never have a car, so I figured I'd never learn how to drive. But now I guess I can!"

"You sure can, my darling is going to be a driving fool!"

"Oh, Billy, thank you!"

"Don't thank me yet, I've never taught anybody to drive before, so this will be a first for both of us." He smiled as he settled in the passenger side, handing me the keys. "Now first thing is to put the key in the ignition and start the car, one foot here." He motioned to a pedal, "And then the other foot on the brake, right here."

Hesitantly, I put the key in the ignition and my feet where he'd pointed. I turned the key as hard as I could, but instead of hearing the humming of the motor, it sounded like somebody was scraping the insides of the car with a coarse metal object. I stopped immediately. "Did I do something wrong?"

"You turned it just a little too far, remember, gently, Sophie gently... like this." He put his hand on top of mine and then very slowly turned the key. Now, the motor was purring like a contented cat. After the car started, his hand lingered on mine, I could feel the electricity from his fingers as they curled on top of mine.

Our eyes met, and with his other hand he tilted my chin up to his face and then kissed the tip of my nose, then my cheek, then my forehead, and then our lips met, and it was like we drank in all of the love that we both felt, our lips brushing against each other again and again. And then his tongue was slowly trailing down my neck. I lay back on the car seat, feeling the weight of him on top of me as he kissed my neck and my throat, and buried his head in my breasts covering me with kisses as he murmured, "Sophie, Sophie, my Sophie."

End Flashback Through Sophie's Eyes
Buffalo, New York, Doctor's Office; 1956

"Sophie Legocki. Sophie Legocki!" I jumped up, back now in the waiting room, realizing that I'd been daydreaming. A woman who seemed visibly annoyed locked eyes with me accusingly "Are you Sophie Legocki?"

"Yes, I'm sorry, I didn't hear you."

She snorted as if not believing it. "I've been calling your name for a couple of minutes. She motioned to a door. "You can wait in there, change into the examining robe and the doctor will be with you in a moment."

I nodded. "I'm sorry, I just...didn't."

But the woman had turned her back to me and was quickly scribbling something on a pad. My words hung in mid-air, making me feel smaller and more uneasy than ever. I opened the door to the tiny room that she'd gestured to, it was just barely big enough for the examining table and the putrid colored green robe hanging on the wall hook. I closed the door, slipping my clothes off and the backless examining gown over my head. I felt both nervous and sick to my stomach at the same time. That seemingly persistent wave of nausea made me fall to my feet, searching for something to relieve myself in. I retched over the sink, but nothing came out this time, I was thinking, "At least I'm in the doctor's office so maybe he'll give me something to get rid of this." Feeling more weak then ever, I barely pushed myself up on the table, the gown slipping off my shoulders. I remembered the last time my shoulders were bare. I remembered his hands encircling my waist...

Flashback Through Sophie's Eyes
Canadian Side of The Falls, Small Motel; A Few Months Earlier

I giggled, my back was to him and Billy's hands were slowly and rhythmically massaging my shoulders, pushing under my sleeveless dress as his fingers moved down my arms sliding the dress off my shoulders, I couldn't help but giggling again, it tickled.

Billy kissed the top of each of my bare shoulders and then as the dress slipped down to my feet, he kissed the small of my back, smiling, "Now what's so funny, young lady?"

Now I really couldn't help but laughing, "Nothing—it just tickles, that's all."

"Does this tickle?" Billy planted a wet kiss on my stomach.

'Uhhhhh, yeah!" And I laughed again.

"How about this?" He kissed me just below my breasts.

I shook my head vigorously, "Mmmmm!!!!!"

Billy kissed me again, this time on each breast, "How about this?"

I felt a shiver go up and down my body and I could barely whisper, "Yes!"

Now he laughed. "I like tickling you." And we both laughed and fell on top of each other, our bodies intertwined as he slipped off my panties...

End Flashback
Buffalo, New York, Doctor's Office; 1956

"Miss Legocki, how are you feeling today?" I almost fell off of the examining table, realizing that I'd completely forgotten about the nausea as I relived the moments of a few months ago.

A tall thin man in a slightly soiled white coat held out his hand to me, "I'm Dr. Evans and I understand that you haven't been feeling well."

I swallowed guiltily, thinking, *"I'm glad he can't read my thoughts."* "No, Doctor, um, I haven't."

"I see we've got a lab report, you came in here last week?"

"Yes, they said that I had to have some blood drawn."

"I see." He glanced over at his chart. "Ok, well let me get the report and I'll be back with you in a moment."

"Thank you," I could barely whisper the words, my mind was still entangled with the thoughts of Billy and me.

He nodded and closed the door behind him. I felt this sudden apprehension again and I started breathing quickly, then a voice inside of me said, *"Calm yourself, Sophie."* I closed my eyes, and with my back against the wall, my feet dangling from the examining table, remembering this same time 5 p.m. only a few days ago with Billy—in his car...

Flashback Through Sophie's Eyes
Niagara Falls, Canada, Restaurant; A Few Months Earlier

Billy parked the car behind the restaurant. He hadn't told me where we were going. He said that he wanted to surprise me. Before I could move, he'd sprung out of the car and opened my door for me. I felt warm and happy all over; he was such a gentleman.

"Thank you."

Smiling appreciatively, he pointed to the view, a complete panorama of the Falls.

"Oh my!" I ran over to the viewing area, leaning over and seeing clouds of what appeared to be steaming water rising high in the air. The sound of the Falls crashing against the rocks was thunderous. Billy came up behind me, wrapping his arms around my waist, I leaned back against his chest. I could feel his heart beating quickly and as I leaned back more, wishing that I could melt into him, he pulled my hair back from my neck and kissed me gently, whispering, "I love you, Sophie."

I turned around, wanting to be at one with him and to merge our souls, "I love you so much, Billy."

"The world isn't ready for our love, Sophie, but every day I thank God for bringing you into my life. I feel like my life is in technicolor and before it was just shades of gray. I can't imagine it without you."

"Oh, Billy." I couldn't say anything else. He encircled his fingers through mine, reminding me of the first time that our hands had touched that day so long ago at Mass when I felt the electricity from him pouring into me.

He put his strong broad arms around me, tilting my face up and kissing it gently, "Let's go inside, it's getting a little cool."

He took my hand, squeezed it again, and led me into the restaurant. It was a small dim place, but it had a warmth to it. The proprietor smiled as we walked in, and I couldn't help remembering the past few months and what we'd gone through, by doing nothing but just trying to live our lives and express our love for each other in a way that didn't hurt anyone but somehow seemed to offend everyone. Billy held my chair for me and then sat down in his own, and put his hand across the table, stroking my fingers. "I thought that since we never go out, not that I don't love being with you in the hotel room, but I wanted to do something special for you. I feel as if I never tell you or show you how much you mean to me, so I wanted to take you some place special. Some place where we could feel comfortable in our love for each other."

"Billy, I don't know what to say. I don't think that I've ever been so completely happy. I know that I should feel guilty."

"No more than I should. We both took the same vows, and we both have chosen to break them for something that is greater than either of us. You know, I think that what I've learned through my feelings for you is that love doesn't judge. True love doesn't judge, and the Father our God, gave us the gift of love and so even though others may look down on us and castigate us and say that what we've done is forbidden by the Church and society, God doesn't judge us because God is love and love forgives all, and knows all."

Tears were now coming down my face, I felt like I would burst with the love that I was feeling for Billy.

He wiped the tears away from my face and then pushed his chair closer to mine. "I want you to have this." He slipped the Rosary that he always wore from around his neck and placed it carefully in my hand. "My mother gave it to me when I was ordained. It was her love that got me through the hard times. And I want you to know that I will always be there for you. Always. Truly. I love you, Sophie."

And now my mind drifted to later that evening. We drove the short distance back to our motel room. And before we even got in the door, my lips were against his, I felt suddenly completely uninhibited. We made love that night with a force and passion that we'd never felt before, and afterwards I wound my body around his and prayed that we would never have to leave.

End Flashback
Buffalo, New York, Doctor's Office; 1956

Now, here in the doctor's office, I clutched the Rosary protectively. It was my constant link to him when we were away from each other. I felt as if his energy inhabited the small crucifix and protected me at the same time.

Suddenly, I heard someone clearing their throat loudly, as the doctor walked back into the room. "Miss. Legocki." I looked up and something in the way the doctor stood in the doorway made my heart jump.

"Yes, Doctor." I almost whispered the words.

"Miss Legocki, you are going to have a baby."

I felt lightheaded and nauseous. I couldn't understand what he was saying. He must be wrong! But he continued.

"You're about four months pregnant, so in late-March or early-April, you should be delivering."

"I'm what? I mean, that can't be. It just can't, I'm 37, I just can't!!!"

He looked at me, his eyes judging me as if I was some errant teenager that had stumbled into his office. "Well, Miss Legocki, I'm afraid that this is the case. Now I notice that you're single and I don't know if you and the.... um...father have plans to marry?"

I was in a daze, I couldn't believe what I was hearing. Billy had never told me that I might get pregnant! But I was. The room was beginning to spin, an even more violent wave of nausea hit me, "Doctor, do you have a bathroom—I don't feel well."

"I understand," he said dryly. "It's this way."

As I stood over the toilet, my head was throbbing, what would I do? I couldn't tell my parents. What would Billy do? For a moment, I was seized with a sense of panic, what if he decided that he didn't want to have anything to do with me and the baby? After all, he had much more to lose than I did. I could just disappear and no one would know or care. But Billy, he had responsibilities, he ran the Parish. He couldn't give up everything for me. And my parents, they would never accept that, this was my mother's worst nightmare that I would end up like the girls on the wrong side of town. And now, at almost 40, her fear was coming true.

I knew I had to stop thinking like this, I had to pray, I had to ask God for guidance. If God gave me this baby, there must be a reason why. I couldn't question his will, I had to accept it. Isn't that what I told the teenage girls who got pregnant and then invariably gave up their babies to the Church, many of the infants in Father Baker's orphanage were from the local girls who'd gotten into trouble. The "fast" girls. Now I was one of them. I tried to fight back the tears, but they kept coming.

As I numbly walked out of the doctor's office, I was hit with an overwhelming sense of dread and a suffocating fear. I brushed against people rushing down the street, everyone with somewhere to go but me. Billy wasn't due for another two days and I was afraid to call him. I wanted to tell him in person. What if I called and then he decided that he just didn't want to see me again? I couldn't bear the thought, but it could happen. And him, a colored priest and me, a white nun.

It was close to twilight and the street was shrouded in deep purple shadows as the sun dipped below the horizon. I didn't know quite where I was going, just walking. Suddenly, I looked up and I saw what seemed to be a flash of light across the horizon. For a moment, it looked as if a star hovered over me. But it couldn't be, it wasn't yet dark, but there was clearly a light sparkling in front of me. I couldn't move, I was transfixed by it and as I allowed the light to flow into me, I was suddenly filled with a sense of calm and purpose. I felt as if I was being hugged and cared for and loved by a force that was greater than me. That same force folded me into its arms, and I thought that I heard it whisper, "*It will be OK. This is what is meant to be. This is good. Your life is good. Have no fear.*"

And I knew instinctively that it would be OK, my heart was still beating wildly, but I didn't feel alone anymore and I knew that whatever happened, it was truly God's will and that He had a larger plan than I could ever imagine for me and for my baby.

CHAPTER

36

Buffalo, New York, Hospital; Present Time

I had gotten up and was staring out the window at nothing in particular, just trying to process everything that Sophie had just told me. When someone tells you how you were conceived, it's a feeling that answers certain questions, but then opens up others. I hadn't really even noticed that Sophie had lain back down on the pillows with her eyes closed tightly. I thought that I could see a small tear trickling down the side of her face. Suddenly, I was hit by a pang of guilt. Was it fair of me to ask her to continue to go down this path of so long ago just to satisfy my own need to know? Did I even have the right to know? If it would cause her such pain, maybe it was better to leave things as they were. I knew enough now to believe truly that my birth parents did love each other genuinely and deeply, and that I was a product of that love, not just some wild night of abandon. For that I was grateful, but I had to admit to myself that something in me still wanted to learn more, still felt as if the pieces had not fallen completely in place yet.

"Joe."

I hurried to Sophie's side as she forced herself up, hastily wiping her hand across her face to hide the tears that had gathered in the corners of her eyes.

Leaning over the bed, I took her hand in mine, massaging it gently. She had gotten so frail that I felt that is if I held her too tightly, she might break, "Sophie, if this is too painful we can stop. You've told me so much, I feel as if I don't know how to say thank you. I've gotten to know you and him in a way that I never thought was possible—but now…"

She waved me off, "I want to do this, Joe, this is for me, too. You are the first person and the only person who really knows what happened, and if this is my time, I want to go knowing that someone else, and especially *you*, knew the real story, that it wasn't just some scandal that the Church tried to bury, that it was more, that there was a reason. And the reason is you, Joe. The reason is you. So, no, I want to tell you, and you have a right to know. Everything."

She settled back onto the pillows and began talking again, slowly and so softly that I had to lean forward to hear her. "When I found out that I was pregnant, I knew that I didn't want to tell him on the phone, so I'd have to wait until the next time that we were getting together. And I tell you, that week was probably the longest in my life. It felt like everybody knew my secret. Even though I wasn't showing, I couldn't help but be afraid that someone would notice something different about me, especially my mother. She watched me like a hawk anyway. But I guess the only good thing was that she was so preoccupied with taking care of my father and so exhausted that she didn't have the time to scrutinize me as much as she normally did. When the day finally came, and I was in the car with Billy, I was seized with such a panic that I could barely get the words out."

Flashback Through Sophie's Eyes
A Few Miles From The Canadian Border; 1956

Billy took my hand and kissed it while smoothly turning the car wheel with the other hand. We were almost to the Canadian border and the air had already turned icy cold though it was only October.

"You're quiet, cat got your tongue?"

He smiled at me and gently stroked my face.

I shuddered in spite of myself. I'd been dreading this moment. "No.... no. I'm just...um...tired, I guess."

He looked concerned as he squeezed my hand more tightly. "You never told me what the doctor said."

"I know. I wanted to tell you today."

He slowed the car down, pulling over to the side of the road and stopping on a small overlook, then gently putting his arm around me. "Sophie, tell me, are you OK? Whatever it is, we can get through this together."

I don't know why I didn't have a better way to say it. I don't know why I didn't have the words rehearsed, but I didn't, so I just blurted out, "I'm pregnant."

For a moment he didn't say anything. Then after what seemed like an eternity, he held me more tightly, gathering me closer to him, but saying nothing.

I sat up, locking eyes with him. "Billy, did you hear me!!!!" I was almost shouting. "I said I was PREGNANT!!!!!"

After a moment, he finally spoke. "I know, I think I knew before you told me. I just—well I just guess I needed to hear you say it."

"So, I said it! Now what?! I'm scared, Billy. I'm really scared!" I had started to shake uncontrollably and a feeling worse than the nausea swept over me. Maybe my fears were coming true, maybe this was the last time that I'd see him, maybe he didn't want me or the baby and he'd just walk away. Tears were now streaming down my face.

"Billy, say something!!!!!!!"

He kissed me on the face for the first time, then held me more tightly than before, "Sophie, we'll get through this. I love you and we'll figure it out."

I started crying again, feeling only confusion, doubt, and the overwhelming sense that something much worse than I could ever imagine was about to happen.

CHAPTER

37

Canadian Side of The Falls, Small Motel; 1956

I painfully opened my eyes. They felt as if they'd been glued together, I guess it was just because I was sleeping so hard these days. It was more difficult for me to get to sleep and then when I finally did, it was like my body was so totally exhausted I could barely wake up. My thoughts were swirling around in no particular order, images of the past few days—the doctor's office, trying to be as scarce as possible at home for fear that my mother might notice something different about me, and then Billy. Instinctively, I reached for him, I touched his side of the bed expecting to feel his warm back, but only air. I bolted up. The day was gray without much light coming in through the heavy drapes. It took a while for my eyes to focus, but as I did, I was seized with this sense of panic. The room was empty, Billy's heavy dark coat was gone, his shoes gone, I ran over to the dresser where he always left his wallet and car keys. Gone, everything gone.

My head was spinning now, and I fell to the floor convulsing with sobs. *He'd left me!* My worst fears were true. I was alone. Completely alone. I couldn't move. I just rolled up in a ball on the floor, clutching my knees, crying out every emotion I'd ever had.

The clock ticked loudly in the background; I had lost track of time. I didn't know whether fifteen minutes had passed or hours. Then I heard footsteps coming closer to the door, my heart jumped, maybe–maybe he'd come back. But as the footsteps continued down the hall, I was seized with another volley of tears ripping through me like a butcher knife. The voices in my head slammed against my brain. "*I knew it! I knew that as soon as I told him he'd leave, and he did. He left me!!!! How could he, how could he leave me—not just me—but us!!!!! How could I be such a fool to think that he'd want me and our baby?!!!!*"

I ran around the room sobbing wildly, not caring if anyone heard me. I wanted to curl up and crawl in a hole. I wanted not to be me. Anyone but me. And I couldn't help thinking, "*Why? Why???*" And I threw myself on the floor, folding my arms into my chest, rocking back and forth. "*He said he loved me, why would he leave me??*" I couldn't stop crying, I felt like I would break in two from the grief.

****

I felt arms around me and heard a voice. "Sophie! Sophie, what are you doing?!!!!"

I knew that I must still be dreaming. I'd fallen asleep on the floor exhausted by the tears and panic. But it wasn't a dream, my eyes were so swollen and red that I couldn't open them, but I felt myself being scooped up from the floor and being laid gently on the bed. I was finally able to open my eyes and I could barely choke out, seeing Billy in front of me, "Why did you leave me? You don't want me anymore! You don't want the baby!!!"

"Sophie! Sophie, my love, how could you think that?! What—what have I done to make you think that I'd leave you, that I'd abandon you and *our* baby? I'd never...never!" And now I felt his tears against my face. "I just went to get us some coffee—I didn't want to wake you...that's all...I thought you'd still be asleep."

Now I was even more angry, my panic and relief, being overwhelmed by a new see-saw of emotions, "Then why didn't you just leave a note????!!!"

He hugged me tighter, "I should've, I'm sorry, truly sorry." Then he pressed his face to mine, whispering, "I will never...never leave you! Do you hear me? I love you and I'll never leave you."

That afternoon, we talked for a long time. We sat on the bed looking out at the empty parking lot that was the view from our small room.

Billy took my hand and put it to his lips. "We're together and we'll always be together, in God's eyes, we're one, we're His children and nothing and no one can ever break us apart, and I give you my word, my vow, that I will be with you always for the rest of the days that I have on this earth. We may not be man and wife in the world's eyes, but in our eyes, we are. I love you, Sophie, and I pledge my love to you, a love that

God has given us and that I accept with a full heart and joy."

I hugged him tightly, "Oh, Billy. I'm so sorry. I just was so scared!"

He pressed his hands gently against my lips, "It's OK. I understand, but I just wanted you to know that you don't have to worry or doubt my commitment to you and to our baby. I've been making some calls, my mentor, the Priest who made it possible for me to study at the Vatican, is retired and living in Cincinnati, and he had told me before of a home for unwed mothers that he helped start many years ago—so I can see if, when the time is right, you can go there. I've met some of the Sisters there. They are very kind. I've told them..." And he swallowed hard, "I've told them that there is a young woman in my Parish who will need their assistance at the right time and they've agreed to make sure that there is room for you. And I will be there, with you. No one has to know the truth, but I will be there with you."

I didn't know quite what to say. So, for a moment, we just sat in silence in each other's arms with only the sound of birds soaring overhead.

I leaned my head against his shoulder, closing my eyes as I began to speak, I tried not to tear up, but it seemed as if these days, that's all I did, was go from one emotional abyss to the next. On the one hand I was reassured that he hadn't left and he said that he was there for me, but I knew that even with the relief that his words brought, I knew that my life had shifted in a fundamental way and that everything that I'd known, the life that I'd had since I was a timid 14-year-old, leaving my family to devote my life to God, would never be as it was. I had to face the fact that I'd broken every vow that I'd ever taken and that guilt and sin would live with me forever. But now, I had to somehow keep moving forward and do what was best for the tiny life growing inside me.

I twirled my fingers around his, saying slowly, "I think that I should take an extended leave of absence, I can't stay there in...well...in this way that I am now. I'm going to tell them that my father has taken a turn for the worse and that my mother needs me full time. I think that I can get some type of job at the factory to make a little money and also be out of the house as much as I can. My mother will just be glad to have the extra help at night and somehow, I'll just have to convince her that I've put on some weight from not being as active as I was at the nursery." At the thought of what lay ahead for me over the next five months, I almost gagged, feeling the nausea rising in my throat, but I swallowed firmly. No more. I told myself. No more. I have to face what I must and go on. I must go on. "So, that's it. That's what I'm gonna do."

Billy pushed my hair away from my face, kissing me gently on the cheek and then wrapping his arms around me. "I'll still come up on Tuesdays. And you call me if you start feeling ill." He looked at me with such intensity, holding me even more tightly, "If anything, and I mean _anything_, happens and you need me, you promise me that you'll call me right away. Don't wait, there's nothing, and I mean nothing, more important to me than you and the baby. Nothing." His words were like a balm for my soul that soothed the conflicting emotions that overwhelmed me, fear, panic, anger and yes love. Because through it all, I couldn't help loving that tiny life growing inside of me.

CHAPTER

38

Buffalo, New York; Three Months Later, February 1957

My back ached and my feet and ankles were swollen, and I felt intermittently hot and cold in the large heavy woolen sweater over my wide skirt that I wore to try and hide my growing belly. I'd been working at this small glass factory since I'd given my leave notice at the convent. Mother Superior had left a few months earlier to work at another convent, and they hadn't named her successor yet, so ironically, I gave my notice to Sister Catherine, my good friend from my early days at the Convent. She accepted it without question.

I longed to sit for a few minutes, but we only got breaks once an hour and my supervisor watched us closely to make sure that we met our quota. The work was mind numbing, but at least it got me out of the house. As I grew larger with each month and I swaddled myself in more roomy sweaters, my mother eyed me more sharply as I left the house. Most of the time she just pursed her lips and continued grimly bathing my father, but this day she blurted out, "Your ankles look swollen, Sophie."

I pretended not to hear her as I stuffed my sandwich in a brown bag, my hand on the door. She shook her head, looking me up and down suspiciously, "Usually they get swollen like that when you're with child."

There was a silence between us. I shrugged, "Mother, please, I'm a nun. You forget that I'm on my feet almost eight hours a day, I *guess* my ankles are swollen." I tried to sound nonchalant, but my heart was beating loudly. I avoided her eyes, as I grabbed my purse, shouting behind me, "I'll see you tonight."

I couldn't help dreading what she'd have to say this evening, maybe I could go to the library and read a few hours before I went home and then sneak in quietly. She was usually so exhausted by the end of the day that she fell asleep in front of the TV by six. As if reading my mind, my only friend there, Andy, walked up to me smiling broadly. He was a cheery Polish kid whose family had come here a few years earlier, but with the help of the large Polish immigrant community, they were already prospering in their own small home and a business that his father had started. He came up behind me, putting his hand on my shoulder. "Eh there, Soph, you're looking a bit tired, why don't I give you a ride home t'night? I got to make a coupla stops, but afterwards I can run you by your place that way you don't have to be takin' the bus."

Smiling gratefully, I gave him a small hug. "That would be great, I don't have to be home early, so you make as many stops as you need and then you can drop me off." I felt like God must be listening to me, I had ridden with Andy before and between running into everybody that he knew, which was a lot of people, and then making all of his stops, I might not be home until eight, and for sure Mother would be asleep by then. I was starting to feel a little less anxious even though the voice inside of me whispered, *"Yes, but she'll just ask you again in the morning."* I refused to think about tomorrow; I just needed to get through one day at a time. Tomorrow would take care of itself.

CHAPTER

39

A few hours later, the loud horn went off signaling the end of the day and immediately the room broke into a frenzy of people pulling off the gray aprons and eagerly grabbing for coats, hats, purses, empty lunch boxes and whatever else they'd brought from home. And the mad dash began to get in the front of the line for the different buses that took the workers everywhere from a few blocks away to miles and miles from here. This was considered a good job for Buffalo especially with so many businesses closing lately. But, for once, I could lay back and take my time packing up my things. And thankfully so, with my expanding waistline and swollen ankles it was getting harder every day to move quickly, so again I silently thanked God for hearing my prayers.

"So, you ready t'go, Sophie?"

"Two minutes and I'll be ready. I just need to stuff this book in my purse."

He leaned over me curiously, "Whatcha readin'?"

I blushed, suddenly embarrassed. "Just one of those silly romance novels, it helps to pass the time at lunch."

He smiled. "I would never have figured you for readin' one a' those books, you seem so serious." He chuckled, "Why if I hadta guess, I'd say you'd a been readin' somethin' like some religious type book, but I guess

I'm not much of a judge." He laughed again, taking my heavy purse from me, "I'll take that for ya."

I smiled weakly, suddenly overcome with panic. Was it so obvious? *Did I have "NUN" written across my forehead, and what if he knew somebody back at the convent? Andy wasn't stupid, he was just too much of a gentleman to say anything about my increasingly obvious condition. My thoughts were now running away from me, what if he'd seen Billy and me? What if...*

Suddenly, I heard a snap of fingers, jolting me back, "Hey there, did I say somethin' to upset you? You look like you seen a ghost and it's not even dark yet!" He smiled again, "C'mon let's get going—don't want to stay here any longer than we need to."

"Right, let's go." I followed him to his car trying to tame my thoughts and the uneasy feelings. I climbed in the passenger seat next to him, barely squeezing my ample belly into the small car. Andy's car was really old and sometimes seemed as if it would hardly make it another day. The doors had to be slammed extra hard to stay closed, and sometimes he had to yank so hard to get them open that it seemed as if the door handle would come off. But no matter how long it took him to turn the motor over, and no matter how much it groaned and shook, it always seemed to come alive just at the moment when you'd lost hope. But today, for some reason, the car must've been in a good mood because it started up almost immediately. Clearly pleased, Andy stroked the steering wheel as if it was an obedient cat. "There she goes, good car, she's a good car."

I laughed, relaxing for the first time. "She sure is."

Now we both laughed, and he turned on the radio, loudly, fiddling with the dial until he got a station with some of that new music that everybody was saying was so scandalous. Andy snapped his fingers and hummed along as he steered the car through the evening traffic.

"Oh darn! I forgot, I told my mum I'd pick her up somethin' from Wilson's, darn." He did a quick U-turn, as I almost slid on top of him. Drumming his fingers on the wheel and glancing at his watch, "We'll have to take the short cut otherwise I'll never make it to my buddy's in time, don't want to get you home too late."

"Oh, don't worry about me." I felt like saying, '*The later the better,*' but instead just said, "Really, I'm fine. I don't have anything that I have to do, you just take care of whatever you need to do."

"Thanks, Soph."

"Thank *you*, if it wasn't for you, I'd be running for the bus."

Without taking his eyes off the road as he gunned the motor, "Now we can't have that can we?"

As we bounced along the road, I noticed that we were coming to a more deserted area of town, I felt suddenly uneasy. "Which way are you going?"

He looked around, "I'm gonna take the shortcut, across the railroad tracks, you remember I took that way one other time."

Suddenly relaxing, "That's right, I remember."

He slowed as we approached the tracks, "Cuts out about 15 minutes, no traffic." And he winked at me as we pulled up next to a sign that clearly read: "NO CAR CROSSINGS."

He stopped and waited for a moment, looking in both directions, then gunned the motor and jumped the car over the track, laughing like a kid. "I love this."

I couldn't help but giggle also, his laughter was infectious as we hurtled over the tracks.

"Hold on, one more to go." He gunned the motor again, but this time the motor choked and then stopped. Calmly, he turned the key again, "Don't worry, she'll start up."

It was very dark now, the only light coming from a broken street light on the other side of the tracks.

"OK, now what's the problem?" he mumbled to himself as he turned the key, but the only thing coming from the aging motor sounded like nails scraping over a blackboard.

I leaned over anxiously, "What do you think it is?" He shrugged, "I'm not sure, lemme see something." He opened the glove compartment and pulled out a rusty flashlight, then shoving his door open, he barely wriggled out. The way that we were positioned over the tracks had blocked his door from opening completely. *"It's a good thing he's thin,"* I thought to myself.

Propping open the hood of the car, he shone the flashlight into the bowels of the motor. "Here 'tis. I think I know what's ailin' her."

"What is it?"

Suddenly, he stopped and became very still, whispering hoarsely, "Mother a' God… We gotta get outta here!"

Then I heard it, too, a long, low whistle in the distance, and through the heavy fog, I saw a light. A train! Going at full speed, barreling towards us. The approaching train was causing the car to vibrate, shaking and rattling as if it would break in two.

He sprinted over to my side, "C'mon, I'll help you out!"

He pulled on the car door, but it was stuck, jammed on the tracks.

"Shit!!!! You gotta slide over to my side."

I pushed myself over to the other side, but the steering wheel was so low that I couldn't get around it. I started hyperventilating, tears coming down uncontrollably as I realized that I was about to die!!!!

The train roared closer and closer, the car now shaking so much that I felt like I was about to vomit.

"We're not going <u>this</u> way! No, <u>we're not!!!!</u>" Andy slammed the hood closed, grabbing the stick shift and putting the car in neutral and then with half his body in the car, and his hand steering the wheel, he managed to edge the car over first one track then another, steering it down over the last railroad tie. The track was on a gentle slope and so with sheer force of will, he was able to push the car off the tracks and to the side of the tracks into the dirt just as the train crashed past us.

First one car, and then another and another and another and another streaking past us, barely a few feet away. I couldn't stop shaking and crying. As he pried my door open and I tumbled out, I clutched him, sobbing, "Thank you, Andy!!! Thank you, Andy—thank you!!!!!!"

****

That night as I lay on my bed, my hand resting on my stomach, I felt the baby move, I couldn't fight back the tears, thinking how close I came to losing everything. And I knew at that moment that there truly was a plan for me and my baby, so as I rubbed my stomach and felt my child shift and turn, I closed my eyes.

CHAPTER

40

I smiled at Billy who was sitting next to me, massaging my fingers anxiously. We were at the train station. The day that I was headed to Cincinnati to the home for unwed girls that Billy's mentor ran. Cincinnati, the place that I was going to have my baby. I'd told Mother that I was going there to help out as a housekeeper in a Cincinnati Catholic Parish. She wasn't pleased, as I'd expected, but there wasn't anything that she could do.

The sound of an infant whimpering floated past me, and my thoughts drifted to earlier that day. I let my hand rest lightly on my stomach, a habit I'd gotten into as my belly expanded, squeezing past the waist of even my most ample skirts. I liked to feel the baby stir inside of me, and when the baby would shift or kick, I'd smile feeling my growing connection to that precious little part of me. Sometimes I'd be dreaming about the baby, feeling the small head against my breast, sensing the peaceful breathing as I gathered my baby in my arms. But then I'd wake up and realize that it was just a dream and I was alone in the same room that I'd been in as long as I could remember.

The hard, narrow, iron bed, the peeling green and white wall paper with images of antebellum ladies at a picnic, I never knew why Mother had picked out that wallpaper. It was so far from the hard scrapple life that we lived. We weren't poor, but I always felt that we were just around the corner from staring poverty in the eye, the same watery stews laden with misshapen knotty potatoes, a few mangy carrots, and the occasional tough, wiry pieces of beef marbled with more fat than meat, filled our cracked white and black bowls every night. The blue and red rag rug that I'd put my feet on so many bone-chilling mornings was thread bare, and the corner of my room, now quiet, but where back then, there always seemed to be a crib with one of my brothers crying loudly, keeping me awake, demanding to be held, diapers to be changed, colicky babies, all of them. Nothing in that room had changed, nothing was different. Except me. The nun, who was no longer the nun. The mother who would soon have to give her baby away. I tried not to cry, but sometimes I'd have to turn away and excuse myself because just as I'd gotten into the habit of feeling my baby moving inside of me, I'd be seized with this sudden feeling of loss when I knew that soon, very soon, I'd be empty. Inside of me would be empty and I'd never see my baby again.

Sometimes I'd fantasize about Billy and me really being together, being married and having our own small home, and raising our child who I knew would be so special because my child was born of a love that defied convention, a love that just was. Neither of us was looking for it, we both had devoted our lives to God and yet, God had something different in mind for us. A twisted road that neither of us would ever had thought would be in front of us. Did I have regrets, did I wish that this hadn't happened? Sometimes I asked myself those questions. What if I'd never met Billy, what if he'd never come to that Parish? He'd told me once that his dream had been to be the pastor in a large Parish in Harlem so that he could be there in the middle of something bigger than himself where he could really make a difference. When he told me about those dreams, I sensed his frustration, I sensed a longing in him for something more than ministering to a small Parish in a backwater town. But invariably, he'd shake it off quickly, stroking my cheek, or kissing me lightly, as if knowing that I'd read his thoughts, knowing that

I'd felt a desire in him that neither I nor the baby could ever really fulfill.

We didn't really talk about what it would be like after the baby…was gone. The past five months had been so focused completely on just living day-by-day, trying not to panic, trying not to let the accusatory whispers and muffled laughter at work sting too hard, trying just to put one foot in front of the other and go on and keep my thoughts on our Father who knew all things, and who loved all things, even a fallen nun and her baby. That's how I thought of myself sometimes, as fallen from what I'd planned for myself. But then I'd feel the baby move inside of me and I'd be flooded with such profound love that I knew came from the Father to the baby and then to me.

"Hey, there, are you OK?" Billy had been holding my other hand as these thoughts ran through my head. This was the day, the day that I dressed slowly and deliberately, something warm but roomy, it was a long ride to Cincinnati on a shaking train to that home for girls like me, except that I wasn't a girl anymore. Billy had arranged everything just as he said he would with his mentor who'd founded the place. They had a room for me with the Sisters of Charity. I couldn't help thinking of the irony— the Sisters of Charity taking care of one of their own.

I thought back again on earlier that day when I folded my clothes. I didn't have much, just three skirts, all in dark blue and brown plaid, an itchy gray wool sweater, a softer pink sweater with small stitching around the neck and pearl buttons. A black and gray striped jacket and my black low-heeled shoes with the permanent scuff marks where I'd tumbled out of the car, scraping against a jagged stone as the train that had almost ended my life whizzed by in a cloud of smoke and dirt, and nonchalant passengers calmly turning the pages of books or scanning the dark, empty countryside from the grimy picture windows.

I carefully squeezed the rest of my things in between the clothes. My favorite of the tattered romance novels, the one that I'd read over and over that swept me up into other worlds, comforting me those lonely months at the glass factory, my rosary and the Bible they gave me when I began as novitiate, a small card from the restaurant that Billy had taken me the first time that he told me that he loved me. This was the day that my life got packed up and moved and changed to what I didn't know. Only our Father in Heaven knew.

I clutched Billy's hand tightly, moving closer to him, trying not to see the faces around me, tired, haggard young women tugging at screaming children, dragging them to the trains past the darkened corridors that smelled of sweat and stale urine. The drunks in the corner, always the same old men, laughing coarsely, clutching their bottles and moving unsteadily, never more than a few feet, their life contained in a dank musty corner where the world passed them by. Billy stroked my back, whispering, "I love you....very...very much."

I nodded numbly because that's how I had to feel. If I let myself acknowledge any of the emotions that were trying to tumble out of me, that wanted me to scream and cry and say *"I don't want to let you go. I don't want to go someplace where I don't know anyone and where I won't see you on Tuesdays and where I'll wake up in a bed that wasn't my own. And where they'll take my baby."* If I let myself feel any of that, I knew I'd break down. So, I was still, very still, trying not to hear the thoughts in my head, trying not to feel the dull pain that was knocking at my temples and forcing my eyes closed.

He nudged me gently, gathering me in his arms, "That's your train."

I nodded, no longer aware of anything around me, feeling only his touch as he lifted my chin to his face, kissing me on the lips. "I love you, Sophie, and I love the baby and we'll make it. I promise you!" And then, reluctantly, he let me go.

CHAPTER

41

The sky was that ugly iron gray when for some reason the clouds stubbornly refuse to let go of their load of frothy powder puffs. The weather forecast had been snow for days, but it never did and now they were saying that it was too cold to snow. When I heard that, I imagined that the baby snowflakes had been frozen in place, stillborn in the sky never to be released to blanket us in icy whiteness. I looked out the window from my bed. My roommate, a young red-headed teen from Cincinnati who looked barely older than 15, was lying on her side flipping through a magazine. They didn't let you have transistor radios here, but she had somehow sneaked one in, and at night when she thought that I was asleep, she'd turn the dials until she found what she was looking for, usually Elvis or one of the other teen idols that kept the young girls swooning.

Minnie, my roommate, abruptly closed the magazine that she'd been looking at, and turned over awkwardly, she was huge, much bigger than me, probably because she was so small and thin that she became all baby. Minnie's red hair was short and cropped to her head, I supposed that she was trying to have one of those chic cuts that you saw in the magazines, but on her it only looked like someone had taken a pair of sharp scissors and haphazardly cut it in no particular fashion. Her eyes were bright blue and very large with dark circles underneath that made her look older and more solemn then her years. I wondered what those eyes had seen. She rarely talked about her parents and never mentioned the father of the child, but on those nights when she wasn't being lulled to sleep by the sound of the crooners on the radio, she was tossing and turning and saying things that I couldn't understand but which seemed to come from a soul tortured by things that haunted her when the lights were low and others slept. I'd never worked with unwed mothers before, only their children, but I knew the demons that crept up in my mind and my baby was one born out of love, what of those others, the children who were the result of some other circumstances that I shuddered to imagine.

She propped herself up on one elbow, "Sophie, can I ask you a question?"

Startled, that she was talking to me, I sat up curiously. Because other than the fact that her parents had also been immigrants, we didn't have much in common and we rarely spoke. The truth was that I was the oldest woman here, usually by 20 years, sometimes more, so I really had nothing in common with any of the girls. Sometimes when I saw the nuns doing their chores, helping the girls and caring for the children in the nursery next door, I thought of my days before this, before Billy. But then I let go of those thoughts as quickly as they came because no matter how hard these past months had been, no matter how many tears I'd shed and how much guilt I felt, the only thing that I would never regret was loving Billy and loving my baby.

As I thought again of my baby, I brushed a tear away. My due date was very soon now, and then as quickly as this all had happened, it would be over, but the life inside of me would go on and this dull ache in my soul would never go away because I knew that I'd probably never see my baby again.

"Sophie...are you awake?"

"Sorry, I was just, well, thinking about something else."

She slowly closed the magazine and then painfully pulled herself up so that she was facing me. "You seem like you know a lot about a lot. I mean you're old, I'm sorry, I didn't mean that you were really old—but you're older than most of the other girls."

"It's OK, what did you want to ask me?"

"Sophie, do you think that God still loves us? Even though we've sinned, because, well because of our babies, we're sinners. And my priest said that I'll probably go to hell, and I just...." She had started shaking all over and tears were coming down. "I just feel so guilty about everything and I don't know what to do, but I don't want to go to hell or die a sinner!"

Part of me wanted to hold her like the child that she was. But the other part of me felt as confused and upset as she, ravaged by my own guilt which tormented me every time I closed my eyes, every time I saw one of the nuns and remembered who I was, and remembered the vows that I'd taken and broken, not once but many times, ending in this, this pregnancy, this innocent child that I'd dragged into my own mortal sin. But I didn't say all that, I couldn't. I just walked over to her bed and gently stroked Minnie's head and tried to wipe the tears away with my hankie, "It's OK, Minnie, don't cry. God loves us all, God doesn't care that we've sinned. God loves us all." I said that as my own guilt felt that it would suffocate me.

CHAPTER

42

I pulled my clothes on quickly, I'd slept much later than usual, the sun, which was mainly obscured by heavy clouds, was high in the sky. After the conversation with Minnie, it had seemed as if all of my own doubts and fears had overwhelmed me and I fell into a deep, hard sleep that I could barely wake myself from.

After hastily dressing, I walked quickly to the one hall phone that all the girls shared, I'd told my mother that I was helping out as a housekeeper in one of the Cincinnati Parishes for a few months. I'd promised to call her once a week and I was worried about my father. He just didn't seem to be getting any better, but in my condition, there wasn't anything I could do. Lately, my mother had seemed to have started to fail also, and it was making her more ill-tempered than ever. So, I'd begun to dread these weekly calls as the operator connected us. The phone rang and rang, and finally my mother picked up.

"Hello...Mother."

"Well, you finally called."

"I'm sorry, I got busy, there's a lot of work here."

"Hmmph,, well anyway, your cousin Dora and her husband are driving through Cincinnati tomorrow on their way to Florida and they want to see you while they're there."

"What?"

"Are you deaf? I said Dora and her new husband will be in Cincinnati tomorrow and they want to see you."

My heart was racing, I had to think of something. I couldn't see them, not now, it was too obvious, even the biggest clothes couldn't hide the pregnancy, "Um, there's a big event and I don't think I can get off."

"What do you mean you can't get off? What are you some kind of slave? You mean to tell me that they won't give you an hour off to see your cousin, what kind of place is this? Why I have a mind to call them myself and tell them that..."

"Mother, STOP!!!!" I was shouting, but I was so upset I didn't care. "Just let me handle it. I'll talk to Mother Superior and see what I can do."

"I think it's just disgusting, what is that woman's name? You never did tell me the name of the Parish. Why I'll..."

"Mother, I will *handle* it. I will call you later this afternoon and tell you what she says."

"You better." And she slammed down the phone.

I felt weak and nauseous, I hadn't thrown up in months, but now I felt like I couldn't hold it back. I ran to the bathroom, barely making it to one of the stalls, and retching over and over again. My hands were shaking, and my forehead was damp with sweat. What was I going to do? If my nosey cousin saw me, she'd know immediately and tell everyone. EVERYONE. I sat on the floor in the stall, twirling my hands nervously around my rosary and at that moment, I seemed to hear a voice that said, "*Pray. Pray.* "

I clasped my hands together and silently prayed to God, "*Dear God, I know that I've asked for your help a lot, but please help me, she can't see me. Dora can't see me."* I don't know how long I sat there praying over and over again to God until I finally pulled myself up and stumbled to my room, collapsing onto my bed. Thankfully, Minnie was out of the room for the moment, so I could be alone with my thoughts. But I was so exhausted that all I could do was to fall in a fitful sleep. When I awoke, I slowly opened one eye, glancing out the window. Huge snow-flakes were beating against the glass, the clouds were belching out enor-mous quantities of snow. I bolted up. Minnie was back in the room, as always nonchalantly flipping through one of the teen magazines.

"God, you've been asleep awhile. Look at it! All the roads are closed, nobody can get in or out, I'm so mad, I was supposed to go to the five and dime, but now I'm stuck here all day!" She angrily grabbed another magazine, throwing down the one that she'd been reading.

Still not sure if it was true, "So you said all the roads are closed and no one can get through?"

She nodded in disgust. For a moment I felt weak-kneed, but I had to be sure, so I tried to smooth down my hair and slipped on my shoes, walking quickly down the hall into the office of one of the administrators, Kathryn was her name. She had light brown hair and was slightly plump, and wore clothes that, if I'd not been a nun, I probably would have worn myself, light-colored dresses with floral patterns and comfortable shoes. She'd always seemed to take an interest in me. I guessed that she was probably around my age, late-thirties, maybe early-forties. But I think that she felt sorry for me, in my condition and all.

And now I'm remembering the first time that we met...when I first got here.

Sisters Of Charity, Kathryn's Office; A Few Weeks Earlier

I stood awkwardly in the doorway to her office, feeling self-conscious. Kathryn, the administrator, had asked me to come and talk with her. As I shifted from one foot to the other, she asked curiously, "You're not the typical mother here, are you? Sophie, right, that's your name?"

Afraid that she might discover the truth about me, I quickly inter-jected, "Sophie Legocki, from New York State. My—um Parish priest arranged for me to come here—given that with everyone knowing me and all, you know, it's a small community."

She nodded sympathetically, "Yes, I imagine that must have been hard. Come in my office, part of what I do is to get to know the girls, we've got some standard information that we need to take down, do you mind talking now?"

I really had nothing else to do, my days were pretty much empty especially compared with the busy life I'd had at the Parish and I couldn't think of any excuse not to talk to her. So reluctantly I followed her into her small cramped office. She nodded for me to sit down on the one chair, a sturdy blonde wooden rocking chair with a blue and white calico cushion that was surprisingly comfortable.

"Would you like some tea?"

"No, I'm um—I'm fine, thank you."

"OK, then. Why don't we start with the basic information, do you know who the birth father is?"

My face reddened, and I felt myself suddenly flush with anger, I wanted to get up and walk out but I knew I couldn't, so I spit the words out, talking more loudly than I probably should have, "Of course, I know him! We love each other. It wasn't like some fling or something! It was real—it *is* real."

I guess sensing how upset I was, she stepped from behind her desk, putting her arm around my shoulder. "I'm sorry, Sophie, I didn't mean to offend you, it's just that—well, we have to ask."

Trying to calm myself and sensing a slow pain radiating from my temples, I started to rock back and forth, hoping that it would help, "Sure. OK."

She looked up at me, raising one eyebrow, writing as she spoke, "So you know the birth father, it sounds like you know him well."

I nodded, afraid to say more.

"OK, so let's continue with the birth father, you don't have to tell me his name unless you want to."

"No. No. He's a very successful business man and…well —very smart."

"Did he finish high school?"

"High school???!!!! He went to college, and a famous one, and then did other school after that. He's very smart—very brilliant—very..." My voice trailed off as I thought of Billy, and I had to swallow hard not to tear up.

She didn't seem to notice and just continued matter of fact, "So, I assume the race is Caucasian." She had started to write that down when I interrupted her. I was torn, should I tell the truth, but with Billy being colored, the baby could be—dark. And then they'd know, so maybe something else other than colored. Maybe that's what I'd say.

I cleared my throat, "Um, he's not...um, white. The father, I mean."

She looked at me incredulously. "Really, and you're sure that he went to college?"

"Yes, absolutely."

"You believe him?"

"Yes, of course, why do you keep asking me that?" I was rocking back and forth faster and faster, nervously wishing that I hadn't even seen her.

She continued, tersely, "So the birth father is not white, so he is—what?"

"He's um, Mexican."

"OK—Mexican." She wrote that down and turned to the next page in her notebook.

End Flashback
Sisters Of Charity, Kathryn's Office

I was thinking of that as I walked into Kathryn's office, we had continued that day, and finally I'd managed to calm myself down and answer the rest of her questions, but now I felt even more guilty than ever. Eventually I'd have to tell them the truth about Billy. But maybe, maybe not, maybe if the baby wasn't too dark. At the thought of the baby, I knocked on her door, remembering why I was there.

"C'mon in."

Kathryn looked up from a book that she was reading, taking off her glasses. "Is everything OK, Sophie are you feeling all right, do I need to call the nurse?"

"No, I'm fine—just fine, I just, uh, wanted to know if the snow is as bad as it looks, I mean um, Minnie mentioned that the roads were closed and that no one could get in or out."

She swiveled her chair around so that she was facing the window, "She's right. I just heard on the radio that the mayor has declared a state of emergency. So, I'm afraid that we'll be stuck here for a few days."

"So, you mean no one can get in? No one?"

"'Fraid not, they've closed all the roads."

Barely able to contain my joy and total relief, "Thank you. Thank you so much."

Not sure what to say, she smiled, "I'm not sure for what, but you're welcome anyway, Sophie."

I felt like kicking up my heels with joy! My cousins couldn't get in! They won't know my secret now. No one will! A huge weight lifted from me, and the heaviness and desperation that I felt after I spoke to mother yesterday was suddenly gone. As I continued down the hall back to my room, I silently thanked our Father, for again helping, for, again forgiving me for my sins and delivering me from far worse. "*Thank you, Father. Thank you, God.*" I whispered over and over. Fighting back tears, but this time of relief and happiness.

CHAPTER

43

March 1957

I don't know how long I'd been sitting there looking out at the gray landscape. The snow that had blanketed the streets in a white frothy covering had iced up and was now gray and dirty. The sun threw out a few weak rays, warming the air slightly and forming the inevitable pools of water as the snow melted. The air was slightly more balmy than it had been, and the surprise late-March snowstorm was now more of an annoyance than anything else as cars groaned and squeaked trying to maneuver out of the partially melted drifts. A slow drip of water was making its way down the window and my eyes followed it from the top of the window sill to the bottom as the dew drop lazily meandered down the glass.

Suddenly, I felt a dampness between my legs and saw that a large dark spot of water had stained my dress, before I could react, another gush of water had spurted out from between my legs. Feeling confused and weak, I barely whispered out to Minnie, "I can't stop peeing..."

Running over to me, she took one look, shaking her head. "Your water just broke! I'll get the nurse!!!" Minnie was all baby and much bigger than me, so she barely wobbled out to the hallway as I fell back onto my bed, thinking, *"Oh my God! It's happening! I'm having the baby!"* I closed my eyes, feeling a sharp pain and then another. I started breathing faster and faster as the pains continued, each deeper than the last. I wanted to scream out, but I bit my bottom lip. After what seemed like an eternity, I felt two strong hands picking me up and easing me into a wheelchair. I remember passing some of the other young mothers as they were being wheeled out of the rooms, some of them screaming out in pain and fear. And now it was me. My head was spinning and all I could think was, *"I want Billy, I want Billy!"* But he wasn't here, and I couldn't call him.

When we got to the ambulance and then to Good Samaritan Hospital, they put me on a bed and one of the nurses told me to start breathing. A doctor came in with a long needle, telling me to sit up and put my head down as far as I could. I gasped as he stuck the needle in the base of my spine, a feeling worse than the escalating waves of pain that were wracking my body. And then my mind started to drift into what they called the twilight sleep. Around me, I could hear voices, but everything seemed to be in slow motion. Through the fog, I could barely see the doctor coming towards me, the nurses gently removing my dress and placing my legs apart, my hands felt heavy and I couldn't lift my head, I wanted to speak to say something, but I couldn't. It was like I was paralyzed, but I could still see everything happening around me. And then I closed my eyes.

****

A bright light shone in my face and I heard the lusty cry of an infant, and someone placed a tiny perfect pink baby on my breast.

The nurse smiled, "It's a boy."

His brown eyes were scrunched close and a few dark wisps of straight hair lay flat on his head. I put him to my face, our cheeks touching, and kissed him gently. My baby. I touched his tiny fingers, caressing each one, wanting to hold him closer to me, but the nurse was taking him from me.

"We'll put him in the nursery now."

And the emptiness that I knew that I'd feel crawled over me, saturating me, hollowing out my heart. I needed to talk to Billy, and as I clutched the side of the bed and painfully tried to hoist myself up, I almost slipped out onto to the floor.

The nurse clucked disapprovingly, helping me back in and tucking the covers under my chin, "You can't get up for a few days, you just had a baby. Now relax, we'll bring your baby back a little later today. You need to get some rest; just sleep now." She handed me some pills and a glass of water.

Shaking my head no, "I don't want to take anything, I just want to see my baby!" But the nurse sternly refused to budge, holding out the pills. "The doctor wants you to sleep, I can give you a shot, if you don't want to take the pills." She held out the pills again and realizing that I had no choice, I reluctantly put them in my mouth and swallowed.

I don't know how long I slept, but I realized that I was in a different room now. There were long rows of beds each one with a girl who, like me, had recently given birth. Most were just starting to wake up from the forced sleep, others were like me earlier, trying to get up and wander around, but like me, after a few steps they realized how little energy they had and fell back onto their pillows. I was trying to prop myself up on my elbows weakly when I became aware of someone standing over me. It was the nurse who had given me the pills.

She raised one eyebrow, suspiciously as she eyed me accusingly, "You have a visitor, Miss Legocki, he said that he's a 'friend.'" I sat up expectantly, hoping beyond hope that it was Billy. I tried to smooth my gown. "We'll take you to the receiving room, we don't allow men in this area."

I didn't know what to say, but I suddenly felt light-hearted and giddy like a teenager waiting for her first date, and here I was a 37-year-old nun who had just given birth and hoping that my lover was here to see me. One of the assistants handed me a thick gray robe and helped me into a wheel chair. As he whizzed me down the hall into the receiving room, I could barely stop my fingers from twirling around the coarse terrycloth of the robe's belt. I was so nervous, thinking, "*What if it's not him, or what if it's him and he sees me like this, and he changes his mind and then doesn't want to see me again or what if he sees the baby and he thinks he's not dark enough...*"

I couldn't stop the runaway thoughts and as we neared the doorway to the receiving room, I started feeling like I could barely breathe, we got to the doorway and as I glanced into the room, I took a sharp breath. It was empty, turning to the attendant anxiously as he wheeled me to the couch and then helped me out, "I thought that I had a visitor."

He shrugged. "That's what they said, alls I do is wheels the girls around." And he expertly collapsed the wheelchair and then picked it up, sauntering out of the room. Now I really felt panicked and instinctively started praying, *"Dear God, please let it be him, let him not leave, please dear God, let him still love me and the baby...please..."*

"Sophie..."

I opened my eyes and saw him standing tentatively in the doorway. I wanted to run up and hug him tightly and press my lips against his. But I knew I couldn't, but I couldn't stop smiling. He walked over to me and sat in the chair facing me. I was thinking of the first time that we sat in the garden facing each other like this and he brought me the books and my hand brushed against his as he carefully turned the pages.

"How are you, Sophie?"

I wanted to touch him and run my fingers against his square jaw and caress his soft wavy hair, but instead I said, trying to sound as normal as possible, "A little tired, but I'm OK. I tried to get out of bed this morning and almost fell. I guess this took more out of me than I realized."

He leaned a little closer, whispering, "God it's good to see you. Sophie—these two months have been hard. Very hard. I wish I could have done more than just call you every week. I wanted to see you and hold you and comfort you."

A tear was slowly rolling down my cheek as I thought back on the loneliness that had too often overwhelmed me since coming here, waiting for Billy's weekly call was the only thing that kept me going. But, I couldn't say that, all I could do was nod and quickly brush the tear away from my face. "How did you know that—that the baby had been born?"

"I asked Father McClellan to keep an eye on you since—as your—Parish priest, I was of course concerned about your welfare. He told me when you went into labor and then when the baby was born. As soon as I heard, I came straight away."

If it hadn't all been so real, I might've smiled in spite of myself, but not wanting to call attention to us, I just nodded.

He leaned forward. "What does he look like?"

Thinking back on the baby's perfect little round pink face and straight brown hair, with his skin with just a tint of olive, "He's beautiful. Absolutely beautiful."

"I really want to see him, but I don't want it to seem suspicious…with me already being here…and well, you know."

"I know, I want you to see him, we have to think of something. You have to see him."

He got up and walked to the window, staring out, and after a moment, saying, "I'll tell them that Father McClellan had sent me to make sure that the child was all right, he'll back me up on it. I can't come here and not see my…" And his voice trailed off sadly.

Then suddenly, in a monotone, almost matter of fact, as if he'd rehearsed this, saying, "You can stay here a few more weeks, up to a month, if you like, I've arranged it with Father McClellan. I've told him that you can't go back right away, and there's a policy that allows the girls to stay up to a month to transition back to their lives, would you like that, Sophie, to stay longer?"

I felt this lump in my throat. I guess I didn't know what to expect him to say, maybe my fantasy that he was going to tell me that he'd decided that we'd keep the baby and get married and run off somewhere where no one knew us and start a new life. But how foolish would that be, how foolish to think that he, a colored priest, could or would give up everything… for me and the baby? So, I swallowed hard, "Let me think about it, to be truthful, I've just been trying to get through these months and I hadn't really thought of what I'd do next."

He came back over, sitting down in front of me again. I could feel his energy reaching out to me and I longed to be in his arms, back on the lumpy mattress in that small room in the Canadian motel, with the sound of the Falls pounding against the rocks in the distance, but instead I was here. Feeling tired and crampy, and no thought, no plan of what was next for me.

CHAPTER

44

Buffalo, New York, The Glass Factory; Two Months Later

It's quitting time!"

The girl next to me, whose name I never bothered to find out, whistled at the same time as the long shrill end-of-day horn, then quickly began shoving her few belongings into her bag and all along the line, grimy men and women repeated the same ritual, untying the dark gray aprons, grabbing sweaters and purses and paper bags and the other odd assortment of things that they'd brought to work. The same job that I'd had months before and now I was back here again—at the glass factory.

I thought back on the month after the baby's birth, the kind, but firm message that the baby was no longer mine. He belonged to the Sisters of Charity and I was little more than a nuisance at this point, me. The mother who asked to see her baby a few too many times, me, the oldest of the girls who didn't want to seem to leave—me, the one who had the colored visitor that I heard the nurses whispering about. The disapproving looks of the staff, Kathryn's sudden condescension as I changed my description of the father from "Mexican" to "colored." Mother's suspicious look as I returned, obviously thinner than I left, and her snort that meant she didn't believe me when I told her about the strenuous work that they'd had me doing working as the housekeeper in the Cincinnati Parish that had allowed me to shed those extra pounds. And, of course, Billy, who I spoke to surreptitiously on the phone and only saw one other time. And finally, my decision, perhaps the hardest decision that I'd ever made, to leave the life that had defined me since I was 14. I sent in my permanent resignation and now, for the first time since I was 14, I was rudderless, no Church, no Sisterhood, just me alone, back in Buffalo trying to put back together the pieces of my life. It had been over a month since I'd spoken to Billy and longer since I'd seen him. I guess my worst fears were coming true. We were drifting apart. At first, when I came home, we'd speak on the phone almost daily. But he didn't offer to come up anymore and Tuesday after Tuesday passed. Now the memories of what we'd had were starting to seem as if they'd happened to someone else. And that someone else wasn't me. It was who I'd been and was no more.

Buffalo, New York, Hospital; Present Time

"Ms. Legocki, we need to take you in for some bloodwork. I'm afraid your visitor will have to leave."

I couldn't believe that, once again, the nurse seemed to have a knack for interrupting just when the good part had gotten going. I cut my eyes at her. I didn't really believe that they needed to do any bloodwork at that point; they just wanted to stick their nose in and figure out what it was that had so entranced Sophie that even the doctor was calling her recovery a miracle. Sophie must have been thinking the same thing, as she said, "Nurse, do we have to do it now? I'm really feeling like I need to rest."

"Rest, hmmph, well if it's rest you need then maybe you'd better stop talking so much." She pushed the button on the bed and raised it up slowly, handing Sophie her robe. "The orderly will be here in a minute—and you…" She said, turning to me, "I'm afraid will have to come back later."

Realizing that it was pointless to argue, I grabbed my coat, "Sophie, I'll be back in the morning."

Gratefully, she squeezed my hand, "Thank you."

That day, I walked through downtown Buffalo, places I'd never really seen before. I'm not sure how far. I couldn't get Sophie's words out of my head and the images seemed to be playing out in front of me, my birth, my father--Sophie, her anguish, but there was something missing. Father Grau's feelings, what had he been thinking, what had he been feeling? I felt restless as if I had more questions than answers. It was starting to turn dark at the edges of the sky and the rumbling overhead suggested impending rain. I turned up my collar and ducked into a small corner bar. Scanning the room, I could see that it was half empty, looked like a local joint, the kind of place the working guys go to unwind at the end of the day, definitely not my kind of hangout, but at this point I just needed somewhere warm and dry to sit out the storm. I was the only black guy in the room, but nobody seemed to notice me as I slid in a chair behind a small table in the corner. An older white woman with badly dyed blonde hair and too much red lipstick ambled over. "What you havin'?"

I was dying for a cognac, but by the looks of this place, I didn't think they'd have my brand, so I said, "I'll take a beer."

"On tap or bottle?"

"On tap is fine."

I could swear that she winked at me, but before I could react, she was over at the other side of the room. That restlessness that had overtaken me since I'd left the hospital was circling back and I felt as if there was something missing, something that I needed to know. I just didn't know what. Leaning back in my chair, my eyes fell on a picture hanging crookedly over the bar. It was of a group of men standing looking straight in the camera, like one of those shots you see in a movie that seems posed and yet candid at the same time. By the look of their dress, the picture was probably taken in the late fifties or early sixties. One guy in the middle was kind of swarthy, he looked Italian, but could have been a light-skinned black guy. In fact, he could've easily passed for someone in Mama's family, good looking with an intense stare. For some reason I was drawn to him, and the more that I stared, the more I couldn't take my eyes off him.

****

And suddenly the room started fading away and I looked down at my hands and saw another pair, thicker than mine, fingers more square than mine, and just a little darker but not much. I looked down at my feet and realized that I was staring at heavy black shoes and I felt the weight of something against my chest, something hanging from my neck. Instinctively, I clutched it, turning it over in my fingers—a shiny silver cross. And at that moment, I knew that I was him, Father Grau. I knew that he had come through me. Again. The thoughts in his head were starting to overwhelm mine and as I looked around me, I could see that I was in what appeared to be a study. The smell of incense hung in the air and books lined the walls. The desk was massive and overflowing with papers, but none of that seemed to matter. I was on the phone talking to someone that I knew and I found myself saying, "Has he been adopted yet? I know it's only been a few months, but I promised the mother, my parishioner that I'd let her know…for her peace of mind, you know. It was difficult for her—but…" And my fingers fidgeted with a letter opener on the desk. "It was difficult for her to make the decision to give up her baby."

And now I was hearing a voice on the other end of the phone, I knew that voice, it was Father McClellan and he was saying, "I don't know if you are aware of this, Father, but the birth father was a Negro. There was a letter in the baby's adoption file stating that, but the child…well the child doesn't really look like a Negro, but he is and so of course, no white family will take him, and frankly we're having as much difficulty with the Negro families because, well, he doesn't really look like one of them either. You understand, Father."

Now I was twirling the letter opener around and around in circles on the desk despondently, "Yes, I understand. But if anything changes, please let me know."

"Of course, Father. Of course."

Now I was laying my head on the desk, and I felt this throbbing pain between my temples. I took a handkerchief out of my heavy robe and wiped away a tear that was stubbornly forming in my eye. The phone rang. I didn't answer it. It kept ringing. I got up and walked upstairs, looking out a window. I heard a key in the front door and a voice calling out tentatively.

"Father, are you there?"

Reluctantly, I answered, "Yes, I'll be down in a moment." I slowly walked down the stairs feeling the weight of Father McClellan's words bearing down on me. My son, I thought. My son who deserved a loving family and yet, no one would take him because—because he was like me—a Negro. And I couldn't help but think back over all of the disappointments—some small, some major—that I'd suffered almost as long as I could remember. I got to the last step and tried to force a smile; had to keep up appearances.

My housekeeper turned to me, leaning on the broom. "No rush, Father, I'll just be tidying up a bit, next Friday's my last day here. I don't know if they found a replacement, but I want to leave everything nice for you so's if it takes a bit a time you'll be OK."

I nod, not really feeling like talking.

Now I'm in my bedroom. I'm taking out a picture, it's of us. Sophie and me—at the overlook, the first place I kissed her. I feel a pain shooting through me. And I realize it's a profound sense of loneliness that I feel. I can't seem to shake it. I want to call out her name; I feel like I want to reach out to her. But I'm frozen in place. I haven't called her in a month. Because I just don't know what to say or what to do. I can't move, but the feeling of emptiness, the feeling of loss of something, someone who was so a part of me, that loss growing, not allowing me to escape the darkness that is closing in around me.

Every time I think of Sophie, I'm wracked with guilt and this desire to make it right between us. But it's more than that, the love that I feel for her is choking me because it can't be satisfied. It's like I'm watching the slow death of a part of me, my soul is atrophying. Now I'm lying down, trying to sleep, but I can't. I'm staring at the ceiling, praying for God to give me guidance. To show me what I need to do. And then it's like a light is starting to break through in the corners of my mind, a plan is starting to form, and a peace is descending on me because I know what I must do.

****

"Hey, you want anything else?" Startled back to present time by the shrill voice of the waitress, I looked around, not remembering exactly where I was for a moment. Then, seeing the blonde waitress leaning over me with her crooked red lipstick and hands on hips, I realized what had happened. For a moment, I don't really know how long. I'd seen inside his life, inside his thoughts. Once again, Father Grau had let me inside of his world, wanting me to know. Running my fingers through my hair nervously, I said, "No, no. I'm fine."

CHAPTER

45

Buffalo, New York, Courtyard Marriot; Later That Evening

he clerk smiled as I walked past the small front desk. The lobby was non-descript with the standard issue brown and rust colored sofas and pressed wood tables. A few plants, probably silk or plastic, were on each side of the door and in the background, I could hear the sound of a sports announcer blaring out from the TV in the adjoining bar.

"Is there anything you need, Mr. Steele?"

I had been here on and off for almost a month and so they all knew me by now. Luckily, with my career as an international consultant, I could work almost anywhere as long as I had a computer connection, and Glenn, bless his heart, had been more than understanding about me taking this time to be with Sophie. But I wasn't thinking about any of that now, I was still trying to shake the feeling of what I had experienced a little earlier in that bar, the feeling of being someone else. The feeling of being him again. Father Grau, my father. I knew that it wasn't my imagination, or the product of feeling a little too relaxed after the beer, no. It was more, it was as if I had stepped into a portal where I was re-experiencing what he had felt, what he had seen more than 30 years ago.

Still shaking, I put the key in the lock turning it and flicking on the lights. Kicking off my shoes, I sat down on the bed, massaging my temples. I could use a cognac about now and I was tempted to forage in the mini-bar, despite the exorbitant prices, and pop open whatever they had in there. But to my disappointment, there wasn't much except for some bottles of red wine from vintners I'd never heard of and a small flask of vodka. Sighing, I lay back down on the bed, closing my eyes, and immediately, I felt a pressure on my chest as if something was bearing down on me. I tried to open my eyes, but I couldn't, but in my mind's eye, I saw Father Grau's face again and I felt what he was feeling, a tightness around his heart.

****

Now I was able to open my eyes, but this time I saw a different bedroom, not the Marriott, but the same heavy drapes and floor-to-ceiling windows that I'd seen earlier. Father Grau's room at the Rectory. I was holding my hand on my chest and breathing quickly, a panic attack, I knew this wasn't the first one that I'd had. I know what to do, I force myself to breathe slowly, deliberately. I hear footsteps coming up the stairs and a timid knock at the door.

"Father, Father, are you OK?"

I recognize the voice, that woman, the housekeeper. Slowly and painfully, I pull myself up from the bed, shaking my arms, trying to get the circulation going. "I'm fine, Mrs. O'Leary—just fine." I opened the door, forcing a smile on my face, "See, no problem."

She looked as if she didn't believe me, but nodded reluctantly, "OK, Father, sorry to bother you so early in the morning, just wanted to make sure you remembered, this is my last day, 'member I told ya last Friday, so I just wanted to wish you the best. Also wanted to wish you congratulations for bein' made the head of the Parish, we were sure sad to see the old Father's passing, but happy for you that you'll be takin' over now. And I wanted to thank you kindly for all you done for me and my family."

"Thank you for your words, it is a blessing to be able to stay here and bring my vision to a place that I've grown to love so. And I do hope that your husband is better in the warmer climate."

"From your mouth to God's ears, Father."

"He always answers prayers of the devoted."

She took my hand in hers, pumping it warmly, "Thank you, Father, now take care of yourself, I hope you find somebody good to replace me, somebody who'll understand what ya' need."

Now it was my turn to smile and say, "From your mouth to God's ears."

And then we both laughed. After she left my room, I walked over to my closet, grabbing a brown pair of pants, a shirt and a light tan jacket, carefully folding them and putting them in a small bag, then slinging it over my shoulder. I walked deliberately, very deliberately, down the stairs, knowing that when I walked out the door, I'd be changing my life forever.

CHAPTER

46

Buffalo, New York, Hospital; Present Time

ophie was sitting up in bed when I came in bringing her a cool drink. I'd slept late that morning, feeling drained and weakened after the past two days of experiencing HIM take over my consciousness, leaving me feeling as if the life had literally been sucked out of me. After the last time, I'd awakened in a start, it was more like a semi-dream state where I was in it and observing it at the same time. Despite the way that it made me feel, I wanted to continue, I wanted to know what happened when he walked down the stairs. It's as if he would only let me penetrate so far into his thoughts because try as I would, I couldn't figure out exactly where he was going or what the next step was for him. I was thinking those thoughts as I sat wearily in the chair next to the window.

"Are you OK, Joe? You look really tired, I think you need a break. Here I'm the one in the hospital, but I feel as if I'm getting better and you're getting sick."

I waved Sophie off impatiently, perhaps a little too impatiently because she looked hurt when I snapped back, "I'm fine. Really."

There was an awkward silence between us. The first time since this had begun, and suddenly I felt guilty at being so short with her, after all it wasn't her fault that I felt the way I did.

After a long moment, she asked timidly, "Would you like for me to tell you more? Or do you think you know everything that you—need to know?"

Smiling for the first time and realizing that this was an opportunity to find out everything, to answer all the questions that had been flirting with me for so many years, I took her hand in mine, "I'm so sorry Sophie, of course I want you to continue. Please tell me the rest, what happened with you and Father Grau after I was born, what was it like after all of those years of being on your own and to suddenly no longer be a nun, and to have had me? It must have been overwhelming."

She lowered her eyes, not looking at me directly. "It was, the guilt in particular. Sometimes it was so stifling that I thought that I couldn't go on another day and I wanted so much to see you, just to know anything about you. I wrote letters to Kathryn, the social worker, and called, but nothing, I got no information."

"And I hadn't seen Billy for almost two months. I didn't know why he didn't call. I couldn't help but thinking that maybe he really didn't love me and the baby, regardless of what he said, because otherwise he would have called me and come to see me, something. But nothing! There was nothing for almost two months." She sighed. "And then as always, just when I thought that I couldn't take it anymore, God heard my prayers. I'll never forget that day. It started like every other, riding the bus to the factory. Taking my place on the line as always, just polite small talk with the other girls. Going out for our lunch break."

Flashback Through Sophie's Eyes
Buffalo, New York, The Glass Factory; Early Summer 1957

The cold had finally lifted, and the early summer tinge of warmth had started to become more intense around mid-day, the first glimpse of the summer heat to come. I'd bought a Coke from the man who sold them on the corner, enjoying the guilty pleasure. For so many years I'd not had soft drinks, but now—now I guess that I could have whatever I wanted. A blessing and a curse. I missed the serenity of the Parish, the feeling that I was doing something with my life. Sometimes the longing for what I had there overcame my reason and common sense and I felt that I would go back, that I had to. But, then I remembered how I'd broken every vow, and I knew that the life that I'd loved could be no more for me.

"Sophie, come on. Sit on the wall with us."

Startled, my thoughts broken into, I tried to perk myself up forcing a smile at Basia, one of my few friends at the factory. She motioned for me to sit on the wall next to her. Like me, her parents were Polish immigrants and she was also a little older than most of the other girls working there, not that there were that many women. Most of the others were in their early twenties, unmarried and happy for the job so that they could have extra money to spend on clothes and parties. They lived at home and once they married they usually got pregnant almost immediately, and then, of course, stopped working. The cycle continued and though the money from a job might have helped, once they had children, most of their husbands insisted that they stay at home and fill the same role that their mothers and their grandmothers had before them. The role that I willingly walked away from at 14, but now at 37, I wondered, had I really changed anything? I was back living at home with my parents and feeling so raw and confused. I wasn't sure what the next step would be for me.

And Billy, was he just a memory? Every time I thought of him and the love that we shared that now lived in our child, I felt a dull pain in the bottom of my stomach. Every time I thought of Billy's touch, his kisses that were now no more, I had to hold back tears. No calls, no letters, it was as if he had cut me out of his life completely. Without him, I felt lost. I had no purpose, and no idea where my life would go next.

I thought of all that as I reluctantly climbed up on the low wall and sat next to Basia. I usually preferred to keep to myself, and other than Basia, rarely spoke to any of the other women there. But, I didn't want to seem snooty, and since Basia had invited me, I felt that I didn't have much choice but to join them. I didn't really care for the other women and they probably had the same feelings about me. There was Jane, a plump curvaceous blonde who seemed to live to gossip, Margo, her constant companion, who hung on every word that Jane uttered and usually repeated them as if they were the gospel truth, and Rosalyn, a tall thin brunette who I always felt looked through me, rather than at me, although I could never figure out why.

Jane leaned over to me, asking teasingly, "So, Sophie, do you have big plans for the weekend?"

I lowered my eyes, thinking of the weekend in front of me, helping my mother with my father. Reading in my room, longing to be anywhere but there, but knowing that I should be grateful to at least have a home to go back to as I'd now left the Convent for good.

Jane sidled closer to me. "You didn't answer my question, do you have something special planned for the weekend?" I didn't really want to engage Jane because it always seemed to lead somewhere that I didn't want to go. Her prying made me uncomfortable, so I said quickly, hoping that she'd move on to another subject, "No, I'll probably just help around the house, that's about it."

"C'mon, Sophie, you must have a fella to take you out." Jane winked at Margo as if they'd agreed on something that I was completely unaware of, but which I was sure would end up with me being the butt of some story that would circulate around the factory floor. Ever since I came back after the baby was born, I'd heard snatches of conversations, people wondering where I'd gone and why I looked so obviously different.

Jane continued, obviously determined to make her point. "I'm sure that Sophie has a fella, or at least *had* a fella," Margo snickered.

Basia frowned disapprovingly at them, "C'mon, Jane, can you just let up? It's a nice day, let's enjoy it."

Staring defiantly at her, Jane spit out angrily, "It's a free country and I have the right to ask a simple question!"

"Yeah, she's right, it's a free country." Margo, as always, Jane's little echo chamber.

I could see where this was heading, "Look, I'm just gonna go back to the floor, I'm finished eating. It's fine, Basia."

Jane stared me down defiantly. "What are you running from, Sophie, why can't you just be honest?"

Margo smirked, "Yeah, just be honest and tell the truth, it's obvious that..." I didn't hear the rest because suddenly I'd noticed a man coming towards me from across the street. And I froze. My heart started beating wildly and my hands started shaking as I saw him, as if in slow motion walking towards me, his light tan jacket billowing behind him and his crisp white shirt and light brown pants seemingly illuminated by the glow of the sun surrounding him. As his eyes met mine, he began walking more quickly and then I found myself jumping down from the wall walking towards him faster and faster. Then we both started running towards each other, oblivious to the open mouths and shocked stares. And then I felt his arms around mine and felt his lips against mine, and I didn't care anymore about anything, and I heard Billy say, "Sophie, I've missed you so."

The last thing I remember as I clasped his hand and walked quickly to Billy's car was Jane's high-pitched squeak.

"Oh my God, her fella's a NEGRO, OH MY GOD, she was with a NEGRO!!!!!! Just wait 'till I tell everybody!!!!!"

But I didn't care what they said anymore. I was a former nun in love with a colored priest, and I'd had his baby. I'd probably lose my job and I didn't know what I'd tell my parents if they found out. But I just didn't care because right now the man I loved was holding my hand and I was holding his. And as he opened my door for me, and then walked over to the driver's side, climbing in and locking both doors, I felt this sense of euphoria. We sped away leaving all of the ugliness of the past few minutes behind us and I realized that for the first time in months, I was truly happy. When we got to a narrow street miles from the factory, he finally slowed the car down and parked. He'd driven the car down a road that was quiet and deserted, a road that we'd traveled so many times.

Turning to me hesitantly, with his eyes so full of love that I wanted nothing more than to live in his smile forever, he whispered, "Sophie, I'm so sorry that I haven't been there for you. I was made the head pastor at the Parish and—well that's not really much of an excuse. I've really got no good excuse except that I just didn't know what to do. But I do know that I can't live without you in my life. I love you and our baby more than ever, and I know that we did the right thing by giving him up so that he'd have a chance to be raised by a good family who will love him as we would have, if we could."

"But society and—well—the Church, and the life that we have now, would only let us go so far. But our love can't be denied. They can't take that from us. I love you, Sophie, even more than before." He paused for a moment, as if mustering up strength for what he was to say next. "And I have a plan. A way for us to be together."

My head was starting to spin, and I grasped his hand more tightly, was he going to ask me to—marry him? To run away together? Was he going to leave everything behind? For us.

He stopped again, tilting my face up to his and kissed me with such passion and warmth that I felt as if every cell in my body was on fire, as if I could lose myself in him, and then he cradled me in his arms whispering, "I want you to come live with me at the Parish."

Stunned, I sat straight up not believing what I'd heard, "But, Billy! I can't!"

He pulled me back, encircling his arms around me, stroking my hair softly, "Yes, you can. Since I'm now the head pastor, I have the right to a live-in housekeeper." He drew me even closer, "Sophie, I need you in my life. God, I love you so much and I can't live another day without you. I just can't. And this is the only way." He kissed me tenderly on my brow, raising my fingers to his lips, brushing them lightly across his face. "I've prayed on this. I've thought about every possibility, we could marry, but then how would I support you? As a colored man, there are no jobs for me, my whole life has been the Church, I couldn't ask you to live like that. But this way, we can be together in the same house. We cannot live as husband and wife in the eyes of God, but we can have all of the advantages of a life in the Church with a home and a way to sustain ourselves."

I fell back on the seat of the car, my thoughts in a jumble. "But what about Mother Superior and the other Sisters, they'll remember me—I can't go back there!"

He laid my head in his lap, "They're all gone now, everyone who was there when you were has left. The Church has moved them to other Parishes. They're all new, no one will know you, even the older parishioners won't recognize you without your nun's habit."

I closed my eyes, it was a way. Maybe this is what God had planned. Certainly, the life that I had now was empty with no future. And at least there, back in the Church, even though not in my former position, I could still be in that world. I could still feel as if I was doing God's calling. And most importantly, I would be with Billy.

So, I turned back to him and knew as surely as I've ever known anything, that this was right. "I'll do it. I want to be with you and if this is the only way, then it must be God's will. So yes, I will be your housekeeper because I love you and I never want to be apart from you ever again." He pulled me up to his lips and as I melted into him, I knew that my prayers had been answered and that I was finally whole again.

CHAPTER

47

Canadian Side Of The Falls, Small Motel; Later That Evening

I propped myself up on one elbow, kissing Billy softly on the cheek. He barely stirred, still sleeping after the passion that we'd shared earlier. His skin next to mine felt warm and reminiscent of the many nights that we'd spent for almost two years in this same motel, the place where our love had conceived a child. And now it was here that we went in this hour of the greatest change for both of us. I couldn't believe that this same day, I'd awoken in my small dim room at my parent's home, the same room that I'd returned to in disgrace. And now, less than 24 hours later I was about to take the greatest step of my life. I was leaving with Billy the next day to be his live-in companion, his housekeeper, but in all respects his lover and his wife. Me, a former nun, and him, a colored Parish priest.

We were defying everyone but God because I had to believe that God had directed this for us. Mary was a virgin when she gave birth to the son of God, our Savior. She, like me, was disgraced and looked down upon, but she followed God's plan for her. And now I knew that God was speaking to Billy and me in the same way. God had brought us together. God had brought us a child, for every child is brought by God and now God was finding a way for us to live in his grace for the rest of our lives. Who was I to question the will of God? I had only to do as he wished. Billy stirred and then reached for me, I snuggled closer to him as his lips met mine again, as his hands caressed me once more, and our bodies locked together once more.

The next day I told my parents that I'd accepted a job as the housekeeper for the Parish priest. I told them I would make more money. When my mother looked at me angrily, accusing me of once again using them as long as I needed a place to lay my head only to walk away again leaving her to the work of caring for my father, I reminded her that I would be sending her money. I reminded her that she had asked me more times than I cared to remember since I came back home, what were my plans, what was I going to do now that I was back here? And now I had an answer for her. I was going to leave and return to the Parish where I'd been. Perhaps not as a nun. But still as a servant of God.

And so I closed the door to my childhood home that I'd first left at 14 and now was leaving again. I walked around the corner where Billy was parked. When he opened the car door for me, I knew that he was opening the door to a much bigger life than either of us could've imagined and one that surely only God could have planned.

CHAPTER

48

Lackawanna, New York, The Parish Rectory; Six Months Later, 1958

I hummed as I polished the statue of St. Martin de Porres, the Afro-Peruvian saint and the savior of people of mixed race. As I ran my cloth lovingly over his smooth brown stone face and down the deep red, flowing ceramic robes, a little chipped with age, and then back around over his arms and his granite hands held out in supplication, I couldn't help but think of Billy. Each time I brushed the dust away from this statue, I thought in awe and wonder of the majesty of God and the perfection of His plans for us. When I found out that I was pregnant, and I was plunged into the deepest period of self-doubt, fear and guilt that I'd ever had in my life, when I sadly walked away from the life that I had known since I was 14, would I have ever believed that a little over a year later I would be back here? No. I would not. Yet, here I was, not as I'd been before, but in a way and in a manner that God had planned so that the love that He had placed in our hearts could flower once again. And now that I'd been here living with Billy for the past six months, I felt, and I believe that he did also, that the love that we had was even stronger than before.

Each time that he crept quietly down the stairs into my small first floor bedroom off the kitchen or when I knocked timidly on his carved bedroom door upstairs and I heard his words beckoning me in, I knew that this was truly what was meant to be. I smiled as I closed my eyes remembering the first day that I'd come here, still unsure...

Flashback
Lackawanna, New York, The Parish Rectory; Six Months Earlier

Billy turned his key and the large dark heavy wooden door of the Rectory creaked open. He stood aside, letting me walk in first and then closed the door behind us.

Looking almost like an excited teen who had the house while their parents were away, he followed me in, stopping awkwardly in the vestibule. "Um, why don't you put your things down here? I'll take them to your room later."

"OK, that sounds fine." Suddenly feeling shy, myself, and not sure what to say, I blurted out, "Is there anything you need me to do—I mean, like um, cleaning or anything?"

"No, no that can wait, sit down—I—um—yes, just sit down."

I smiled nervously, feeling even more unsure of myself, "OK." I started to sit in the straight back chair that was for visitors waiting for an appointment with him, but he jumped up.

"No...no, not here, in there, in the living room. I'll be right back."

I walked tentatively into the parlor and settled into one of the burgundy brocade chairs. I realized that all the time that I was a nun, I had never actually been in that room. Whenever we met, it was usually in his office and, more often than not, we generally spoke when I was doing my duties at the nursery or helping out some of the older Sisters. So, now, really for the first time, I was able to look around me. The room had three narrow floor-to-ceiling windows with paned glass partially covered by heavy burgundy drapes now closed tightly, blocking out most of the late afternoon sun. The drapes were the same color as the armchair that I was sitting in. Next to my chair there was a wide, deep mohair covered mustard yellow couch with embroidered pillows of scenes of our Savior. There was an ornate cherry wood table in front of the couch, and on the table were three fine pieces of cut glass crystal reflecting the few rays of sunlight that seeped in through the drapes. On the floor was an enormous oriental rug with scenes of children playing in a garden and flowers and vines crawling up the sides.

I felt like I had walked into another world of wealth and privilege that before this had been closed to me. I remember hearing that a rich parishioner from a neighboring Italian Parish that had just redecorated and didn't need the furniture, had donated it to the Parish and so the rather simple wooden pieces that had been there before were replaced with this, giving the room an air of opulence and majesty, much grander than I had ever seen.

Feeling even more uncomfortable than before, I felt doubt creeping in. Maybe I hadn't made the right decision, maybe this was all too much for me. I thought of the small narrow house that I'd grown up in, with the worn plaid brown couch and chairs, everything frayed at the edges, and the simple gray and green linoleum floors that you could never really seem to get clean—nothing like what I saw before me. Maybe I should tell Billy that I was wrong, that I loved him, but that this wasn't the right thing to do after all. And the more I thought of it, the more the demons in my mind chattered loudly, telling me—*I should get up now and leave, go back to where I was supposed to be.* I heard them whispering in my head—*My mother would be happy, she'd have someone to help with my father.* So, I should leave this place.

Small beads of sweat were starting to break out on my forehead and I felt my breathing becoming more and more shallow. I'd made a mistake, this wasn't God's plan, it was only my own selfishness. I didn't deserve to be happy, after all I had sinned so many times. I needed to pay for my transgressions with penance, it wasn't right for me to have happiness, even with Billy who I loved so much. I needed to be punished. Yes, that was it. I needed to be punished. I was a sinner and I needed to be punished by God. I had made up my mind, I wasn't staying.

I closed my eyes leaning back against the chair, trying to calm my breathing. Now that I'd made my decision, I had to figure out how to tell Billy. I was just so tired, after the drive and all of the stress of dealing with my parents, my mother hissing at me angrily as I walked out the door not looking back, feeling her accusing eyes boring into me. I was just so tired, but I knew now that my mother was right to be angry, that I didn't deserve anything but punishment and I had to accept that willingly and try and go on with my life.

****

I felt fingers stroking my hair, and as I slowly opened my eyes and looked up, I saw Billy behind me smiling as he gently ran his hands over the top of my head. I smelled something warm and fragrant and I saw a cup of steaming tea in front of me. I couldn't help but smile, but then as if something wanted to snatch any happiness away from me, I remembered the thoughts playing loudly in my head from before. I realized that from sheer exhaustion, I'd fallen asleep in the living room, but that now that I was awake, I had to remain steadfast in my resolve to accept God's punishment willingly and to leave here.

But, in spite of the thoughts in my head, I couldn't stop smiling as Billy walked in front of me, kneeling and then taking my hands in his.

"You fell asleep and I didn't want to wake you."

Trying to shove the guilt away, I said, "I know, I'm sorry. I shouldn't have. I know that you must have things for me to take care of." I thought that even if I was only here for a few days before I went back to my parents, I should at least have the decency to be helpful and to do the work that I was being brought here to do.

He massaged my hands in his, whispering, "Will you forgive me for not being there for you these past two months?"

I nodded through my sleepy eyes, squeezing his hands and hugging him tightly. "Yes, yes—I forgive you."

He smiled, "I have a surprise for you." He took my hand, leading me out of the living room and into the dining room. I could see that I must have slept for several hours because all of the lamps were lit and on the table, the flames from long narrow white candles that had been placed in a delicately etched silver candelabra flickered back and forth casting shadows of light that danced across the table. I caught my breath as I saw what lay before me. The enormous oval table was covered in a cream-colored damask cloth and there were two place settings, each with wine glasses and shiny silver flatware. Billy led me to a chair, pulling it out for me, smiling lovingly, "My dear—your chair."

I was completely swept up in awe and wonder. I knew I didn't deserve all of this. I was a sinner.

"Now close your eyes, c'mon, Sophie."

"I don't know what to say, Billy! This is all so…incredible. I don't deserve this."

"You most certainly do, my love. Now close your eyes and don't peek!"

I had to laugh in spite of myself. I'd never seen this side of Billy, this playful, wonderfully spontaneous side.

And as I closed my eyes tightly, as he'd insisted, my senses were overwhelmed by the aroma of roasted meats, and herbed vegetables and tart warm apples, and so much more. I heard a plate being placed before me and the smells were so inviting, it took everything that I could to keep my eyes firmly closed. I heard more rustling and liquid being poured into the glasses, tinkling against the sides of the fine crystal goblets. I heard heavy dishes and felt steam curling around my nostrils as dishes were being placed on the table, making a soft thud as they were laid on the cloth. I heard Billy's chair scraping against the wide wooden floor boards, and his hands resting on the table.

"Now you can open your eyes."

I couldn't stop smiling as I looked around at the feast in front of me, "Oh my Lord, Billy! This is beautiful!" On my plate was a fine piece of beef roast with a sprig of parsley on top, soft boiled potatoes dripping with butter, and savory carrots. The apples that I smelled were in a casserole in front of me with cinnamon and sugar dotting the top, and a plate of crusty white buttered bread was next to it. Deep, lush red wine was in my goblet. Billy held his glass up, softly touching his to mine, saying, "To us."

I felt tears coming to my eyes, and even though the voices in my head were loudly telling me that I didn't deserve this and that I deserved nothing but misery, I took his hand, lifting it to my lips, kissing it with all of the love and passion that I felt for him.

He smiled broadly, but I could see that he, too, was struggling to force back tears. "We've been through a lot together, Sophie, and I wanted to show you how much I love you and that I know how much that you're giving up to be here with me." He squeezed my hand tightly, "I wanted you to know that I truly appreciate everything, and that I truly love and appreciate you, I'm so happy that God has made a way for us to be together." And then he choked up, barely able to force out the words, "Because I realized those months that we were apart, that my life...well...that my life just wasn't...I guess what I'm trying to say is that I love you, Sophie, and I don't ever want us to be apart again. You are my life, my love, and the mother of our child."

And then I shut the door on the voices in my head and ran to him, laying his head on my breast, wiping away his tears with my hands and covering his face with kisses.

****

Now, I'm remembering back after we both composed ourselves and eagerly dug into the scrumptious dinner that he had prepared, as he told me proudly how his mother had taught him to cook, and that these were some of her favorite dishes, recipes that she'd brought with her from Ireland. And I thought that I would burst with happiness. And I remembered after dinner, in my mind, seeing Billy and me lovingly washing up together and then Billy taking my hand saying, "Close your eyes again."

And this time I eagerly closed my eyes, ignoring the voices that still seemed to want to block any joy that I could have.

He led me through the kitchen and I could hear a door opening, then he turned me around and said, "Now you can open your eyes."

Seeing the room before me, I threw my hands around his neck, kissing him again and again, my eyes traveling around the room to the small bed covered in a deep purple bedspread, to the dresser with a vase with red roses in it, to all of my things had been hung up in the armoire, to the pair of pink fuzzy slippers next to the bed. As we fell into each other's arms, I felt myself easing down gently on the bed with him running his fingers across my face and hearing his voice whispering, "I love you, I love you so much."

And hearing myself say, "I love you, Billy, and I'm so grateful, I never want to leave you. Ever."

End Flashback
Lackawanna, New York, The Parish Rectory

And now, six months later as I shook myself back to where I'd been when I drifted off while polishing the statue of St. Martin de Porres, I glanced at my watch and realized that I'd been daydreaming for almost an hour. I had work to do; some of the white priests from other Parishes in the area were coming over tonight for their monthly poker game. I'd heard about this ritual from Billy, but this was the first time that it was being held here since I'd moved in. I secretly wondered if he didn't want them to see me and that was why all of the others had been at the other Parishes, but I brushed those thoughts out of my head. Now was not the time to let those meddlesome voices take over. I needed to finish the dinner so it would be ready, and then set the table. I didn't want to disappoint Billy by not having everything exactly how he wanted it to be.

I laid out the places on the dining room table and put down the trivets for the hot dishes. Back in the kitchen, I opened the oven, carefully removing the double roaster that held two perfectly browned chickens. I spooned some of the drippings over the top and then set the roasting pan on the table. The large pot of mashed potatoes was on the stove warming through and the steamed broccoli was in another pot. I'd also made rolls and I'd already put them in the bread basket tightly wrapped with a cloth to stay warm. As I turned, I saw Billy coming into the kitchen rubbing his hands together.

"That smells delicious, you've out done yourself, Sophie." He kissed me on the lips and rubbed his hands over my back, massaging out all of the tension like only he could do, then whispering, "I hope the poker game goes quickly."

I blushed and smiled, feeling completely and totally happy. He was about to kiss me again when the loud chime doorbell rang. Reluctantly, he let me go. "I guess I better answer the door."

"OK, I'll get the drinks ready." Billy had told me that it could be a hard-drinking crowd with whiskey being the drink of preference, so I had already taken out the large bottle of Jack Daniels and the soda water and ice. I could hear the doorbell ringing several more times and laughter and loud talking from the living room. I could also smell cigar smoke coming in from the living room. It was hard to believe that these were priests who were so solemnly giving Mass on Sundays, because if I didn't know better, I'd have thought I was back in my parent's cramped house with some of my dad's drinking buddies.

And then the little voices in my head whispered, *"And who'd think you used to be a nun?"* I was suddenly flushed red with guilt as I thought back on Billy and me embracing earlier and on waking to his touch every morning—my greatest fear being that some nosey parishioner would wander into the Rectory and see me creeping out of his bedroom in my nightgown, but I had to put those thoughts away. It almost seemed as if every time that I was starting to relax and be truly happy, those voices would remind me that I had no right to be happy and that my sins would forever haunt me.

I shoved the thoughts away and took out five whiskey glasses, filling each one up almost to the top with just a dash of soda and ice in each one.

As I pushed the swinging door open that led to the dining room, carefully balancing the tray that held the drinks, I was careful to avoid eye contact with any of the priests, just smiling quickly as I served their drinks.

"Thank you, Miss Legocki." I turned, almost startled. Billy had never called me that before, but I guess that we had to keep up appearances, so I just nodded in acknowledgment and then quickly retreated back to the kitchen. The other priests seemed to barely notice me, of which I was thankful because at this moment, I would have liked nothing more than to have been invisible.

Billy came into the kitchen a few minutes later, smiling, "You're doing great, Sophie, but I think they all need refills."

"OK, Father Grau." I figured if we were play acting, I needed to get in swing of things also. He winked at me as he left the room.

I took out the bottle of whiskey, trying to compose myself as I entered the living room. The five of them were sitting and laughing. I filled each glass up, and one of the priests said playfully, "Now there, young lady, don't be stingy with the whiskey, fill 'er up to the top, I like my whiskey strong and my glass full." He then broke into laughter.

Father Doheny, a loud red-faced priest, who was practically bursting out of his ample robes, bellowed out, "Hey, did you hear the one about the nun and the priest?"

Father Mahoney, one of the younger priests winked at me salaciously, "Naw, tell me, but wait, I think I need another refill over here." He held up his glass to me and feeling suddenly uncomfortable, I quickly I filled his glass, "Would you like soda water, Father?"

"Naw, I like mine straight."

I could see what Billy meant by hard drinkers, the bottle of whiskey that had been full when they came was now more than half empty.

Billy signaled me and understanding that he was ready for dinner, I said, "The meal is ready if you'd like to go the dining room." They all still held tightly to their glasses of whisky, getting up one by one and filing into the dining room.

"Sure."

"Why not?"

"Let's go."

Quickly, I hurried back to the kitchen, bringing out the chickens first, then the side dishes. As I put them on the table, I inadvertently knocked Father Mahoney's napkin on the floor, bending over quickly, I handed it to him and as he took the napkin, I felt his hands linger a little too long. And I don't know why, but at that moment, I almost felt as I had as a 14-year-old when the boarders in our house brushed a little too closely to me. Feeling embarrassed, I walked into the kitchen, but not before I could hear Father Mahoney's booming voice from the dining room.

"So, Father Grau, do you ever get tempted?"

I could hear the silence in the room and then Billy's voice saying clearly and loudly, "Oh no. She just works here."

Laughter and snorting, Father Mahoney, his mouth obviously stuffed with food, "And she even cooks, how about we trade, you can take my Mrs. McGregor and I get yours. I can guarantee that you won't be tempted by mine, but I can't say the same about yours." And then he laughed loudly and coarsely.

Billy's voice had that forced nonchalance as he said, "She's *just* the housekeeper, now why don't we finish up so we can start the poker game."

I couldn't believe what I'd just heard, my cheeks were burning hot. So, that's all I was? He didn't even defend me from that boor, he just said I was no one, nothing. I felt numb with anger and the voices inside my head were triumphant. "*Leave,*" they said. "*We told you not to stay here. Leave and show him you don't need him.*" Maybe I *should* leave. I won't be treated like this, I won't. And as I cleared the rest of the plates, avoiding all eye contact, then I washed up, hearing the voices of the men as someone pulled out a pack of cards and started dealing.

Suddenly, I knew what I had to do. I grabbed my coat and my purse and walked out the back door. I wasn't sure if this was the right thing to do, but I couldn't stay here and just be nothing—I couldn't. I walked and walked, weighing my options. I could go home, I didn't really have any-place else to go. But at least I did have some money now. The bus station loomed before me with the bums lined up out front swaying uneasily in the dark. But for once, I wasn't scared, I think I was still too angry.

Walking up to the counter, I glanced at the bus schedule and realized that I'd missed the last bus by five minutes, the next one wasn't until 5 a.m. the next morning. But I didn't care. I was going home. "I'll take a one way to Buffalo." The clerk glanced at me suspiciously, probably wondering what a woman on her own was doing here this time of night. The *other me,* before the baby and before I'd broken every vow I'd ever taken, would have cared. But that me was gone, I'd already descended as low as I could, so the snide look of a clerk couldn't hurt me. The only thing that could hurt me had already. I couldn't forget Billy's words, his scorn. I could feel my face flushing again, a tear trying to force its way down my cheeks. So, I grabbed my ticket and walked over to the other side of the station.

CHAPTER

49

"Sophie, Sophie!" I turned, seeing Billy walking quickly towards me, he'd taken off his collar, and his eyes were ringed with dark circles. He ran over to me, sitting next to me. And for a moment, neither of us said anything. I was still so angry at him and then I spit out, "So why are you here? I'm nothing, right? Just the help, just the housekeeper."

"Sophie, what else could I say?!"

"I don't know, but you didn't have to act so—I don't know, like how could I ever be *anyone* that you'd be interested in—like I was just some nobody."

"Sophie, I'm sorry, I'm so sorry. When I realized you'd left, I told them all that they had to leave. And Sophie, I'm getting out of the poker night, this is it, this is the last time. I don't want to do anything to cause you pain. Nothing. You're my life. Please, please understand that. Please come home. To *our* home. Sophie. Please."

The voices in my head were screaming, *"No, NO!!! It's a trick, he doesn't love you. Leave now."* And I hesitated, but then my heart won out and I took his hand and let him lead me home, back to our home.

Buffalo, New York, Hospital; Present Time

Sophie's sudden cough propelled me back to the now, her hospital room, the incessant chattering of the nurses in the hall, punctuated by the sound of steel carts clattering with an assortment of IVs and other equipment lumbering past our door. I had been so completely swept up in her story, the story of the two people who were responsible for me being in this world, that I felt almost lightheaded. The sensation of uncovering a part of you that had been hidden so long was almost intoxicating, but at the same time a little unsettling, an odd combination, but I can't really explain it any other way. Realizing that she was still coughing, I grabbed her cup and filled it with water from the jug at the side of her bed, placing a straw in the glass. She took it gratefully, taking a few sips and then handing it back to me.

"I'm OK now. Just a little coughing spell, that's all."

"Are you sure? Maybe I should call the doctor." I reached for the nurses' call button, but she put her hand gently, but firmly, on mine, saying, "No, I'm OK. I don't need to see the doctor."

Still not convinced, "Look Sophie, you have given me so much these past few weeks, the last thing I want is to do anything that's gonna compromise your health, I think I should go and let you get some rest, I can always come back tomorrow."

Suddenly, looking very small and frail, she barely forced out the words, "But what if there is no tomorrow Joe—what if this is it?"

"OK, now I am calling the doctor."

She propped herself up weakly on one arm, suddenly very weary, "No doctor can save you when the Lord calls you home. And I'm not saying I feel like I'm going to die right this minute, but I just feel, no I just KNOW that HE wants you to know everything right to the end and he doesn't want me to stop until you do. So, let me do this for him, for me, for all of us. Let me finish. I'll be OK, but I just need to finish."

Feeling completely overwhelmed and emotionally torn, I reluctantly sat back down, wanting desperately to know, but at the same time, wracked with guilt if getting all of this out would somehow place Sophie in such a precarious position that she'd never recover.

As if she could read my thoughts, she sat up straight, looking re-energized, "Relax, Joe, and let me do what I need to do." Then, as if she was no longer speaking to me, she began softly. "It was maybe a year later when I found him in his office..."

Lackawanna, New York, The Parish Rectory; Fall 1958

I opened his study door quietly, normally I would never have gone in without knocking because even with all that we shared, I felt as if there were times when he needed to be alone to deal with everything in his own way. He was never unkind to me, in fact, during those times when he'd withdraw within himself to another place, he was particularly gentle, but distant. And I knew that until he came for me, it was my turn to give him the time and the space that he needed. But this day, he'd been in his study for hours and I was starting to worry, ever since a few months ago when he'd fallen unexpectedly and we were there together in the doctor's office after he'd finally been able to pull himself up, complaining of unbearable shooting pains in his feet, but refusing an ambulance...

Flashback Through Sophie's Eyes
Lackawanna, New York, A Doctor's Office; A Few Months Earlier

Remembering that day, my hands fidgeting, my heart racing as we waited for the doctor to see us, and when he did, the inevitable quizzical look, who was I, why was I there? A white woman with a colored man.

"So, what is your relationship to Father Grau?"

Without hesitating, "I work for him in the Rectory."

Interjecting himself, Billy said firmly, "She's my housekeeper and she manages my affairs, that's why I asked her to come. Now, doctor, I don't really think that's why I came here to discuss my staff, so tell me what is it, what's wrong with me?"

I could tell that Billy was trying to sound braver than he felt—Billy who was always so strong. Billy, the one who made the hard decisions, who was my rock, now looking unsure of himself and apprehensive as he waited for the doctor. Because the truth is, I could tell that he hadn't felt well for a while, sometimes at night he'd toss and turn in the bed so much, getting up several times an hour, massaging his feet with his hands, thirsty always, and sometimes unable to sleep for hours. I'd drift off and then wake up hours later and could see that he was still awake and that he hadn't slept. But until he fell, he'd refused to go to the doctor, claiming it was nothing, it would pass, but somehow, we both knew that wasn't true.

Looking at Billy, almost with contempt, the doctor said, with no compassion at all, "You have diabetes, and a pretty severe case. You're going to have to make some radical changes in your diet, no sweets of any type including alcohol, and based on your blood sugar, you're going to have to start on insulin shots immediately. The numbness in your feet was neuropathy, you're lucky it wasn't more advanced, or you might be looking at a possible amputation."

At his words, I jumped, up, "No, Doctor, what are you saying?!"

Completely unmoved, he continued, "Your 'Father'" and his words rung with sarcasm, "is very ill, and needs to make some significant changes to his lifestyle." He took out his prescription pad and scribbled something down. "This is for the insulin and some other medications that I want you to take." And as nonchalantly as if he'd just said the sun is shining, he asked, "Any questions?"

Billy, looking numb, shook his head, "No, thank you for your time, Doctor."

End Flashback
Lackawanna, New York, Parish Rectory

So ever since that day, I haven't wanted Billy to be alone. I keep having visions of him falling again and me not being there, or worse. I shoved the thoughts out of my head, clutching my rosary and praying fervently, *"Lord please keep Billy well, please Lord, please don't take him from me, I know that I've sinned, but please make him well."*

And then, as if my prayers had been answered, I heard his voice coming from his study as I slowly pushed the door open. "Sophie, is that you?"

"Yes, it's me. Are you OK?"

"I'm fine—c'mon in."

He got up from his chair and moved some papers on the red velvet couch that had become more of an extra filling cabinet then a fine piece of furniture. He sat down and pulled me gently down next to him, putting his arm around me, usually we were more discrete, even during the day because you never knew when someone might walk in the Rectory, but he didn't seem to care for once, and he took my hands in his, kissing them. "It's happened."

Drawing my breath in sharply and afraid of what might be next, I was frozen in place unable to speak.

He squeezed my shoulder. "It finally happened, they found a family for our little boy."

He was smiling as if all of his sleepless nights and prayers had been heard. I was flooded with a feeling of joy and relief, but still a small tinge of sadness. I think that maybe in the back of my mind I had always fantasized about us, Billy and me, somehow figuring out a way to have our son with us, even though we both knew that it was impossible.

"He's almost 18 months old, but my contact at the orphanage said that a very nice older Negro couple who also have a little boy, and who had fostered our son briefly, now want to adopt him. Evidently they're good people and they love him."

I hugged Billy tightly, whispering, "I'm so happy, now we'll know he'll be OK, because God found just the right home for him." And I couldn't help thinking of Billy and me, sitting day after day in his office, waiting for the call that our son had been adopted, but only meeting disappointment as his contact explained how difficult it was proving to find a family who wanted our baby. He looked almost white, with pale skin and straight hair, but he had "Negro" on his birth certificate, so no white family wanted him, and he was so fair skinned that a lot of the Negro families didn't feel comfortable with a child who looked so unlike them. But evidently this family didn't mind, and so after 18 long months, our baby finally had a home.

That night, Billy slid into my bed next to me and kissed me with all of the passion that he had the first time that we'd made love and as he eased my light cotton gown over my head and buried his lips in my warm skin, and I clutched his strong arms feeling him inside of me, I knew that God had a plan for all of us and that this love that Billy and I shared was part of the plan and that it didn't matter what anyone thought, society, the Church, our families, none of them mattered in God's eyes because God had brought us together, and what God has joined, no man can put asunder.

CHAPTER

50

Lackawanna, New York, Parish Rectory; Three Years Later, 1961

I was thinking of that night when we made love so passionately and deeply after we found out that our baby had been adopted. I remembered the sense of peace that I'd felt knowing that once again, God had answered our prayers and that, surely, God had blessed our union, even if unholy in the eyes of man, it was ordained in the eyes of God and no man could break us apart. So why was I so nervous? I was setting the table carefully, but my hands trembled. I had brought out the best silver in the Rectory and the fine china, and crystal water glasses, there were two places at the table. This seemed like the most important day of Billy and my life together.

His favorite sister, Mary Charles, who ironically was also a nun, was coming to town and she was having dinner with Billy. I, of course, had to maintain the fiction of his housekeeper, so I'd prepare the meal and serve them, but would eat alone in the kitchen. But even so, I felt like somehow I'd be at that table in spirit because this was the sister that Billy always talked about. The one that he seemed to have been closest to as a child. Their mother loved them both fiercely, and according to Billy at least, favored the two of them over her other raucous boys and girls who seemed to gravitate more naturally towards Billy's stepfather, the German immigrant. Billy had told me years earlier stories of his childhood, not an unhappy one, but not really warm and loving, except for his mother who he missed still. But this sister, his youngest, was his heart, they both had answered the call of God, devoting their life to service and it seemed as if even as children they shared a special bond. She was now a nun in Ohio, and rarely left her Parish, but this day she was traveling with a group of other Sisters from her Parish and was only a few miles from our Rectory, so of course she'd have to see her brother.

Nervously, I checked my watch, she'd be here in about 15 minutes, Billy had driven to the bus station to pick her up. I looked at myself critically in the mirror, smoothing my hair and running my hands down my simple blue and white dress, trying to pull out any wrinkles. I didn't know that much about her, but I felt instinctively as if I needed to make a good impression. I took one last look at the table, rearranging probably for the tenth time, the delicate pink lilies that I'd placed in a vase on the table. The grandfather clock in the parlor ticked loudly, and with each tick, my heart beat more wildly. The little voices in my head who had been quiet for so long, had taken hold again, whispering wickedly, "*What if she doesn't like me and says something to Billy that makes him want to not have me here anymore, or what if somehow she guesses the truth and feels that it was her duty to tell the Church? Billy was her brother, but you never know, or what if…"*

But before the voices could spin any more dire scenarios, I heard the key in the front door and Billy's warm, booming voice, "We're here, Sophie."

I took a deep breath and hurried from the kitchen to the parlor, not sure what to expect. She was standing next to him, and even though he was colored and she of course white, I immediately saw the resemblance, she was very small in stature and the nun's habit seemed to swallow her up, making her look even more petite, but she and Billy had the same eyes, the same warm smile that filled her face crinkling the corners of her light blue eyes. I liked her instantly and when she took my hand, shaking it, saying, "So good to meet you Sophie. My brother tells me that you're an excellent cook, so I'm looking forward to what I know will be a fine dinner."

I blushed, not expecting this, "You're—you're very kind. Billy exaggerates, I'm an OK cook, but I appreciate your confidence." That sounded so stupid, but I was feeling so unsure of myself, I couldn't think of anything else to say. "Um, can I bring you something to drink before dinner?"

"Oh, perhaps just some cool water. I'm a little thirsty."

"I've also made some appetizers, nothing really fancy—but I, um…"

She smiled again, "That sounds perfect. I'd love some."

I felt a little better, maybe she wouldn't hate me after all. "I'll get them and your water, too, and B…I mean, um, Father Grau, what would you like?" I suddenly felt sick to my stomach. I had almost called him Billy, what was I thinking, she'll know for sure now. I hurried into the kitchen, my eyes starting to fill with tears, *I'm so stupid, stupid, Oh my God.* My hands trembled as I filled her glass with water and then pulled the pig-in-a-blanket appetizers from the oven. I'd slaved over them all afternoon, carefully rolling out the dough and getting the perfect Vienna sausages, and now it didn't even matter.

CHAPTER

51

J was running my hand under the cold water in the kitchen sink, trying to stop the stinging from where I'd burned myself taking the appetizers out of the oven. I'd been so rattled that I hadn't completely covered the hot pan with the potholder and had singed my fingers pulling the dish from the oven. I lowered my head in shame as I heard Billy's footsteps entering the kitchen. Slowly turning, expecting to see him angry or worse, disgusted at my slip of the tongue, instead he walked up to me, tilting my face up to his and then kissing me lightly on the forehead, whispering, "It's OK, she didn't even notice."

Unsure, but relieved, "Are you sure?"

"I'm sure, now c'mon, let's get dinner started, I'm starving, and you know how I love your meatloaf." He winked at me conspiratorially, it was the first meal that I'd ever made for him and it had a special meaning for us. Feeling suddenly like a weight had been lifted from my shoulders, I carefully, this time, slid the meatloaf from the oven, placed it on a white china plate and arranged the boiled potatoes around it. I also had steamed carrots and spooned them in a chafing dish. The rolls were warm and dripping with butter, and I'd also made a green salad of crisp iceberg lettuce, juicy tomatoes and generous slices of firm cucumber. I put everything on the table, proud of my meal and hoping that she'd enjoy it and then maybe she'd say something good to Billy about me.

I leaned down over her plate, with the flat spatula poised over the meatloaf. "Would you like me to serve you?"

"Yes, Sophie, that would be very nice. I'm quite hungry and this smells delicious, my brother can tell you that I've always had a hearty appetite, especially for well prepared food."

I blushed. "Thank you. I hope that you enjoy it."

She watched eagerly as I carefully spooned the food onto her plate, "Oh, I'm sure I will, yes a little more, that's perfect and I love steamed carrots. I'll take a big helping of those—and the rolls-—yes, two of those."

Billy was beaming, and I could tell that he was pleased. "Sophie, I can dish up my own." He reached for the meatloaf platter and cut a large piece, then a generous spoonful of carrots and salad. Because of his diabetes the doctor said that he shouldn't eat bread, so these days I never made rolls, but he'd insisted that I do so for his sister who he knew loved homemade parker rolls. Reluctantly, he passed on the bread and once they were both served, he bowed his head. *"Dear Lord, I want to thank you for the bounty that you have bestowed on our table and for the love that you give us always, our life is devoted to your grace and goodness and we thank you for this meal that you have laid before us...in the name of the Father, the Son and the Holy Ghost...Amen."*

Feeling suddenly uncomfortable, I turned and headed back to the kitchen where I'd made a small plate for myself.

Suddenly his sister put her fork down, looking me directly in the eyes, "Sophie, aren't you going to join us?"

Now really not sure what to say, I barely mumbled out, "No—no. I'll eat in the kitchen. I've got my plate there."

She smiled at me in a way that said that she wasn't taking no for an answer. "Nonsense, bring it in here and sit with us. I insist."

This feeling of dread had seized me, this was it, all of her seeming kindness was just a trick, she wanted to get me at the table so that she could embarrass me and prove to Billy that I wasn't worth being here. I felt this sudden nausea, but knew that I had no choice but to join them. I looked at Billy and surprisingly he didn't seem the least bit surprised or upset.

Billy nodded his head as if signaling that it was OK. "C'mon, Sophie, you can eat with us."

"Ok—um. I'll be right back."

I hurried into the kitchen and walked over to the sink, my hands were shaking as I splashed some cold water on my face and stood there for a moment trying to get myself together. *"It will be allright...it will be all right...he loves me even if she tells him to get rid of me...he won't."* But I didn't really believe it. I took my plate and walked slowly into the dining room, feeling almost like a prisoner with her last meal. I stood up awkwardly, not sure where I should sit, normally my place was next to Billy, but that was of course when we were alone, and frankly most of the time we ate our meals together at the large table in the kitchen.

"Now, Sophie come sit next to me, don't worry I won't bite." She laughed merrily, almost like a young girl instead of a grown woman. "The meal is delicious, my brother certainly wasn't exaggerating when he spoke of your culinary skills."

I lowered my head, still too traumatized to say much, except a mumbled, "Thank you." I was hoping that we could just eat in silence or at least that the two of them would talk so that I wouldn't have to risk blurting out something that would let her know for sure that Billy and I were a couple.

But unfortunately, she seemed to have other ideas and she leaned forward meeting my eyes levelly. "So, tell me about yourself, where are you from? Billy tells me that you met a few years ago when you were a parishioner at the Church."

"Uh, yes, I was."

"Are you from this area?"

"No—no. I'm from Buffalo."

"So, were you working down here?"

I gulped not sure what to say. I looked at Billy frantically, but again he seemed not to be the least bit bothered, and then sensing my panic, he interjected smoothly. "She was one of the lay assistants in the nursery, helping out the nuns with the children."

I sighed in relief. Billy to the rescue!

"Oh, I see." She took another small bite of meatloaf as if contemplating her next move. "So, then you've been around the church for some time?"

"Yes, I guess you could say that."

She took another spoonful of carrots. "So, do you keep up with some of the reforms that Pope John is proposing, some of them are quite forward thinking."

"I had heard, but I'm not really familiar with the details."

"Well he's instituting a lot of new policies, some say too radical, others say it's time the Catholic Church came into the new way of thinking, I mean since the War all sorts of things are happening, women are starting to work. Now, we Sisters have always worked so in a way you could say that we were almost the standard bearers for these new movements that are taking place."

Billy nodded his head in agreement, "I think that it's all positive, as a society we can't afford to deny access to education, or job opportunities because of gender—or race."

His sister squeezed his hand, as if sensing some of the challenges that her brother had faced over the years. "Here! Here! I am in total agreement. This country has to change in many ways."

She took another sip of her water and then smiled as if thinking of something. "Who knows, maybe someday women will even be priests."

Billy laughed, "You never know."

And from that moment, I relaxed and started to enjoy my dinner. We talked about a wide range of subjects from the Church, to some of the horrific things that were happening in the South with the terrifying lynchings, to some of Billy's travels. I never tired of hearing his stories of Italy and France and he had us both enthralled as he described one of the key battles in the War where he'd lost many of the men that he'd grown to love.

Billy looked at his watch, and then took his sister's hand in his. "Well, this has been a wonderful dinner, but I think that unfortunately we better leave. I don't want you to miss your bus."

She nodded in agreement. "No, that would not be good. Mother Superior would be quite displeased."

And as she said that, I couldn't help remembering my years as a Sister, I still missed those days sometime, but shoving those thoughts from my head, I pulled out my chair and hurried to get Sister Mary Charles' coat.

As I handed it to her, she embraced me warmly, pulling me closely to her and then saying softly, so only I could hear, *"Take care of my brother, he loves you very much."*

I was literally at the edge of my seat, "So, did she know???"

Sophie leaned back on her pillows, smiling at the memories, "I think so."

CHAPTER

52

"o, not yet! Not yet!!! Please, not yet! Please, please—please—no—please, God!!!!!"

I bolted awake, hearing Sophie's cries. I realized that I'd been dozing in the chair. I'd gotten in the habit the past few days of staying later into the night and not wanting to drive back to the hotel. If I was too tired, I'd usually take a little cat nap in the chair in her room before I'd hit the road. I'd even gotten used to the constant noise in the hallways. I was particularly exhausted that day after a series of lengthy conference calls for work across multiple time zones coupled with the inner roller coaster that I was experiencing as Sophie told me more and more about her and Father Grau. I had mixed emotions as she recounted their anguish around my adoption, on the one hand, so grateful for Mama and Daddy, but at the same time angry that an innocent child could languish in the system and almost not be adopted because of what's written on his birth certificate. But I shoved those thoughts out of my head, leaning over Sophie's bed. She was sitting straight up as if she'd seen a ghost.

"Sophie, Sophie, are you all right!" I held her thin shaking hands in mine and quickly poured some water into the plastic cup by her bed. "Here drink this!"

She took the water, sipping weakly from the straw, I turned on the light and could see tears glistening in her eyes. They'd left dry tracks down her pale cheeks and she was breathing heavily.

Feeling panic setting in, I pushed the nurse's button firmly, "I'm calling the doctor."

This time she didn't protest, just collapsing on her pillows. I pushed the nurse's button frantically again, but afraid that they wouldn't come soon enough, I ran out to the hallway, rushing over to the nurse's station where one of them was animatedly telling some story about a patient. I interrupted them, receiving icy looks as I suppose he was just getting to the "good part." "Can one of you come into Sophie Legocki's room, she woke up suddenly yelling and I'm afraid there's something wrong!"

The head nurse followed me into the room, quickly striding over to Sophie's bedside. He checked her vitals and then put a thermometer in her mouth. Sophie numbly closed her eyes and I noticed the tears starting to come down again. The nurse leaned over her kindly, "What's wrong Ms. Legocki, are you in pain?"

She shook her head no wearily, unable to speak with the thermometer still in her mouth. The nurse took the thermometer out, reading it quickly. "Well the good news is that she doesn't have a temperature, sometimes if there's a high temperature delirium can set in. And..." He hesitated, checking the machines next to her bed again. "Her vitals are normal." He plumped up her pillows and then smoothed the sheets around her neck. "Ms. Legocki, was it a bad dream?"

She shook her head again, still not wanting to say anything.

The nurse turned back to me. "Well, we'll watch her and if she gets agitated again, I'll call the doctor. "

"Thank you." Not really knowing what else to say.

I sat down gingerly at the edge of her bed, wanting to comfort her but not really knowing what to do. For a moment neither of us said anything, then she began talking, almost in a whisper so that I could barely hear her. I leaned closer.

"He was so happy—that's what I remember most..."

Flashback Through Sophie's Eyes
Lackawanna, New York, The Parish Rectory;Three Years Later, 1964

I had just finished dusting the furniture in the living room and was about to run the vacuum cleaner when Billy burst into the room, smiling broadly. "It's happened! It's really happened this time."

He rushed over, twirling me around in a circle, "My dear, you're looking at the next head priest at St. Mark the Evangelist's Parish in Harlem! I just spoke to Father Gregory and he said that it's all but a done deal. They just have to verify some of my paperwork and the classes that I took at the Vatican, and it's done! We'll be moving to New York City!"

I didn't know quite what to say, Billy had mentioned casually a few months ago that there was an opening in that Parish and that he was going to apply, but he never spoke of it again and since it wasn't the first time that he'd tried to get a position in one of the Parishes in New York City, I didn't want to say anything for fear it would dredge up the disappointment that he'd felt the last two times that he'd tried to move up. Because truth be told, Billy had so much more experience and knew so much more certainly than any of the other priests in this area, but despite that, year after year he'd be passed over when a position at a larger Parish opened up.

I hugged him, "Billy, that's wonderful! I'm so happy for you!"

He kissed me lightly on the tip of my nose, "Happy for US!" We'll have so much more freedom in New York, and I've already verified that I can bring you with me as my housekeeper. You know I wouldn't leave here if I couldn't have you with me. As the head Priest, I have the right to bring my staff and what's more…this position may have some international travel, I might finally be able to get back to Italy—and even Paris. We can't travel together, but I can get a ticket for you and we can meet over there. Oh, Sophie, this is what I've been waiting for, for so many years!"

He rubbed his hands together in delight, pacing around the room excitedly. "Sophie, do you know what this means? I can finally do the work that I've been dreaming of ever since I became a Priest. I can finally minister to my people and make a difference. Ever since I was a seminarian in Italy, I knew that I wanted to be a Priest, but I felt lost like I wasn't sure what God wanted my work to be and then just that chance meeting with that young fellow, about my age, but he was so directed and so full of fire and not just the desire but the determination to help the Negro race, that it was infectious, and from that moment, I knew what I wanted to do as a Priest. I told you about him, the young man that I met in Paris, didn't I?"

"No, you didn't, you mentioned that you'd gone there a few times when you were studying in Italy, but that's all, so tell me!" Billy's enthusiasm was buoying me upward higher and higher, and the thought of a whole new life with him in the most exciting city in the world was making me feel giddy, like an excited teenager.

We sat down together on the couch. I pushed the vacuum cleaner away and we held hands as he laid his head back on the couch, smiling to himself, remembering back then...

Flashback Through Father Grau's Eyes
Paris, France; 1931, Age 26

I don't know how long I wandered, my thoughts clouding any sense of direction or time, but I found myself drawn to a tiny street sandwiched between two wide avenues. On both sides of the street, cars were lined up, parked on the sidewalk, some almost on top of the others. Music rippled through the air, jazz, American jazz, but not the sometimes somber contemplative side, but Dixieland jazz, the kind that made you tap your feet in spite of yourself and before you knew it, you were whirling someone around the dance floor, both caught up in the reverie of the moment. That jazz, the kind that could only be played by the Negro musicians, like Louis Armstrong and others who were taking Europe and France, in particular, by storm.

A car honking jolted me out of my thoughts, "Bougez!" A man driving a silver Packard stuck his head out the window and I realized that he was shouting at me trying to get me to move. As he expertly maneuvered the long car down the narrow street, barely missing the line of cars on both sides and even more narrowly missing the clumps of people lingering outside the door of what I realized was causing all of this commotion, a club where all of Paris seemed to be trying to get in. I looked over the doorway and saw "BRICKTOP'S."

Everybody knew Bricktop's, the most popular nightclub in Paris. It was owned by an American Negro woman expatriate, Bricktop. I'd never been there before, but somehow I had absentmindedly managed to find my way here.

A loud voice rang out in heavily accented French that sounded more like English with a slightly forced French accent, "Excusez-moi!"

I turned and found myself face-to-face with a large Negro woman, light-skinned, about my color, with red freckles and a mop of thick red hair. "You speak English?" She said to me.

I nodded yes. She had a long red feather boa wrapped around her overflowing bosom and her clothes, while obviously expensive, were just a little too tight for her ample form.

She looked me up and down, in a way that made me slightly uncomfortable, "Well, aren't you a cutie, how did you get so far from home?"

Not sure what to say, I just shrugged, "I don't know, I just found myself here."

She laughed raucously, "You just found yourself in Paris? Now that's a new one, heard of finding yourself in lots of places, but not Paris, everybody I know *plans* to come to Paris!"

Embarrassed, I fumbled with my words, "I didn't mean that exactly, what I meant was that I found myself here—at—this place."

"Well, I don't know if I like that any better, nobody just finds themselves here 'cause this is definitely the place to *be.*"

Realizing that I'd made an even bigger gaffe, I tried to recover, "I didn't mean…"

She laughed again, obviously amused at my embarrassment, "Shucks honey, don't worry about it, I was just teasin' you!" She sidled closer to me. "Well now that you *found yourself* here, I bet you wanna have a good time."

Her eyes traveled over me again, as if taking in every inch.

Not sure what she had in mind, I just smiled, almost afraid to say anything else that might be misinterpreted again,

She looped her arm through mine, "Well I'm going to help you out, you ever been to Bricktop's?"

"No, I haven't."

She walked to the door, winking at me coyly, "Well honey, come on in!"

The door swung open as if she'd said, *"Open sesame!"* and the crowd surged forward. Suddenly, people from everywhere engulfed us, or more accurately her, kissing her madly on both cheeks, "Bricktop, you are here—we wait all night for you!"

And then I realized that I'd been led in by the famous Bricktop herself, but before I could turn and thank her, she was pulled away by one of her many admirers and I found myself standing somewhat awkwardly in the middle of a horde of people, all dancing, drinking, arms draped over one another, some shouting loudly over the raucous jazz band. I almost felt as if I had been dropped into the middle of an island where I was the odd man out, where all the natives were partaking in the customary rituals and I was observing from afar, except that I was in the middle of it all.

I felt someone tap me on the shoulder and I saw a young colored man, about my age, gingerly balancing three drinks, one looking like it was about to tip over at any moment. "Hey there, be a sport and take this for me. I'm bringing this drink to my girl and the other one to my buddy, but I'm about to spill one of them. Can you take this for me, my group's over there in the corner." He laughed, "The loud ones, you can't miss us."

Not sure what else to do, I followed the young man across the room, dodging wildly dancing couples as I criss-crossed through the crowd, finally finding myself squeezed behind the young colored man whose drink that I was still holding, and his two friends who were lounging in the corner. One, I guess his girl, a dark-eyed French woman wearing probably one of the most unusual looking dresses that I'd ever seen. It had a low waist that was popular with all the young ladies my age, it was dark green with a virtual riot of sequins in the shape of a snake, from her shoulders to her hem. This was a far cry from the clothes that I'd seen in Cleveland, even in the windows of the finest shops, I don't think I'd ever seen a dress that sparkled so much. He looped his arm around her waist proprietarily; maybe he thought that I was staring too much. I smiled to myself, thinking, *"Wonder what'd he do if he knew that I was a future Priest."*

He broke into my thoughts, suddenly, "So sport, what brings you to Paris?" Before I could respond, he held out his hand, "By the way, I'm Albert, and this is my girl, Giselle—she doesn't speak much English, but then…" And he nuzzled his face in her neck, pecking it lightly. "We don't really need to talk much." He winked as if I should be in on the joke. "And this is my buddy, Emory."

I shook his hand, and Emory's nodding to Giselle who barely seemed to notice me. "I'm William, good to meet you." Emory nodded, but like Giselle, his eyes hardly met mine and I could see that he was scanning the room, perhaps he had a girl that he was looking for, his "Giselle." As if to confirm my thoughts, he turned quickly, his eyes following a young woman across the room, "I'll be back." And with that, he was gone, seemingly swallowed up by the crowd.

"That Emory," Albert chuckled to himself as if not surprised. "So, William, right? What's a colored man like you doing in the most beautiful city in the world?"

Not really wanting to say much, I said nonchalantly, "Oh just a little vacation. I'm studying in Rome."

"Really, what you studyin'?"

Without hesitating, I blurted out, "Religion."

He nodded, "I like that, a colored man studying religion in Italy with the Pope I'd guess," and he laughed at his own joke. I didn't have the heart to tell him that he wasn't too far from the truth, "Not exactly…"

"How long will you be there?"

"Probably a couple more years."

"And then what?"

"I guess I'll be heading back to the States."

"I figured that—but I didn't mean that. I meant, then what are you going to DO? As in really DO with your life, for us—the colored race. We fought like the white boys in the Great War and what did we come back to, not a hero's welcome with ticker tape parades, but race riots across the country 'cause the crackers thought we'd take their jobs."

He suddenly became very intense, leaning forward, "It's up to folks like us, the ones who've been given a chance to do something with our lives, to give back so that all Negroes can prosper. Hell, we were slaves for 150 years and we never got our 40 acres and a mule, so now it's a new day, a new century, and we've got to make sure that the colored race keeps moving forward. That's what I'm gonna do when I get back, I've decided that I'm headed to Harlem, that's where it's all happening, I'm gonna open up my own store and I'm only hiring colored folks, that's what all the rest of 'em do, ever seen an Italian store with anything but Italians working there, or a Jewish place with anybody but Jews working there? Well, that's what we colored folks have to do, hold out our hand and help our people. We've got to make our lives mean something, William, 'cause if we don't, then who will?"

And in that moment, the confusion that I'd been feeling since I got to Rome, happy to be there, but sensing that there must be something else, some larger reason why I was given that opportunity. It all became clear now. I, too, would go back and help our people, maybe not in the same way as Albert, but after all what was more important than your spiritual life, what could mean more than helping our colored people welcome the grace of God into their lives, because with God, miracles could happen. And I could do even more. I could help our folks learn life skills so they could get better jobs, the kind that Albert was talking about providing. And having spent all my life up to this point in Cleveland, where colored folks always seemed to be relegated to the scraps that the whites didn't want, I knew in my heart that my ministry and what I could teach would change lives and would make a difference.

I was so lost in my own thoughts, that as I turned back to say something more to Albert, I realized that he'd disappeared on the dance floor with Giselle. I smiled, it didn't matter, I'd gotten the message that God had for me and the path for my life had never seemed clearer.

End Flashback
Lackawanna, New York, Parish Rectory Living Room; 1964

"Oh, Billy, what a story, I can see how that changed you." I gazed at him, seeing him as I had the first time, with all of the same awe and admiration. "I'm so proud of you, Billy, you don't realize what a difference you've made already! We may not be in Harlem yet, but you've made things better for the people right here with the classes that you've given, showing the colored and Spanish men how to organize to get those good union jobs. You should hear them, everyone speaks of you with such respect, why you know so much more, then the other Priests, you speak three languages! And look how you've grown this Parish. When I came, we could barely fill the Church and the nursery, now there's a waiting list for the nursery and every Sunday Mass is packed, even the 6 a.m. service! Billy, you just don't know what you've already done. But I do, and it makes me love you even more!" Billy gathered me in his arms kissing me gently on the lips, then saying, "I've got an idea, let's drive up to our favorite place by Niagara Falls, just for the day, we can't stay the night because I've got a call with Father Gregory tomorrow morning, but we can at least spend a few hours there."

I clapped my hands, suddenly feeling that child-like joy that fills you up when something really special happens, "Oh Billy that would be wonderful!"

CHAPTER

53

I leaned over Billy, teasingly running my fingers through his curly hair, still jet black with only a few traces of gray. Behind us Niagara Falls thundered loudly, and a rainbow peeked over the rocks. But for once, I wasn't really focused on the scenery. I whispered coyly, "Remember the first time you let me really drive by myself. You were so quiet and just looking straight ahead! I remember saying, '*Billy, how'm I doing?*'"

He circled his arms around my waist, whispering into my ear, "I was praying! When you went over the curb at full speed, I knew that it was time to call in the higher powers." Billy winked at me and I tapped him playfully.

"I wasn't that bad, was I??"

Mischievously grinning "Well, since I'm a man of God, I cannot tell a lie—You were *definitely* that bad!"

"Oh stop!" I giggled remembering the look on his face as I careened around the corner and the car jumped over the curb. "Well, remember the time you just *knew* where you were going and refused to ask directions and we ended up in the middle of nowhere and then when you finally decided that you had to ask someone, that poor little old lady that you tried to wave down. Oh my! She looked like she'd seen a ghost!"

He laughed heartily at the memory, "I guess I did kind of scare her coming out of the shadows like I did."

"We've had some great times." I snuggled closer to him. My face was damp from the spray coming off of the Falls. He wrapped his arm around my shoulder, lifting my face to his lips. "And you know what?"

"What?" I kissed the tip of his nose. "Tell me what."

"I love you more than ever."

He pressed his lips against mine and we kissed deeply.

I was remembering that kiss from earlier that day, feeling his lips burrowing into my neck and my face and my hair, and his hands roaming down my back. Now it's hours later and we're back at the Rectory in my bed.

I turned over, expecting to feel him next to me curled up against my back the way we were every night. We'd gotten home much later than we planned, and he insisted that I get in bed and he'd join me shortly. My mind was foggy, trying to get my bearings. My bedroom was always very dark with the heavy drapes tightly closed. Fumbling for my glasses, I turned on the night light, noticing for the first time that he wasn't there. His side was untouched.

I pulled myself out of bed, surprised, calling out softly, "Billy, are you still upstairs?"

Silence. I pulled my robe around my shoulders. "Billy…"

Something made my heart jump, "Billy!!"

I ran down the hallway peering into the bathroom, nothing. Then I bounded up the stairs. Then I heard a rustling in his bedroom. My heart pounding, I rushed into the room. One light was on, and then I saw him, slumped over in his chair.

Running over to him, "Billy!!!! Billy! Are you OK? Tell me you're OK!!!!!!." He moved slightly, but as I tried to prop his head up, his eyes rolled in the back of his head and then his body convulsed in pain. I screamed, "BILLY!!!" Tears coursing down my cheeks, I fumbled for the phone, shouting to the operator, "Send an ambulance—to the Rectory—QUICKLY!!! NOW!!!"

I held his head in my hands, trying to massage color back in his face, but other than the shudder he'd had, he was still. Not knowing what else to do, I rocked him back and forth in my arms, refusing to believe the worst. *"God, don't take him from me—not now—don't take him from me. No, not yet! Not yet!!! Please, not yet! Please, please—please. No, please—not yet!!! God, you've never let me down, you've always an-*

swered my prayers. Please, Father! I know I don't deserve happiness, but please-—please don't do this—not now. Not yet!!!"

I heard a pounding on the door, "Ambulance—Open up!" Laying his slump body down gently, I tried to brush away the tears that wouldn't stop. "He's in here." I was shaking, my whole body was trembling. Running into the room, they brushed past me, one of them opening up Billy's shirt, the other cupping his mouth to Billy's, trying to force breath into him.

But after a few minutes, they stopped. "I'm sorry, Ma'am."

No sound came from me and I dropped to the ground, not seeing or feeling anything.

End Flashback
Buffalo, New York, Hospital; Present Time

Sophie had choked on the tears flowing down her cheeks, "I almost couldn't bear the funeral—having to pretend to his family that I was no more than a—housekeeper—I couldn't bear it—the memory of that loss and the pain that has never gone away."

"Oh, Sophie." I ran over to her and held her in my arms, and we comforted each other. I was there a long time that night. It was past midnight when I headed back wearily to my hotel room.

****

The last thing that I thought of as I lay my head on my pillow were Sophie's words, "I'm done now. I did what he wanted me to do." I remembered that she'd closed her eyes, her face now dry from the tears that had dampened her cheeks earlier as she recounted her last moments with my father. It's funny, I never thought of him like that until this moment. Until this moment when he became more than a name or an abstract concept. Until this moment when he became my father. He wasn't Daddy, nobody could ever be Daddy and I still missed him. But the man who gave me life was someone whose life I had lived thanks to Sophie and the time that we'd spent together re-living a time that gave me a window into my past, into who and what I was. Thanks to her, and I believe the grace of God, William Grau, or Billy as she still called him, was now real for me. He was my father.

****

Sophie died a few weeks later on January 28, 2007. She never left the hospital.

CHAPTER

54

Buffalo, New York, Funeral Home; A Week Later, 2007

I checked my watch anxiously; the priest was due there shortly. Sophie had wanted something simple. She'd laid it all out in her will. Her few belongings going mainly to her nephew, a man about my age, who I'd never met and frankly never thought I would until now. As the executor of Sophie's estate, it was I who had to reach out to everyone.

"Joe." I whirled around, surprised to hear my name. I was the only spot of color in this sea of whiteness. Her relatives and few friends had started to stream in the small parlor of the funeral home.

"How are you, Joe?" I hugged Dorothy tightly, she was an older white woman, about Sophie's age, with one of those wise faces that misses nothing. Her graying hair was neatly combed in a bun and she always seemed to radiate warmth. She was a small woman but with great force of character. She reminded me a little of some of the strong, loving women in my own family and extended family in Cincinnati. I believe that Dorothy guessed the truth about who I was even before I forced Sophie to tell her. Dorothy had always been kind and supportive of my relationship with Sophie. I hugged her tightly, I appreciated her familiar face. Because frankly, although I was "kin," I think I'd never felt like more of an outsider. Everyone was looking at me suspiciously, like I was some dark alien who'd dropped into their Polish world.

Dorothy looked at me with the concern of a mother focused on the well-being of her child. "Are you OK?".

"I'm hangin' in there." She squeezed my hand. I hugged her, and my eyes locked into those of a man probably about my age, pinkish face, dumpy with greasy brown hair, a rumpled dark suit and scuffed shoes. A mousy woman wearing a severe black dress that hung off of her coat hanger-like shoulders hovered behind him. He just kept staring at me like I was some strange animal in a zoo. Finally, as if he could stand it no longer, he made his way over to me. Stopping, I held out my hand, "I'm Joe."

He ignored my hand and I quickly pulled it back.

"Who *are* you?" His eyes were accusatory, as if I'd stolen something. For a moment, there was silence.

Then I said, "I'm Sophie's son."

His face turned bright red. And he quickly turned his back to me, his wife shuffling behind him dutifully.

Those were the last words we spoke. I knew from pictures that he was her nephew, the one that she'd left most of her few possessions to. But as far as he was concerned, I didn't exist.

****

I had the dream again. The dream that Sophie and Father Grau, and I were somewhere very light and very bright. I think it may have been near Niagara Falls, because I hear water in the background. We're talking and sharing a laugh. And as the sun goes down, he takes her hand and they both turn towards me smiling and waving goodbye. I want to follow them, there's so much more that I want to say. As they disappear over the horizon, I realize that they're not gone, just hidden for a moment, because there will be other sunsets and other valleys and we'll be together again. But for now, I sleep deeply, remembering those days and that time when I was given the gift of me.

THE END

1. Aunt Callie (left) with husband, Otis "Pops" Wilkinson (center) and Florence Steele (right) celebrating with Joe after his Harvard graduation.
2. Joe with Otis "Pops" Wilkinson.
3. The "Brothers" (back row) Glenn Tunstull, Tony Carr, Joe and David Foley; (front row) Bill Steele, Jr. and Billy Steele Sr.

4. On their wedding day, Joe and Glenn Tunstull.
5. Author, Lisa Jones Gentry with Joe at a Harvard reunion.